Praise for *The Illum*

"*The Illumination Code* helps us overcome the two fundamental fallacies of the modern age: that the world we experience with our eyes and ears is all there is, and that it is basically random, happening without rhyme or reason. The truly real world is not random but highly tuned — oriented to its own evolution and so to the evolution of all things in it, ourselves included. The world of the quantum sciences is a 'natural miracle.' The key to comprehending it lies within us. Einstein once said that there are just two ways we can live our life: as if nothing is a miracle or as if everything is. This book tells us that everything is a miracle — a 'fathomable' not an unfathomable miracle. Kim Chestney's codes bring you closer to the comprehension of a reality that was wholly hidden prior to the quantum discoveries — and is now only partially hidden. What we learn in this book about the real world — which is not the world of everyday sensory experience but much more — is a true 'aha experience.' We have intuited something like this in our moments of insight and revelation, but now the miracle is offered to us with a scientific background. The revelations of the sciences are strange but not new. Insightful people have always known them. We are the greatest miracle — each of us a miraculous conscious being in a miraculous consciousness-imbued and consciousness-radiating universe."

— **Ervin László**, author of *Science and the Akashic Field*

"*The Illumination Code* is a dynamic guide to self-discovery and spiritual growth. This is not a passive self-help book but one that encourages the reader to be proactive. Each of the seven keys involves engaging exercises designed to expand the reader's intuitive abilities. One of the many virtues of this book is that it is not written from a fluffy, New Age perspective but from a down-to-earth, rational perspective. Kim Chestney expertly incorporates quantum physics not as a cold, distant exercise of academia but rather as a very up-close-and-personal force that both touches and connects all of us. I highly recommend this book."

— **Mark Anthony**, JD, Psychic Explorer® and author of
The Afterlife Frequency, Evidence of Eternity, and *Never Letting Go*

"Kim Chestney, the queen of intuition, has crafted an extraordinary masterpiece with her latest book, *The Illumination Code.* This is a transformative treasure chest filled with profound perspectives that will challenge any outdated beliefs and elevate every spiritual journey. It equips readers to embrace their power, trusting in their innate abilities and embarking on a transformative journey toward higher consciousness. With a unique blend of personal experiences and profound perspectives, Kim weaves a beautiful tapestry that goes beyond a mere reading experience. Its powerful lab tools further amplify its brilliance, igniting a spark that illuminates every aspect of life. *The Illumination Code* is undeniably a gift to humanity and an absolute must-read!"

— **Vibecke Garnaas**, channeler, producer,
and host of the *Spiritual Quest Podcast*

"Kim Chestney brings intuition into the mainstream by weaving together Western science and Eastern philosophies. Like Kim herself, her books are engaging, authentic, and life-changing. I highly recommend both!"

— **Carin Lockhart**, yogi and author of *Joinings*

"In *The Illumination Code* Kim Chestney has taken the foundational intuition principles she established in *Radical Intuition* to the next level. She has written a master class on how quantum physics and natural laws unlock the transformational power of intuition for everyone."

— **Barron Cato**, founder of Natural Way Consulting

"Kim Chestney takes us on a journey to embrace a whole new way of living that is full of wonder, guidance, magic, and empowerment. *The Illumination Code* is a remarkable book that bridges the worlds of science, spirituality, and the New Age seamlessly: a true work of quantum activism."

— **Jemma Skye Champeau**, transpersonal and grief counselor

"*The Illumination Code* is true to its name: it has illuminated a path for me to feel connected and one with the universe and the loving guidance that it contains for me. By supporting ancient spiritual teachings with a scientific foundation, especially recent discoveries in quantum physics, Kim Chestney has opened a portal to accessing and mastering one's intuition and feeling connected with the infinite."

— **Rabbi Neil Schuman**, spiritual leader, Manetto Hill Jewish Center, Plainview, New York

The
ILLUMINATION CODE

Also by Kim Chestney

Radical Intuition:
A Revolutionary Guide to Using Your Inner Power

The Psychic Workshop: A Complete Program
for Fulfilling Your Spiritual Potential

The
ILLUMINATION
CODE

7 Keys to Unlock
Your Quantum Intelligence

KIM CHESTNEY

Foreword by Peter Smith

New World Library
Novato, California

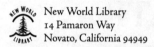 New World Library
14 Pamaron Way
Novato, California 94949

The material in this book is intended for education. It is not meant to take the place of diagnosis and treatment by a qualified medical practitioner or therapist. No expressed or implied guarantee of the effects of the use of the recommendations can be given or liability taken.

Text design by Tona Pearce Myers

Library of Congress Cataloging-in-Publication data is available.

First printing, April 2024
ISBN 978-1-60868-862-3
Ebook ISBN 978-1-60868-863-0
Printed in Canada on 100% postconsumer-waste recycled paper

 New World Library is proud to be a Gold Certified Environmentally Responsible Publisher. Publisher certification awarded by Green Press Initiative.

10 9 8 7 6 5 4 3 2 1

To the part of you that knows everything

Be a light unto yourself.
— Buddha

Contents

PART I: THE DEEP DIMENSION

PART 2: FIELD WORK

Foreword

I feel it was inevitable that my path would cross with Kim Chestney's. We are in the same field of work, though I feel there are times when our very thoughts are quantumly entangled.

Scientific circles champion the concept of peer review, wherein those who have a professional understanding of what you are talking about can critique, disagree with, or even dispute your findings. In my view, that process can be limited by competition and ego.

The field of work that Kim and I are in doesn't have the same pitfalls. In the area of human consciousness and how it can be explored through a quantum lens is a landscape of limitless possibility. This is a field of exploration that is starting to explode, and we welcome those who truly "get it" into a community of emerging thought leaders who collectively have come here to change the world. There is no doubt in my mind (or even beyond it) that Kim is one of these people.

Getting the message across about the limitlessness of you, which has been hidden for so long, requires three steps.

The first is to assemble a tapestry of collective thoughts from various trailblazers that cover science, consciousness, and even philosophy, and then add your own.

The second step is to translate all this into a narrative that can pique the human interest in a way that allows the reader to feel resonance with the information shared. Between the words are vibrational frequencies, urging the reader to remember their magnificence.

The third step is to make the narrative real through stories, examples, and personal experience — to open new neural pathways that lead to change, insight, and ultimately a personal knowing of the concepts. If you are successful, the reader will then understand that they are a metaphysical being living in a multiverse of divine design...and they have taken on a human disguise to do something of importance.

Kim Chestney is one of the few people I've found who can traverse all three of these steps and offer a path to the end point that can change your life. There are too few people in the world who can grasp this metaphysical landscape enough to write a book like the one you are about to read.

As I moved through the manuscript I found myself saying out loud, "Absolutely!" and "Well said, Kim!" as well as "Wow, I never looked at it that way." The further I moved into the book, the more I moved into coherence. You will hear more about that from Kim....

You will be learning about the seven keys of the illumination code. All of them resonate with me and my own understanding of our place in the universe. If I had to nominate a favorite, I would choose "Illumination Key #6 — I Am Extraordinary."

If I could, I'd buy a T-shirt for everyone on this planet with that printed on the front and back and make them wear it until they believed it. This reminds me of a time when one of my own clients struggling with anxiety and depression said to me many years ago, "I just want to know that I'm normal." My response was a simple one: "Well, it's best you understand that would be a lie, as you are in fact paranormal or even supernormal, and it's time you knew." After you're finished reading Kim's book, an understanding of what I'm talking about will come.

These past few years I have come to know Kim, and her presence has always left me both inspired and in a higher vibration than before the conversation began. We are indeed kindred spirits traveling as two particles in the same wave. That wave is human consciousness, and we are heading in a specific direction, chasing higher frequencies.

I encourage you not just to read this book, but to absorb it into your own field of consciousness. Allow the intentions of the author to permeate your being, as she has a pure purpose behind the words she is sharing. Please work through the exercises that draw you, as something greater at play is creating that attraction. Most of all, keep going. It takes courage to move into the metaphysical landscape and leave the conditioning of our society behind.

The reason I like Illumination Key #6 so much is that it goes against everything we've been told about ourselves through our societal conditioning, our education systems, and most likely our formative years. You may have been told you are "ordinary," but you are about to discover so much more than that. Isn't it incredible how five letters can change the entire universe? So go and be *extra*ordinary.

I'm grateful to be able to write this foreword; in fact, it is an honor. Those of us bringing this wave of change for humanity need to connect to make that wave stronger.

I'm so glad Kim's and my paths have crossed in the field of unlimited possibility, and the following quote, attributed to Pierre Teilhard de Chardin, comes to me: "There is an almost sensual longing for communion with others who have a larger vision. The immense fulfillment of the friendships between those engaged in furthering the evolution of consciousness has a quality almost impossible to describe."

May this book bring you illumination!

— **Peter Smith**, founder of the Institute for Quantum
Consciousness, author of *Quantum Consciousness:
Journey through Other Realms*, past president of the
Michael Newton Institute for Life Between Lives Hypnotherapy,
and current member of the MNI Advisory Council

The Final Frontier
Is the Inner Frontier

Spiritual practitioners don't use sophisticated research instruments.
They use their inner wisdom, their luminosity.... The practice
of mindfulness, concentration and insight can purify our mind
and make it into a powerful instrument with which we can
look deeply into the nature of reality.

— Thich Nhat Hanh

Step inside and learn the future. These words set in motion the chain of events that brought you and me together today. It all started on a brisk and starry October night in northern England, on opening night of a centuries-old Yorkshire tradition: the illustrious Hull Fair, Britain's largest and oldest traveling carnival. Returning each autumn since 1279, this celebration is like no other. Rung in each year by the Lord Mayor of Kingston Upon Hull, the festivities herald a weeklong jubilee — rich with exotic food stalls, whirling rides, and candy snaps — all imbued with the nostalgic charm of yesteryear. In this particular year, 1991, it was my turn to be enchanted by the inviting glow of festival lights and the pageantry of the fair's seemingly endless parade of carnival attractions.

Of course, no proper traveling carnival would be complete without its crown jewels: the fortune-tellers. Wandering through rows of bejeweled, twinkle-lit caravans offering palm and crystal ball readings for five pounds, my friends and I couldn't wait to get a sneak peek into what might lie ahead. We met a friendly woman with long, flaxen hair who welcomed me with a sparkle in her eye; the sign above her door read "Step inside and learn the future." I obliged and sat down at a small table draped in red velvet. I looked around in wonder. The walls were ensconced with strings of beads and lace curtains and countless antique framed pictures of this mysterious woman with famous people — celebrities and royalty.

After chatting a bit, she took my palms in her hands and began to extract from the ethers small, yet strangely accurate, details of my life. As she continued to read my palms, I realized something curious: she wasn't looking at my palms at all. She spoke, looking into my eyes, just like we were having a conversation. I don't even think she looked at my palms once; she didn't use a crystal ball or tarot deck either. She just smiled and effortlessly poured out a stream of information about my life. She spoke of ordinary life things — of lovers, fathers, mothers, and daughters — but then she said something simple but most extraordinary: "In 1994, you will be in a foreign courtroom. It may be uncomfortable, but you will be doing something that will help."

I paused. *Did she just predict an exact date?* Yes, she foretold an event with a specific date and time in the future — three years ahead. During all my dabbling with psychic readings, never had anyone been so clear or confident enough to share such totally ver-ifiable information. Who would dare? If they were wrong, they would be instantly discredited. But there were no gray areas in her words: this was going to be right or wrong. Either I was going to court in 1994, or I wasn't.

Two years later, in 1993, I was about to find out the answer. Time had passed, and I moved back to the States, the prophecy from that starry night now faded into the back of my mind — until one afternoon when I found something interesting in my mailbox: a federal jury summons. How unexpected. I was only twenty-two years old and had never known anyone who got called for jury duty. As I held the summons in my hand, in a strange, quiet moment, *something clicked.* It all came rushing back — the prediction, her words, the dates. And I was suddenly overtaken by what I can only explain as *knowingness* — an absolute certainty — that this was the beginning of what was foretold to me years ago. I knew I would be selected for that jury; and I knew the trial would not happen until 1994.

At the time, I could not explain why I felt what I felt. It wasn't just that I believed the prophecy; it was like I was connected to the information on my own. Somewhere inside, I suddenly *knew it for myself.* When I went to jury selection, I knew I would be selected; I talked to each lawyer, and I could not shake the feeling that they were going to pick me. I felt a complete alignment with the process, and I played my part.

Within days, I was selected to serve on that jury. But would it happen in 1994? She didn't say it would happen *around* 1994; she said *in* 1994 — which was months away. Finally, in the summer of 1994, it all came to pass, and the vision foretold on that distant night in a distant land unfolded just as predicted: I spent two weeks sequestered in a United States courtroom, serving for a trial that was intense and uncomfortable — but also an opportunity to do good. Somehow, someway, the woman at the Hull Fair knew exactly where I would be and when something would happen, three years ahead of time. She did something that should have been impossible, but it wasn't.

It is possible to know the future. How could I deny it? It happened. I personally experienced it. I felt it. I even *knew* it myself, in the end. My mind was alight with curiosity and wonder. If it was possible to predict the future, what else was possible? What other secrets did this mysterious world hold? I had to know more. My breakthrough experience defied the boundaries of my reality and made me question all others. Though history itself was rich with stories of extraordinary experiences like mine, I knew it then for myself. I no longer wondered *what if* things like this were possible; I wondered *how* it was possible. I felt like I had stumbled upon a big secret. And I was on fire with the desire to get to the bottom of it.

Impossible things are possible.

If the woman at the Hull Fair can do an impossible thing, can't we all? Can't I? Can't you? The answer has to be yes. Yes, we can do many things that, as children, we were taught no one could ever do. In our own day and age, science is proving it too. Thanks to the quantum revolution, a new understanding of the universe is emerging. Though most of us grew up understanding the world as a cause-and-effect universe of three-dimensional space and time, we now know that this "real" world is not a real world at all. Our physical reality is just our local interface with a much greater world — an immaterial quantum world. This is the place where subatomic reality becomes our supernatural reality, where past, present, and future are interconnected, where you can speak to someone without saying a word, and where the answer to a problem simply arrives without working to figure out the solution. Quantum reality is a world of meaning and magic, where impossible things become quite possible.

I never forgot that extraordinary day at the Hull Fair. Fast-forward twenty years — it still had one more gift for me: while conducting genealogical research, I discovered that, previously unbeknownst to both myself and my family, my maternal ancestors originated in the very same part of Yorkshire that I called home in 1991. Most fascinating of all, my grandmother Wakefield's eighth-great-grandfather was Edward Wakefield, the Lord Mayor of Kingston Upon Hull in 1581. My very own ancestor rung in the Hull Fair four hundred years before I was led back there.

Life is meaningful, and there is no such thing as a coincidence.

In a final act of synchronicity as I was putting the finishing touches on this story, I received yet another unexpected surprise: Robert, one of the long-lost friends who accompanied me to the Hull Fair on that evening in 1991, reached out to me for the first time in over thirty years. We had not seen or heard from each other since I left England in 1992. For some reason, he had the random idea to contact me now as I was writing our story.

An Invitation to the Deeper Dimension

This moment is an invitation to embrace a new understanding of reality — to step across a threshold into the unknown. It is a call to expand your mind and fulfill your greater potential as a human being. Have you ever witnessed something that should not be possible in this world? Have you ever known, felt, or sensed something that defies rational explanation? Have these kinds of mysteries moved you to seek a deeper understanding of life — one that doesn't deny the unexplainable phenomenon of the universe? Many people, like you and me, have been called to the hidden truth so that together we can share in the discovery of a deeper, inward reality. The future — the final frontier — isn't *out there*. It's inside you.

The Illumination Code is a guide for personally experiencing the magic of the quantum universe. It offers the missing pieces of the cosmic puzzle, revealing how the seemingly vast, impersonal laws of physics are, in actuality, supremely personal. All of it was built for you — every scientific principle, every rule, field, force, particle, and bit of information is alive within you, working to support your existence. As you begin to activate your latent powers of intrinsic awareness — the innate intuitive function that connects you with the quantum dimension — you can step beyond the textbook knowledge systems to touch the magic of the microcosmic realities from the inside.

Yes, it is absolutely possible to know the future. Yes, it is possible to connect with other people beyond your location in time and space. Yes, you have an inner guidance system that shows you the way. And, yes, all these things are supported by our emerging understanding of quantum physics. In a world of relativity, where there is really no such thing as objective time, why shouldn't you be able to know the future? Everything that has ever happened or will happen is happening right now. All the information is out there; you just need to learn how to access it.

Whatever truth you are looking for, you can find it in the intuition-accessed inner dimension of reality. But don't take it from me; experience it for yourself. Know it for yourself; feel it for yourself. Do it for yourself. This is the only way to be sure. The keys, experiments, and practices in this book are designed to give you learnable and repeatable firsthand evidence of your quantum nature. This is an invitation to move past outdated scientific concepts and social conditioning to find your own personal truth in the illuminating code embedded in a deeper dimension of reality — the place where supernatural mysteries, strange coincidences, and unexplained happenings are just part of the magic of living in a quantum world.

The quantum revolution is revealing an enchanting universe — imbued with a deep magic that we are just beginning to discover, or maybe one that collectively we have forgotten. Throughout the ages, mystics and wise ones from cultures all around the globe have been reporting the wonders of the metaphysical world; today, scientists are proving those wonders are real. What an exciting time to be alive, as we open up to the great beyond and new scientifically validated concepts like:

- Quantum physics has a personal application to your life and purpose.
- Unexplained psychic phenomena are actually byproducts of proven quantum systems.

- Your interface with the quantum field allows you to do things like:
  o Know the future or the past.
  o Nonverbally connect with other living beings.
  o Receive guidance, creative ideas, and insight for your life path.
  o Expand your awareness beyond perceived limits of time and space.
  o Activate synchronicity and recognize personal signals from the universe.
  o Awaken to the true nature of reality and existence.

The universe is always speaking to you. Through serendipitous events, moments of inspiration, gut feelings, epiphanies, and intuitive knowingness, life has a fundamental system of communicating in a deeply personal way. Our ancestors knew it; artists, geniuses, innovators, teachers, and gifted intuitives of all kinds still know it. I think you know it too.

Though many concepts in this book may seem radical, they are grounded in our emerging understanding of physics and are validated by the research of groundbreaking physicists. I am not a physicist, but the ideas in this book are built on the genius of great thought leaders who have created a scientific foundation for a renewed understanding of the physical and metaphysical universe — one that also validates many ancient wisdom traditions. Life is coming full circle as we witness the old aligning with the new, and we have the unique opportunity to participate in the reunion of mystical, ancient teachings with modern-day empirical knowledge.

The Illumination Code Experience

The Illumination Code is a manual for the exploration of your inner world. Its purpose is to activate your latent powers of intrinsic knowing, or *quantum thinking*, and teach you to consciously work with the psyche on a quantum level. Signals from inner space flow in a constant data stream that can be downloaded only by your intuition. With this book, you can crack the code of your intuitive mind and learn to speak its language.

The book is divided into seven chapters, each based on an illumination key designed to unlock a personal experience of the universal truth manifesting as quantum phenomena. Each key is supported by investigations, experiments, and labs that apply the leading-edge principles of modern physics to your life. Some of these foundational concepts include:

- Intuition is a quantum phenomenon.
- There is a nonlocal field that invisibly connects you to everything and everyone.
- The holographic nature of the universe gives you inner access to all information.
- Relativity shows us there is no such thing as absolute time or division in space.
- Particle-wave duality is part of the creative power of your mind.
- You are in sync with others through quantum entanglement.
- You live in a multiverse with countless other forms of interdimensional life.
- The state of universal coherence allows us to become one with the universe.

Each illumination key takes you progressively further into these mysteries and calls you toward new, expanded states of awareness. I recommend reading the chapters ahead in order one by one as the information and practices build on one another as you go, continuing to unlock more sophisticated facets of the hidden dimension.

The Seven Illumination Keys

The keys in this book are designed to open the locked dimension of your inner awareness field, giving you access to progressively deeper facets of reality. Each key is an intentional affirmation — a code of its own — created to deprogram a conditioned aspect of your consciousness and open your mind to the beyond. Every key comes with its own activating practice to put it into action in your life and prepare you to work with it. As the keys successively unlock elements of your quantum dimension, you get to personally explore, investigate, and experiment with the nonlocal and interdimensional realities of the universe.

Illumination Key #1 unlocks the gateway
to your quantum dimension.

Illumination Key #2 reconnects your inner
information highway.

Illumination Key #3 expands your awareness
beyond the limits of reality.

Illumination Key #4 opens your mind to the
timeless wisdom stored in the cosmos.

Illumination Key #5 teaches you the secrets
of quantum intelligence.

Illumination Key #6 empowers you to
do impossible things.

Illumination Key #7 guides you to the ultimate
truth of who you are.

Investigations, Experiments, and Labs

The book provides multiple ways to explore each key's power in your daily life. Through personal investigations and simple experiments, each chapter has interactive exercises designed for you to apply the truths you discover. At the end of every chapter, you will find an intensive exercise, called labs, to develop your quantum intelligence. A lab is a place where you can research, experiment, and discover — all of which is essential for your inner world investigation. The only way you can fully comprehend the potential you hold within you is to experience it for yourself. The interactive work throughout this book gives you firsthand evidence of quantum phenomena, such as the following:

- Downloading bits and bytes of nonlocal information
- Connecting to others beyond time and space
- Decision-making with your quantum intelligence
- Using your metasenses to process input from the quantum field
- Understanding signs that the universe uses to communicate with you
- Remote viewing other places, times, and lives
- Becoming aware of other worlds and alternate realities
- Reuniting with universal consciousness

These activities also include a variety of meditations and inner reflections to attune your mind with the resonant vibration of the knowledge-infused deep dimension.

Preparing for Your Inner Exploration

The Illumination Code is an interactive book filled with exploratory practices, so consider gathering or creating some of the items below to facilitate and record your discoveries:

- A new journal or notebook for your practice sessions and insights
- A quiet space in your home where you can go within undisturbed

- Intuition-activating tools and card decks
- A regular time to practice developing your intuition on a consistent basis

The Illuminator's Kit: An Illumination Code Companion can be downloaded at the link below and includes a printable workbook, Insight Card Deck, sacred seeing boards, and an array of intuition-enhancing tools.

ADDITIONAL RESOURCES

Download the Illuminator's Kit: An Illumination Code Companion at KimChestney.com/illuminationcode.

Practice with the Illuminate! Interactive Card Deck at KimChestney.com/insight-cards.

Join a community to practice developing your intuition at Intuition-Lab.com.

There is a whole universe of information within you — truth, knowledge, wisdom, all the things you have ever looked for — a treasure trove waiting to be unlocked. At last, human beings have the information to crack a code that has eluded us for so long — the illuminating code of the universe. With the new science, *you* have the capability to consciously tap into the cosmic information and energy that has been secretly moving you all your life. And it's easier than you think.

PART 1

The

DEEP DIMENSION

CHAPTER ONE

A Part of You Knows Everything

Intuitive realization is the king of sciences, the royal secret....
It is the first perception of truth — the imperishable enlightenment.

— THE BHAGAVAD GITA IX:02, THE SONG OF GOD

Imagine that one day in your life you experienced something extraordinary. Maybe you caught a glimpse of something unexplainable — something that didn't fit with what you have been taught about reality. Maybe you had an intuitive revelation, or a dream or vision. You could even have noticed an impossible coincidence or an undeniable sign from the universe. Or maybe, just for a moment, the illusion of reality lifted just enough for you to recognize something from the magnificent, hidden dimension underlying our world. Maybe it happened again, maybe it didn't.

Imagine that this experience became part of the very fabric of your being — that even though you couldn't explain it, you also couldn't convince yourself that it wasn't real. Maybe it continues to silently call to you, even though the world tells you that it could never have happened. Maybe you have searched for an explanation in religion, science, philosophy, or psychology, discovering clues and pieces of the puzzle along the way. If you were fortunate, you were able to find others who also know what you now know, becoming part of a silent revolution of witnesses to a deeper level of existence — those who know there is something more going on in this world.

Imagine that you are one of the many seekers and free-spirited adventurers playing your part in the greatest investigation of all time: the quest to understand what we are all doing here in this world. What is the purpose of our lives? What are we meant to do or learn here? How can we discover the truth about our human nature and our ultimate reality? Some of the greatest minds in history have participated in this ongoing investigation — scientists, philosophers, theologians, mystics, mathematicians — stretching back as far as we know, to the dawn of our civilization more than six thousand years ago. Now, it's our turn.

For the first time in history, you and I have access to revolutionary scientific information that reveals an entirely new way of understanding the world. During a great paradigm shift over the last century, quantum mechanics has shown us that our reality can no longer be seen as a mechanistic cause-and-effect system; classical physics explains only the surface of reality. Today, science is lifting the veil of empirical reality to reveal a deeper, exponentially more powerful inner *quantum reality* that creates the world we call home. Beneath the surface of all the objects we touch and feel is another reality — one that is alive with unseen interconnectedness, brimming with energy and phenomena that seem like nothing less than magic.

If you look closely, you can see the magic everywhere. Since the day you were born, an invisible, intuition-accessible code has been infiltrating your reality. What if this code is embedded deep within the quantum dimension to be read by an expanded version of your mind — with a purpose to inform and guide your life? What if this code contains all the answers you seek but exists on a level that is out of reach for your thinking mind? What if your intuitive mind is the ultimate quantum computer — able to process an entirely different kind of information — if only you knew how to turn it on *and use it.*

Intuition Is a Quantum Phenomenon

Many have said that any sufficiently advanced technology is indistinguishable from magic. Could your consciousness hold the world's greatest technology, designed to do impossible things? Could everyday people, like you and me, be able to participate in a magic that is meant to be discovered not only by scientific formulas and technological instruments but also by personal experience — through our most extraordinary information-processing system, our power of intuitive insight?

Insight — the remarkable power of the mind to instantaneously receive information from the quantum realms — is poised to become humanity's most advanced form of knowledge acquisition. With scientific discovery we learn from the outside world; with intuitive discovery we learn from the world inside us — not just in terms of age-old ideas like our inner wisdom or inner guidance but also via the real, quantifiable information processing of quantum relationships. The task of the future is to build on centuries-old traditions of *external education* with the emerging possibilities of *internal education*.

Through the faculty of insight, you have direct access to the code of the universe itself — the program that is running silently in the background of what we call reality. You can read the code of the past or the future, of your own life or other people. You can access knowledge that exists outside this particular moment in time and space and beyond the limitations of the linear thinking mind. Your faculty of insight is a built-in technology that gives you intrinsic access to an inner matrix of information and energy, the very building blocks of this world. Our scientific experiments show us how quantum mechanics work, from the outside looking in; but it is through intuitive insight that we personally experience it — from the inside looking out.

The only technology you need to interact with the quantum

world is your intuitive mind. By reimagining intuition as the means to navigate a deeper reality, we can understand it as a kind of *quantum thinking* that naturally extends beyond the limits of the intellectual mind. Fundamentally, every human being has intrinsic access to all information in all places and times. This power of insight gives you — and every other human being — the potential to learn from the inside, from the microcosmic reality that is constantly informing your life. Your consciousness itself is the ultimate information system — wired, through inner access only, to a connection beyond the limits of physical reality.

The Lost Code of the Cosmos

Every day, every moment, the universe is broadcasting billions of signals — subtle forms of information and energy that interpenetrate your whole world, even though they are virtually undetectable in material reality. Some of these signals are for the world at large, and some of these signals are just for you. With modern technology — like cellphones, remote controls, radio, television, and even the internet — you can pick up on all kinds of imperceptible information; but there is a whole universe of signals out there that don't require a material technological interface. These codes of information are meant to directly interface with your conscious mind.

A part of your mind has been receiving these universal signals for your entire life. They have been providing you with information about the world around you — invaluable data that speaks to your intuition, your instinct, and other feelings, while your thinking mind remains unaware. On occasion, these signals break through into your consciousness in moments of insight, epiphany, or sudden awareness — when your inner receiver tunes in to unexpected bits of important information. The processing of this secret code can feel like an aha moment or a revelation; it can give you a gut feeling or a sense of inner knowingness. These experiences are manifestations of a universal intelligence transmission system that your mind processes as intuitive sensations, thoughts, or feelings.

Every day of your life, the cosmic information system is guiding you from the inside out. With the rational mind, you process information linearly, based on codes from the macrocosmic world outside you; conversely, the insightful mind, like a quantum computer, interfaces with the microcosmic inner dimension and holds the magnificent power to process information simultaneously — to know everything all at once. For example, to solve a problem, the thinking mind must go through the formula — for example, figuring out $1 + 2 + 3 + 4$ to get to the answer of 10; but, with the quantum intuitive mind, you can get from the question to the answer in an instant of intuitive knowing, without thinking at all. Your intuitive mind is connected to a worldwide web of information that you can download and apprehend in an instant.

We used to call people who could read the secret universal code or tune into a wider signal bandwidth *psychic*. But, today, we are realizing that everyone is psychic. In America, about 75 percent — three out of four people — believe in the reality of supernatural phenomena. Furthermore, 67 percent of Americans say that they have personally experienced a supernatural phenomenon. More people believe in psychic abilities than don't; and more people have experienced them than haven't. Whether these people are encountering their extrasensory perception, telepathy, precognition, or good old-fashioned intuition, impossible things are becoming a way of life. With each decade that passes, we are waking up new inner potential as the magnitude of our extraordinary nature comes into focus.

Are we, then, gods with amnesia? How did we forget about — or have to rediscover — the illuminating magic of the quantum dimension? Legends, myths, and sacred stories throughout history remind us of the power it holds; the supernatural is integral in ancient wisdom, with prophecies, miracles, and revelations commonly accepted beyond question. Our ancestors had no idea about quantum mechanics; to them, our metaphysical nature was a natural part of life. Only in recent times did we begin to use the word *psychic* to pejoratively label the observable but unexplainable manifestations of life in a quantum universe — a technique to diminish what our rational minds are unable comprehend.

Quantum physics turns out to be the magic behind three thousand years of mystery and misunderstanding. The laws of the subatomic universe defy the logic and reason that have been the foundation of our understanding of reality and instead function in a way that feels supernatural. At the quantum level, entities can communicate despite vast distances, appear out of nowhere, defy all sense of time, and even be in two places at once. When we apply these laws of physics to the mind, we can see how those unexplainable experiences were explainable all along — we just didn't have the knowledge to know it at the time. But now we do. We don't have to live in the dark anymore; we all have the potential to expand our bandwidths and open back up to the great, cosmic information broadcast.

There is no such thing as a psychic person or psychic phenomenon; *all people are psychic, and we live in a psychic universe* — or as Ervin László, Nobel Prize nominee and physicist, described it, a consciousness-infused universe. To be psychic is an intrinsic quality of all consciousness. It describes our ability to connect with information beyond our position in time and space, something that appears to be impossible from the materialistic worldview. How can separated objects possibly interact? We now know that something is connecting them — an unseen force that unites all things. Like the water that connects all beings in the ocean, every object in our material world is bound together in an invisible field of information. In fact, we are part of that information; not only are we *in it*, but we are *made of it.*

All along, we have been looking for the truth in all the wrong places — in physical form and in the laws of the material world; but now, the new science reveals that everything — your body, matter, energy, atoms, protons, electrons, quanta — everything that you know in the world is actually *made of* consciousness-infused information. Everything you think, do, or interact with is an exchange of information. The desk in your office is made of information; an itch on your arm is information; a creative idea is information; a memory is information; your dreams are information; your thoughts and emotions are information; the energy in the ethers around you as you go about your day is full of information. On a microcosmic, intuitive level, you are processing information 24/7.

 Information codes are the building blocks of the universe.

In the words of visionary physicist John Archibald Wheeler, "The most fundamental feature of the universe is information — other physical quantities are more like incidentals. Information is present throughout space and time, and it is present at the same time everywhere." Everything is information. Cosmic information is building, connecting, and guiding all the world. Wheeler notoriously coined the phrase "It from bit" to explain how tangible physical reality (it) is ultimately made of information (or bits). Everything you see, touch, sense, think, or feel is a part of an extraordinary code of intelligence that programs all creation.

László's work takes this idea one step further, making a case for intuition as an essential part of our information-based universe: "The world 'runs' on information, but on what it runs is not the garden variety of information we think of when we read a newspaper or talk to a neighbor. The world runs on 'in-formation.' It runs on information that is correctly spelled with a hyphen. The concept of in-formation comes from quantum physicist David Bohm. In-formation is an active impulse that acts on, 'in-forms' things and events." Information on the quantum level arrives from the *inside*, implicitly — not from any observed, external event but from a "cosmic impetus."

Human beings process information in two primary ways from our relative position in the universe: our thinking mind processes information from outside us (the macrocosm), while our intuitive mind processes information from inside us (the microcosm). You process garden-variety information while you go about material reality, responding to stimuli from the cause-and-effect world. But the other kind of information — *in-formation*, derived from the inner world through the process of insight — has one uniquely identifiable trait: it has no observable information source in this world, not even in your own mind. You don't *think it up*. It is of cosmic impetus; it arrives seemingly from nowhere.

In-formation — or insight — arrives instantaneously, in a flash, often out of the blue. Like the stroke of genius that answers the problem you were struggling to solve or the big idea that pops into your head, it is a sudden awareness, an instant knowing, or a gut feeling that guides you, even when you have no idea how or why. In-formation is a code of invisible truth that seems to arrive from nowhere because it arrives from beyond our reality.

Luminous Mind

The realization that we live in a world of information (a.k.a. in-formation) is a first step into the mystery of the deep dimension — the key to understanding how it is possible for a part of you to know everything. If cosmic intelligence is everywhere, how can we get more of it? Where can we find this treasure trove of inside knowledge? Where is it stored? Though we will explore this question extensively in chapter 4, the answer is tied to one important property of our universe: light.

From the dawn of history, light has had a distinguished role in our world, signifying the presence of the divine or most revered truth. The archetype of a guiding light is practically a universal truth. The Egyptians worshipped the sun as the light of life. In Christianity, light is associated with wisdom, holiness, and God's presence — Jesus called himself "the light of the world" (John 8:12). Hindus celebrate Diwali, the Festival of Lights, each year to honor the triumph of light in the world. Buddhism teaches the pure state of the "luminous mind," where the perception of light endows the mind with luminescence. The twelfth-century mystic Saint Hildegard von Bingen bestowed light with the highest honor of all: "God was and is light and radiance and life. And God said, 'Let there be light,' and so were the light and the radiant angels created." On some level, we have always known that light is more than a biological necessity — it is the key to life itself.

In science, too, light is at the center of the magic. The holographic principle suggests that fundamental cosmic information is stored in patterns of light that can be read like a code, revealing the underlying workings of the universe. According to Deepak Chopra, "The photons that make up light have no mass, but they do carry energy and information" and are well known to transmit information in the form of digital signals. Technology has already harnessed the power of photons — or quanta — to carry information through innovations like fiber-optic cables, solar cells, medical imaging, and computer technology. Quanta are the smallest units of energy in the universe, and they underlie the behavior of atoms and subatomic particles — hence the term *quantum* physics.

When viewing the quantum dimension through the lens of

information and consciousness, quantum reality is our inner reality. To *go within* means to explore the quantum intelligence that informs our existence through the information and energy transmitted by our inner luminescence. Light is at work in your mind and body — all the way down to the deepest levels of your consciousness and into the fundamental cells, atoms, and particles that compose your being. Underneath the illusion of solid matter, we are all living bodies of light; we perpetually radiate, communicate with, and are informed by the glowing dance of an electric world.

EXPERIMENT: THE INNER LIGHT SHOW

When you look at your physical body, it's hard to imagine it being built of light. To the naked eye, it all seems dense, heavy, solid, tangible. But when you shut your eyes and look within, things begin to change. Closing your eyes is the one act that allows you to see part of your body from the inside. If your body was made of matter, you might expect to see nothing but darkness when you shut the light out from the external world; instead, what you see is light.

Let's try it now: wherever you are, take a moment to close your eyes and observe what happens.

When you close your eyes, you don't see actual darkness — you see an inner light show with patterns of energy flowing across the screen of your inner vision, morphing colors and shapes, often even geometric and kaleidoscopic patterns. Visually impaired people also report this kind of psychedelic light show, which is generated by phosphenes — the dynamic visual perceptions of light that have no reference to the external environment. When no light from the outside world is present, your inner world is still alive with luminous energy.

How fitting that we use light-themed words, such as *enlightenment* and *illumination*, to describe the experience of heightened awareness or understanding. Being in the light is, both literally and figuratively, being in a place of clarity and vision — a state of being where truth is revealed. Light is the carrier of cosmic intelligence and the harbinger of wisdom. As you walk your life path, the light of your consciousness receives, saves, and shares the illuminating information codes that are perpetually being broadcasted by the universe. Through these codes of light, life itself informs and guides you. You are wired to intuitively pick up its signals with the purpose of moving you deeper into truth and reconnecting you to your wholeness of being.

 The illumination code is cosmic information embedded into your inner light and programmed to guide the expansion of your consciousness.

Through codes of illumination, life guides you from the inside. Every living thing has access to these inner codes of wisdom; the intrinsic knowledge of life manifests in many ways — from human intuition to the instinct of migrating birds or the ability of lost pets to know when their owners are about to arrive home. You and I — and all the life on this planet — are wired into the vast information-light-energy-filled expanse of the deep dimension, giving us the ability to know the unknowable, touch the untouchable, or witness the impossible becoming possible. But these extraordinary parts of life do not have to be isolated experiences or beyond our control. With attention and intention, you can more consciously participate in this universal information exchange. As you venture onward, into your deeper dimension, your inner light language can begin to illuminate hidden truths and invite you further into the boundless field of inner wisdom.

A Part of Me Knows Everything

*A new concept of the universe is emerging.... All that happens in
one place happens also in other places; all that happened at one time
happens also at all times after that. Nothing is "local," limited to where
and when it is happening. All things are global, indeed, cosmic, for all
things are connected, and the memory of all things extends to all places
and times. This is the concept of the in-formed universe, the view of the
world that will hallmark science and society in the coming decades.*

— Dr. Ervin László

The first key to understanding your intuitive connection with the
universe is recognizing that your individual consciousness is an
implicit part of the great consciousness that holds all cosmic information and transcends time and space. On a fundamental level,
you are not separate from anything. In the quantum universe, information — not objects or things — is our point of reference.
This new model of reality is redefining the relationship between
our minds and the world we live in; our potential is no longer
bound by the laws of material reality — it is expanded by the new
frontiers of quantum mechanics. There, in the invisible ethers of
the microcosm, a worldwide web of light-energy-information is
available to us through life's limitless intelligence system.

In your everyday life, you may appear to have access to limited information — to the objects, people, and situations that you
personally encounter — but, as you will discover in the chapters
ahead, this is an illusion of the thinking mind. A deeper part of
your mind has access to information beyond your local reality;
it knows what is happening in other places and even in other
times. It knows everything that is going on around you behind
the scenes — what your friends are doing when you are not with

them, how that new job is going to work out, whether it's going to rain tomorrow. The deeper part of you knows all of that and so much more.

When I was in my thirties, I realized that I had a super-power — one that you may have too: the ability to wake up before the alarm clock goes off. As time passed, I realized that not only could I intuitively wake up to avoid the weekday morning cacophony of a blaring alarm, but I could also wake up *anytime I needed to*. No matter what time I needed to get up the next morning, I would naturally wake up just when I was supposed to do. I had no idea how it worked, only that I always did. I built so much trust in this ability that I didn't even set an alarm for a 5 a.m. flight. It may not be the world's most interesting superpower, but I still use it every day — and I haven't set an alarm in nearly twenty years.

This was one of my early clues that a part of me knows everything. A part of me always knows what time it is and what is going on in my life. My inner timekeeper knows the difference between weekday and weekend; it knows holidays and when I can sleep in; it even knows when I need to check on a sick child in the middle of the night. It knows even when I consciously don't. If a part of me could know all those things, couldn't it also know so much more? Was there anything it couldn't know?

Living in an interconnected information-made universe, it's no wonder that we can access information beyond our local place and time. You are made of intelligence with the ability to know all other intelligences. Even when your thinking mind is distracted by other things, a part of you always knows what time it is; a part of you knows what you are looking for; a part of you knows what awaits on the path ahead. A part of you knows every little bit of information stored in the eternal universe.

A part of you knows everything.

When you let that sink in, many of life's mysteries begin to make more sense. For example, have you ever played with oracle card decks or tarot cards and wondered how they always give you the right message at the right time? How do you always manage to pick just the card that you need when you can't see what's on the other side of the cards? When you accept that a part of you knows everything, you realize that a part of you knows where every card in the deck is; it knows where the card you need is — and it intuitively guides you to pick it.

The whole of life functions in this way. If you ever had the thought to bring an umbrella to work on a sunny morning only to have it rain later that day, you can thank the part of you that knows everything. If you ever felt love at first sight for someone who brought good things into your life, the part of you that knows everything recognized them from the start. If you ever felt a nudge to take your car to the auto repair shop just before a dashboard alert came on, that was the part of you that knows everything looking out for you, as it always does.

All the little nudges, insights, and bright ideas that pop into your head out of nowhere are signals from your all-knowing dimension. These intuitive bits can be mundane, or they can be life changing. Sometimes you may notice them, and sometimes you may not. Sometimes you might listen to them, and sometimes you might disregard them as nonsense — and later regret it. The key is to recognize them — and act on them — more often. Cultivating a lifestyle of *insightfulness*, of living by the intelligence of your inner dimension, is the ultimate life hack for living extraordinarily.

EXPERIMENT: BOOK HACKING

Book hacking is a fun and insightful practice to tap into the part of you that knows everything. For centuries, people have been practicing bibliomancy, or Lectio Divina (divine reading), to hack into their inner guidance system using randomly selected passages in a book of wisdom or inspirational text. You may have done this already if you ever intuitively opened a book to any page for direction or guidance.

Here is how it works: Since the intuitive part of your mind has access to all the information in the universe — including the contents of every page in a book — when you randomly open to a page in a book, there is nothing random about it. Just like there is nothing random about choosing the right oracle card. Your deeper mind is choosing for you, informing your mind and body as it guides you to the perfect message for you at that moment in time.

To try it, simply pick out one of your favorite wisdom books — one that you go to for guidance and support. This could be a book of daily spiritual readings, an inspirational guide by your favorite author, a sacred text like the Bible, or, one of my favorites, the I Ching. Hold the book in your hands and set an intention for guidance in this moment; then, without thinking, let your intuition move you to open the book to any page. Notice the words that first catch your attention on the page, and begin reading there. How do these words apply, literally or metaphorically, to your life at the moment? Is there a hidden message in the text that is speaking to you on another level? Often, you are taken right to the information you need. That's the part of you that knows everything in action!

Whatever you do and wherever you go in life, you are in a constant state of interplay with this all-knowing part of your being. It's your secret best friend, always there for you, nudging you, inspiring you, pointing you toward the things that expand your mind and guide you through your inner dimension — the quantum realm that sustains your life from the deeper realms. Learning to recognize and process the codes of information that flow into you from the great cosmic intelligence is the first step on the journey toward true self-discovery and reunion with life.

> ## ILLUMINATION KEY #1
> *unlocks the gateway to your quantum dimension.*
>
> Once you accept that a part of your mind has access to all the information in the universe, a whole new world of knowledge opens to you. With this inner wisdom, you can know the unknowable and experience the impossible.

A wellspring of guiding intelligence awaits you at the new frontier of quantum consciousness. If you are ready to boldly go where few have gone before, this vast new horizon holds unimaginable wonders — and everything you are looking for. It holds the secrets of illumination, the meaning of life, and the first key to becoming the one you are destined to be.

When you live in the flow of this new unfolding of being, life aligns; you begin to live with ease, in unity with all that is. Everything changes when you start listening to the universal information broadcast that manifests as your inner voice and finally learn to speak its language.

Key #1 Activation: Reprogramming the Mind
A Part of You Knows More Than You Know

Let's begin our inner journey with a simple act of trust — a trust that life has been communicating with you all along and that, on another level of consciousness, you have always known it. Think back to a time in your life when you knew something, even though you had no rational explanation for knowing it; this has happened to us all one time or another. Here are some examples:

- You meet someone new, and, for some unknown reason, you have an aversion to them. This person might know all the right people, wear all the right clothes, or say all the right things, but a part of you is not comfortable with them at all, no matter how much you try to talk yourself into it. As time passes, you then learn that this person has some undesirable personality traits — and a part of you knew it from the start.
- You get a big job offer and you just know it's the right job for you. Even though this new job is scary and will require you to take some risks and make some changes, some part of you tells you to go for it. Despite your reluctance, and even some resistance from other people around you, you take the job — and it ends up starting a whole new exciting career path for you. A part of you knew that job would be just what you needed, even when you were unsure.
- You are deciding to make a new purchase — let's say you are buying a new car — and get a bad feeling about it. The salesman points out a car to you, and your immediate thought is *Nope*. But as he goes on to tell you all the great things about it, you talk yourself into it. You buy the car, only to have it break down a month later.

To build a greater awareness of the part of you that knows everything, *you first need to accept that it exists*. Only then can you begin to comprehend how deeply it is at work in your life. The next time you know something without explanation, you will know why. When those sudden insights or gut feelings show up, you will be more likely to honor them instead of ignoring them. This is how you begin to cultivate a dynamic with the all-knowing dimension of your consciousness. And the more curious you are and the more you venture into its unknown fields, the stronger it becomes.

Living by your intuition is a total mindset shift. It requires deprogramming a lot of information the outside world has fed you. Worldly data shows you your limitations — what is possible and impossible in a material world; but intuitive information, mined from the deep quantum dimension, shows you what is possible. A powerful mental shift occurs as you affirm that your mind is designed to access intelligence that exists beyond the grasp of your linear thinking mind. Your intuitive mind, what some call the "right-brained" mind, is the inner technology that grants you access to a worldwide inner net of boundless information. Here are some ways to start training your mind for the shift into limitless wisdom and possibility:

1. **Reminders:** Create daily reminders for an intuitive mindset. Remind yourself to trust the *part of you that knows everything.* You can post notes on your fridge or bathroom mirror or write it on your whiteboard — anywhere it might fend off any limiting thoughts of the mind. When you are tempted to doubt yourself, remember your limitless nature.

2. **Reprogramming:** To anchor the mind in its unlimited dimension, create a mantra that affirms this new way of thinking. It could simply be "A part of me knows everything." Repeat it to yourself in quiet moments, during meditation, before you fall asleep at night, or whenever you need validation. You can even use malas or prayer beads to program this truth into your mind until it becomes second nature.

3. **Reflection:** Create an uplifting piece of art or graphic, such as a poster, screensaver, or cellphone wallpaper, featuring your mantra or the words "A part of me knows everything." Place it somewhere that will inspire or

encourage you in moments of reflection, or gaze at it during meditation. You can download some art I created for you in the Illuminator's Kit at KimChestney.com /illuminationcode.

The next time you question the magic of your quantum dimension or any of its seemingly unexplainable manifestations, fall back on these reminders. *A part of you knows everything.* Trust it. Honor it. Follow it. Allow it to inform and complement your rational thinking mind. Together, using your whole mind — fusing the knowledge base of the microcosm and the macrocosm — you can find the truth that sets you free.

LAB #1
AWAKENING YOUR QUANTUM INTELLIGENCE

Learning from the Inside

It's time to start thinking with both sides of your brain. The duality within the hemispheres of your brain is not unlike the duality between quantum mechanics and the classical mechanics of physics. The left side of your brain, like Newtonian physics, processes the behaviors of macroscopic objects in physical reality — where the mind is linear, predictable, and measurable; the right side of your brain, like quantum physics, processes the behaviors of the subatomic realm of reality — where the mind is nonlinear, uncertain, and intuitive. Only when we embrace both natures within us can we fully grasp the wholeness of the world around us.

The quantum intelligence that is alive within you gives you access to a whole new way of thinking — a way to go beyond the limits of the left-brained mind. Forget your pros-and-cons lists, deductive reasoning, and formulas for problem-solving — the quantum mind has no use for them. Though your everyday mind needs time and effort to figure things out, your quantum mind functions at lightning speed — instantaneously delivering you the information at hand. Quantum information arrives from the microcosm in a flash of insight, sudden awareness, or intuitive epiphany — faster than your regular thinking mind could ever process information.

Your intuitive thoughts arrive faster than your regular thoughts because your consciousness instantly receives intrinsic intelligence before the logical mind has time to process it. This is why we have the saying *first impressions never lie* — because the part of you that knows everything instantly apprehends what your mind is trying to figure out. You have experienced this in action regularly throughout life, like when you might instantly feel an aversion to a stranger with ill intentions, or immediately know that job offer is the right one for you, or sense you shouldn't buy that lemon of a car right from the start. With quantum intelligence, you learn from the inside. Regardless of what information the world outside is sending you, truth always comes from within.

How to Start Learning from the Inside

Inside learning is the acquisition of knowledge from your inner, microcosmic database as opposed to information gathered from the macrocosmic world around you. When you give authority to your inner information source, you can live life with a deeper sense of clarity and meaning.

Step 1: Trust Your Inner Authority

Quantum intelligence offers a new order of thought: *intuition first, intellect second.* You receive the intuitive truth first, then use your analytic mind to process and apply that truth to your life.

We have been conditioned to skip the first step — to view the creative, imaginative world of intuition as somehow unreal, or at least unreliable. Knowing what we now know about the quantum universe, we have reason to confidently honor intuitively derived truths first, then let our thinking minds support that truth. From this day forward, make your inner authority your first authority. Set a conscious intention to honor your first impressions and those moments of insight that deliver information before you have a chance to rationalize it.

Step 2: Practice Thinking with Your Quantum Intelligence

Follow these instructions and use the framework in the workbook below to practice recognizing and working with information from your inner dimension:

- Grab your journal and a pen. (You can also download a printable 8.5″ × 11″ Illumination Workbook at Kim Chestney.com/illuminationcode.)
- Follow the prompts to encourage insightful information processing — one by one. Honor the first answer that comes into your mind, *no thinking necessary.* Just write down the first word, phrase, symbol, or idea that pops into your head for each prompt.
- Before you get started, be sure to settle into a quiet place where you won't be disrupted. Take a moment to clear your mind. Take several relaxing breaths.
- When you are relaxed, read the first prompt and write down the answer without thinking about it, right or wrong. A word or phrase might come to you instantly or after a short pause. Continue this process for each prompt until you are finished.

Lab #1 Workbook: Flashes of Insight
Recognizing the Truth That Arrives before You Can Think

Inner Learning Practice #1: Sudden Insight

Write down in your journal or workbook the first thought that arrives in your mind for each prompt below:

1. What is the most important challenge in my life right now?
2. What is my best quality?
3. What is my purpose?
4. What is my greatest accomplishment?
5. What is needed for me to grow and evolve?

After you have completed all five prompts, look back over them. Did the answers come quickly and easily? Do any of them surprise you? Do they point to any potentially deeper insights? Take a moment to reflect on your responses. This activity creates an opportunity to be totally honest with yourself. Sudden insights often point to truths that touch something deeper within you — and you may not always agree with your responses at first. Ask yourself why these answers came today. The part of you that knows everything is likely pointing you toward a greater awareness. This exercise helps get your critical mind out of the way and explore the truth behind conditioned thought patterns.

Note: When you are getting started, you may notice nonsense thoughts — impressions that make no sense or are silly or strange. Simply disregard them and carry on. This is just your thinking mind creating resistance to the process. Real insights will resonate with you in a meaningful way and continue to abide as you tune into them.

Inner Learning Practice #2: Insight for Your Life

The above exercise was just a warm-up. Let's try it with your own questions — with prompts that can guide or inform you in this moment. You can use any kind of simple questions, including the following:

- How can I solve the problem of _____?
- What is the truth about _____ situation?
- How can I improve my relationship with _____?
- How can I grow my business?

Use the same process as before, but this time write down a list of five personal questions about your life right now. Don't worry about the answers. Just release any attachment, and let the universe deliver you its guiding code. The code can show up as direct answers, phrases, symbols, pictures, feelings, or any other impressions that instantly flash into your consciousness.

This time, take a little more time with your answers after the initial impression drops in. Open space for more information to flow in and give you clarity. Write down any secondary insights that come to mind — any additional thoughts, feelings, or messages of guidance. Continue to journal for each answer for as long as you need to find clarity for your answer, using the following format:

Question: _____

_____

Insight: _____

_____

Here are some examples of questions you can ask yourself and insights you might get in response:

Question: Where should I travel to this year?

Insight: A palm tree popped into my head, then sunny skies and waves lapping on the beach. I felt a sense of joy as I beheld sweeping views of an ocean. I was debating between the mountains or the ocean, but now the ocean feels right.

Question: What is my purpose in life?

Insight: The phrase "use your gifts" just came to me, then the thought to help other people with my talents came rushing in. As I continued to journal, I received words of encouragement like "You can do this" and "Don't be afraid." To me, this feels like a validation of my plans to change careers.

Once you are finished, take a moment to process any interesting insights. How did your intuitive impressions unfold? Did they show you a picture? Or tell you a story? Did they offer you empowering guidance? Even if you don't like the answers you received, push through the discomfort. Is there a deeper message about yourself your intuition is pointing you to? As you reflect on your various answers, notice how the information you received makes you feel. Does it resonate more deeply as you get closer to understanding? Was there an aha moment when the meaning clicked? When you get to the truth, you will know it because *it feels right.*

The practices in this lab teach you how to receive bits of intuitive code and unpack their deeper meaning. With time, you will learn to easily recognize the flashes of insight that drop in before you can think, and know the truth by the way it feels. Through this process, you can mine deep wisdom from the inside. You can take it beyond this exercise and live by it every day. Trust your first impressions. Think with intuition first. Then, all the world will fall into its right place.

CONCLUSION

Activating Key #1 of the illumination code awakens
the part of yourself that knows everything.

The first key unlocks your quantum dimension with the realization that you have intrinsic access to a universal database — one that includes personal, guiding information for your life.

Key Principles

- All the world is made of information.
- All the information of the world is embedded in light and energy.
- You have access to all that information through your power of insight — also known as inner learning, intuition, or quantum intelligence.
- That information is delivered to you at lightning speed when your critical mind doesn't interfere with it.
- You can intentionally access the universal database of information-light-energy to gain awareness and inform your life.

Key Applications

- Start your Illumination Workbook or record your findings in this book.
- Look for insightful first impressions and flashes of insight that are the hallmark of your quantum intelligence.

When you accept that a part of you knows everything, you stand at the threshold of the deeper dimension. Next, let's learn more about how your inner reality works and ways to expand the information-receiving bandwidth of your quantum intelligence.

CHAPTER TWO

The Field of Intrinsic Awareness

*Nonlocality…is an expression of an underlying and outflowing
information-filled field which connects and inextricably links
every part of the universe with every other part in no time.…
[It] could be the most profound discovery in all of science.*

— PAUL LEVY, THE QUANTUM REVELATION

If there is one idea that makes sense of the universe's great mysteries, it is this: there is an invisible field that connects everything in the world to everything else, linking every bit of information in the universe with every other bit of information. For millennia, mystics have been seeking it, and scientists have been theorizing about it. Finally, science is offering empirical evidence that it truly does exist. This discovery is the missing link between the universe and your mind — the seen and unseen realities, the physical and metaphysical worlds. It unites the disparate forces of the universe and brings all life together in shared interconnection. Today, scientists call it the *nonlocal field*.

The term *nonlocal field* is used in both physics and spirituality to describe a theoretical field of energy and consciousness that exists beyond the boundaries of space and time. It is the universal consciousness that connects all things — the reason a part of you can know everything. This energy-information field invisibly surrounds us and penetrates all aspects of reality inside and out. This medium holds all of creation, coalescing outer space and inner space, connecting all intelligence, and uniting all things big and small no matter how far apart they are in time or space. The non-local field is the great information highway of the universe, flowing within and all around you at all times.

Imagine that the whole world is interconnected and that there is no real distance between anything. Imagine that, like a worldwide web of consciousness, our individual minds are linked — accessible and touchable to each other in an instant from any place in the world. Imagine the potential of living in ever-present connection with all kinds of quantum information stored in the universe itself. You can do more than imagine this ever-present information-filled field; you can intentionally and meaningfully interact with it. This nonlocal, universal databank is the missing piece of life's puzzle that we have always been searching for. And we no longer have to question *whether* it exists, only *how* we can access it.

The addition of a quantum-based interpenetrating field to our understanding of reality makes much of the unexplainable explainable. Supernatural phenomena and intuitive abilities — like telepathy, remote viewing, precognition, and telekinesis — finally have a rational explanation as a manifestation of the nonlocal information exchange. This field brings the magic of the quantum universe to each and every one of us personally. It can touch us because it is part of us. When we learn to intentionally access the nonlocal connection within and between us all, we open the gates to a whole new dimension of the human mind.

The Missing Link between Mysticism and Science

It is often said that mystics experience what scientists later prove. Since the dawn of civilization, ancient religions have pointed us to an invisible dimension of reality — a fundamental, interconnecting essence of the material world, which the Hindu religion called *akasha*. Similarly, Buddhist traditions teach the idea of Indra's net — a metaphor created to explain the interconnectedness of all things — by describing the world as a vast net, or web, that stretches to infinity and contains everything that exists, will exist, or has ever existed. Even in Christianity, the concept of God is associated with a universal consciousness that connects all beings, with the Holy Spirit being a manifestation of the nonlocal field.

The emergence of a unifying nonlocal field revolutionizes the relationship between physics and metaphysics. For centuries, mystics have been seeking the oneness of all creation; the nonlocal field gives us that. For over a hundred years, scientists have long been looking for a unified field — the mysterious ether that fills all voids and makes sense of the world's apparent disconnectedness. The nonlocal field also gives us that. These once disparate worlds are coming together like never before. With each discovery of the magic-like qualities of the quantum universe, the line between the scientist and the mystic blurs even more.

For centuries, mystics have been ahead of their time. They experienced the nonlocal field long before science could conceive of it. Hindu philosopher Swami Vivekananda explained that the whole world is made up of only two materials: akasha (information), or the material of motionless, "omnipresent, all-penetrating existence," and akasha's physical form, prana (energy), or the vital force and manifesting power of the universe. In the late 1800s, the Theosophists popularized the concept of the *akashic records* — a library and filing system of all manifest thoughts, deeds, and events of all time. Carl Jung created a model of the unified, all-knowing inner dimension called the "collective unconsciousness" or universal mind. Even popular psychics, like Edgar Cayce, the "sleeping prophet," gave evidence of this nonlocal reality with extraordinary abilities, such as being able to access hidden information about people's lives and the future.

Many scientists throughout history conducted their own investigations in the nonlocal field. Thousands of years ago, the Greeks introduced the idea of *aether* or *ether* — the invisible substance that fills the heavens. Plato called this "the most translucent" fifth element. Since medieval times, ether has been used to describe the invisible material that fills and permeates all space. Then, in the late nineteenth century, physicists took it one step further, conjecturing that ether gave light the ability to travel through the vacuum of space. They were certainly on to something. Nikola Tesla, too, was fascinated by the potential of ether as an energy source, calling it the universe's "original medium" — similar to the light-carrying akasha, a kind of force field that becomes matter when cosmic energy acts on it. French physicist Olivier Costa de Beauregard even went so far as to say that "today's physics allows for the existence of so-called 'paranormal' phenomena of telepathy, precognition, and psychokinesis.... The whole concept of 'nonlocality' in contemporary physics requires this possibility." The word *metaphysics* simply means "beyond physics" — and the concept of nonlocality is not beyond physics anymore.

Before the discovery of quantum physics, indications of a nonlocal field were there, even if we didn't yet have the scientific sophistication to prove it. Along with our own intuition, the historic canon of spiritual and religious experiences tipped us off to its existence as the medium that facilitated great prophecies, holy visions, and miracles of all kinds. The supernatural world begged for a scientific explanation that only nonlocality could give. But it wasn't until the quantum revolution that God, truth, and the oneness of the universe had a bonified role in scientific theory — a role that begins with the understanding of a zero-point field.

 The nonlocal field is the universal consciousness that creates, connects, and informs all things.

The invisible field that surrounds us has many names, such as the unified field, the akashic field, and the zero-point field. The latter term stems from the fact that this realm is the ground state of the universe, the lowest energy state, the cosmic womb. It is nonlocal — everywhere, at all times. It exists all around us and within us in a state of pure potential, a coherent sea of vibrational oneness. The field contains the source code of all creation. It is the silence out of which all things emerge.

Dr. Ervin László is one of the world's foremost researchers into this groundbreaking field, introducing a new understanding of a spiritual science:

> Mystics and sages have long maintained that there exists an interconnecting cosmic field at the roots of reality that conserves and conveys information.... Recent discoveries in vacuum physics show that this Akashic field is real and has its equivalent in science's zero-point field that underlies space itself. This field consists of a subtle sea of fluctuating energies from which all things arise: atoms and galaxies, stars and planets, living beings, and even consciousness. This zero-point [field] is the constant and enduring memory of the universe. It holds the record of all that has happened on Earth and in the cosmos and relates it to all that is yet to happen.

The Nonlocal Universe

Nonlocality is one of the most revolutionary concepts in the way we understand the world. In a nonlocal universe, you have an implicit connection with the whole world and all the information it holds. You don't have to go anywhere or do anything to find it — it's already a part of you. The field isn't out there somewhere; it is within you everywhere. It is embedded in you, and you are embedded in it. You and the field are part of an inextricable union, continually exchanging energy and information.

"Science calls it the unified field, but mystics throughout the ages have called it the mind of God, divine intelligence, the spirit of nature, the life principle, the kingdom of heaven, Universal Mind, the Great Spirit, the Creator, Allah, Brahma, the All, or the Father," wrote Simone Wright in her book *First Intelligence*. "More contemporary names for the field are superconsciousness, source, the divine matrix, the universal grid, and the force. The names are as varied as the languages, cultures, and belief systems that identified them, but all are alike in describing a singular powerful ground in which we all 'live, breathe and have our being.'"

This cosmic field is part of your very essence. It is a dimension of who you are. You can think of it as your higher self — the all-knowing facet of your consciousness. It is your field of intrinsic awareness, a boundless cloud of knowledge, wisdom, and information that you have implicit access to through the law of insight. You can even think of it as your God-self — your Self with a capital S — what we call divine, sacred, or the truth, the latter of which is fitting because, as the source of all information, it is truth by nature. Nothing in the field is hidden from the part of us that knows everything.

VARIOUS NAMES FOR YOUR FIELD OF INTRINSIC AWARENESS

Nonlocal field	Akashic field
Inner field	Cosmic void
Superconsciousness	Higher self
Zero-point field	Omnipresence
Quantum vacuum	Ground state
Universal consciousness	The force

Much of the field, however, seems very hidden from the part of us that *does not* know everything — our everyday thinking mind. You can't think your way into this field of inner wisdom; you just need to open up and receive from it. This kind of truth isn't learned, it is revealed. It simply *is*, and you must become aware of it. You don't have to find it; it just comes to you. Information is taught; insight is caught. The code of information from the universal field is naturally picked up by your inner receiver through your innate processes of insight.

 Universal intelligence is inner access only.

Your intuitive mind is designed to explore the immaterial world deep inside you; your intelligent mind is made to explore the material world and all its workings outside you. These two complementary faculties give you full access to the universe, inside and out — relatively speaking, that is. In reality, there is no real inside or outside world; there is only our relative perception amid a wholly unified existence. From the point of view of a human being, the physical world appears to be outside us and the metaphysical world inside us; one is macrocosmic, and one is microcosmic. But this duality is an illusion of our subjective point of consciousness, when, in fact, it is all part of the same unified system. In the nonlocal field, there is no duality — only oneness.

The collective, interconnected inner world is subtly influencing the seemingly disconnected world around you; if you pay close attention, you can see it all around you. I noticed it early in my life when I was working retail at a record store. Day after day, I watched the ebb and flow of the shoppers' traffic patterns — periods when the store was quiet, followed by big rushes at the register all at once. I wondered what was causing this phenomenon; it was like everyone was acting together, even though they were total strangers, not communicating verbally at all. I had no way of knowing then that every person in the store was locally entangled with the collective energy of the whole group of shoppers; once one person was ready to go, anyone else who was nearly ready to go felt an inner nudge to be done as well.

Do you remember a time when you were shopping at a store, and nobody was in line to check out — until you got there? Then, of course, everyone in the store miraculously showed up at the same time! That's the power of the field at work.

EXPERIMENT: FLOWING WITH THE FIELD

Next time you are at a store or restaurant, try paying attention to the traffic flows as groups of people arrive and leave in waves. When you are shopping, be cognizant of any prompts from your inner codes, nudging you that it's time to leave; if this happens, pay attention to what others are doing. Are other people beginning to line up to check out? Or did you beat the rush? Are you in flow or out of it?

Here's a fun way to play with the field:

- On days when you are in the flow — those good shopping days when you find all the things you are looking for or are just having a good time — see if you naturally beat the rush. When you are in a state of ease and alignment, your inner receiver is more open to the field's guiding inner codes, and they may give you a heads-up so you don't have to waste time or be late due to pesky lines.

   Remember, these codes intrinsically plug into your consciousness, so they feel like your own thoughts. Don't expect to hear a booming voice telling you it's time to check out; the idea to check out just comes to you like any other thought. This gentle nudge is easy to miss if you aren't looking for it.

- On days when you aren't in the flow — when you are in a rush, feel frustrated, or can't find what you are looking for — the noise of mental friction can interfere with the reception of your guiding codes, and you may find yourself at the back of a long line.

Of course, both dynamics are a natural part of life. Some days are front-of-the-line days; some aren't. Either way, this can be a fun way to witness your inner field at work.

The evolution of modern-day physics has led us to a powerful realization: there is a vast network or matrix of energetic connections between the infinitude of interrelated particles, which exists as an indivisible embodiment of an ever-present universal consciousness. This means that, on some level, you are energetically connected with the consciousness of all things in the universe — all is one and one is all. Furthermore, you are energetically connected to all *the information* of the universe — every creation, every event, every place, and every action that ever was, is, or will be.

Though your local, physical reality is your home base, it is interpenetrated by the nonlocal energetic reality that, like a great cosmic ocean, contains you and everything else, whether you realize it or not. With time and attention, you can begin to expand your awareness into deeper participation with the nonlocal quantum reality. It starts with little things, like waking up before your alarm, getting in line to check out at the store before everyone else, or finding an empty parking spot in a busy lot. As your awareness of the quantum reality expands, so will the extraordinary nature of so-called supernatural experiences.

All of creation is infused with various states of conscious energy — rocks, trees, animals, and human beings alike are built of tiny sparks of consciousness. Every particle that is born out of the quantum vacuum, womb of creation, zero-point field of cosmic awareness — whichever you want to call it — is alive it its own right. We are all made out of points of light in the boundless universal mind that creates and knows all things. The ideas, epiphanies, solutions, and knowingness that so often fall into our minds out of nowhere are a byproduct of our connection to that omnipresent inner field. Our glorious universe isn't just connected by fields of energy or information — it is connected by thought.

Reconnecting with Your Inner Space

If we live in an ever-present field of information that flows all around us, why are we not more aware of it? Why don't we simply know everything all the time? The answer is simple: you can't receive information from the field when your mind is in a state of disconnection from it. How can we intentionally connect to something if we don't recognize that it exists? Our fixation with the material world drowns our inner signal; our intuitive wifi goes down. We focus on this world so much that we forget about the other side of reality. We can easily get lost in the illusory self we call *me*. The more we live in the *me*, the less we live in the *we* — the collective connectivity with the unified field.

This disconnect not only impairs our intuitive ability but also fuels the human existential crisis, often making us feel separate and alone. Despite unprecedented amounts of technological interconnectivity, we still feel disconnected inside. Never before in history has humanity wrestled with a crisis of mental health as we do today — with feelings of anxiety, depression, fear, sadness, loss, loneliness, and confusion on the rise. Recent studies show that 58 percent of Americans suffer from loneliness. Why is it possible to feel so isolated while living amid an intrinsically connected universe? Because we have lost our inner connection. In many aspects of our lives, and especially over social media, we spend more time trying to *appear* connected than actually doing things to genuinely reconnect. We build lives that look good from the outside instead of ones that feel good on the inside.

The more energy we put out there — posting for followers and likes or trying to make it in the world — the less energy we have for our inner reserve. The chasm between the outer and the inner grows, as does our feeling of separation. This belief that we are separated — from each other, from life, from our true being, from the inner unifying field — is the source of our pain, suffering, and, most of all, aloneness. The world outside you is imbued with an illusion of separateness that can cause great despair if not counterbalanced with the inner union of life itself. In truth, you are never alone. And you are never truly separated from those you love. When you embrace the aliveness of being that flows from your inner dimension, all the dark and empty spaces start to fill with light.

 The source of suffering is the illusion of separation from your inner dimension.

Though the field is an integral part of who we are, if we aren't tuned into the intuitive and creative spaciousness of our inner reality, we can feel blocked — shut off from our deep power. Day after day, the din of overthinking drowns out our ability to listen to how life is speaking to us. "The compulsive thinker, which means almost everyone, lives in a state of separateness," Eckhart Tolle explained in *The Power of Now*, "in an insanely complex world of continuous problems and conflicts, a world that reflects an ever-increasing fragmentation of the mind. Enlightenment is a state of wholeness, being 'at one,' and therefore at peace." This wholeness — the inner peace and oneness — is the hallmark of the zero-point quantum dimension.

The expanse of your inner field embodies the sacred stillness of being. You can find it in the silence — in the spaciousness beyond thought. Only while in the quiet is your mind fully open to receiving the universe's guiding codes. This gentle, nurturing inner wisdom calls for you to stop what you are doing or thinking and just listen. Be still and listen. Let the cosmic intelligence pour into you. When this happens, you *feel* it. You know it. It changes you — lifts you up, heals you, reassures you, offers you a path forward. The field fills your heart and mind with its eternal flow energy and awareness.

Spaciousness is the secret to crossing the inner threshold. The more stillness you create in your life — the more space you make between all the things you do and think and say — the more openings you create to merge with your quantum dimension. When you create spaciousness, you shift out of the thinking mind and into the nonthinking and insightful mind. In the quiet moments, you enter the dimension where the stillness speaks. The information held there — the guidance, inspiration, ideas, and wisdom — touches you personally and guides you to fulfill your highest potential.

PRACTICE: DO NOTHING LIKE IT'S YOUR JOB

We have a responsibility to our daily tasks, but we often forget our responsibility to our self. Creating spaciousness in your life is not just a self-care luxury — it is a necessary part of your life balance. When you open space for intuition, insight, creativity, ideation, and imagination, you can think with your whole mind. From this state, you do everything better. You think more clearly; you relate to others with empathy; you work smarter and with a sense of vision. When was the last time you had a great idea while you were checking emails or working diligently at your desk? That's not where the ideas flow. The magic arrives in moments of spaciousness, when you are aimless or relaxed into the flow of life.

To fully immerse yourself in the flow of your inner field, the most important step you can take is the act of making space for its information to download. The simple practice below will help you open up your bandwidth and get you into the insight zone, where nonlocal information can flow openly and freely into your local consciousness.

Step 1: Slow Down

Set your intention to open space for your intuition. Remember that the heavy energies of stress, overwork, illness, and busyness create vibrational barriers to the subtle energies of the inner field, so make a conscious effort to create more empty space on your calendar and spend time alone with yourself. Your simple, quiet moments are the sacred space where extraordinary insight can arise.

Step 2: Spend More Time with Yourself

Add more "white space" to your daily calendar. Whatever you do alone, do more of it: walking, running, practicing yoga or qigong, meditating, dancing, or just being still in the moment. Any activity that gives you uninterrupted, mindless time with yourself serves as a gateway for quantum insight to pour through. The more spaciousness you create, the closer you become with yourself.

Step 3: Let Your Intuition Flow

Notice the thoughts and feelings that pour in from your inner space. Pay attention to any ideas, reminders, or creative energy that comes to you during aimless activities. Time in the white space opens up your mind for intuitive information to guide you and inspire you. Honor the inner impressions that arrive from the sacred nowhere void. Trust any truth your intuition drops.

The simple act of creating space opens your inner connection and gets you into the flow of intelligence from the quantum field.

The stillness, and the inflow of energy that pours out of it, is the harbinger of reconnection. It can be an awakening, a homecoming, a rapture of the spirit. In connection, you feel whole again and more alive than ever. With your inner wisdom, you can see clearly that which has eluded you for so long. Living in a state of union with your inner field, your heart overflows, and your mind is at peace. The saints, gurus, and wise ones throughout history have told us about this state of illumination and enlightenment. The reunion with the all-knowing part of yourself can be the most important experience of your life.

Paramahansa Yogananda, the Hindu and Christian spiritual teacher whose work brought together science and spirituality, taught that the recognition of your true, whole being is found in intuitive *self-realization* and that the quantum intelligence of your intuition is nothing less than "the soul's power of knowing God." If ever there were a medium for the divine wisdom or the love between us, the field would be it. What else could carry the energy (love) and the information (truth) of the highest of high? What else could unite us with the loving presence of all being? As the New Testament said, "The kingdom of God is within you."

The idea that enlightenment is the return to a state of intrinsic oneness pervades the great writings, theology, and teachings of history, regardless of any particular faith or religion. This includes a most sacred role for intuition as a means of revelation, prophecy, and inner guidance. As Richard Rohr wrote in his book *The Universal Christ,* "Do you then also see the lovely significance of John's statement 'It is not because you do not know the truth that I write to you, but because you know it already' (1 John 1:21)? He is talking about an *implanted knowing* in each of us.... The prophet Jeremiah called it 'the law written in your heart' (31:33), others call it the 'Indwelling Holy Spirit.'"

Your field of intrinsic awareness is a network of quantum information and energy that is available to you at all times in all places. You enter into it through the present moment, and you navigate it with your faculty of intuition. Whatever name you call it — the nonlocal field, the zero-point field, or the field of universal consciousness — this field of intrinsic awareness holds the keys to a new, unified way of life. When you make the intentional shift to live by its guiding forces, what was once separate becomes whole. The make-believe wall between you and the rest of the world comes tumbling down.

ILLUMINATION KEY #2

TRUTH IS WITHIN ME

I take refuge in the seminal point which is the union of expanse and awareness...of radiance and emptiness...the indestructible chain of inner radiance that is intrinsic awareness.

— THE TIBETAN BOOK OF THE DEAD

The implications of nonlocality are revolutionary, but they are not wholly unfamiliar to us. You might be thinking, *So we are invisibly* connected with everyone all over the world? We can communicate with them no matter where they go? And it all happens instantaneously, in no time at all? Yes, these are all attributes of a field-connected reality; but they are also attributes of modern-day technology. The internet and your cellphone are streaming all kinds of information. We are no longer shocked at the ability to pick up the phone and have a real-time conversation with a friend who is on the other side of the planet. A global, electronic infrastructure is part of our reality now. Why should it surprise us to think that we have a similar quantum infrastructure within our microcosmic reality?

Our modern-day internet does not sound all that different from the centuries-old idea of Indra's net — the worldwide web of consciousness. The main difference between the two is that the internet uses computer technology, while Indra's net uses the technology of the human mind. With the internet, we share information through fiber-optic cables (which transmit light!) and wifi signals; with the nonlocal field, we upload and download information through the quantum information highway of illuminating codes. Just like you are connected to all the information on the internet through your phone or computer, you are connected to all the information in the universe through your consciousness.

As Wright explained in *First Intelligence,*

> All these principles of intelligence can be revealed mathematically and are regularly used in the fields of electronics, telecommunication, aerospace, and laser technology.... They allow us to speak to someone else on the other side of the planet and watch our favorite television show on our computer or cell phone. All the foundational elements found in this ocean of potential, which support these physical technologies, are not beyond the range of human awareness and perception. In fact, reality is as Einstein imagined: a universal ocean of possibility existing as a

timeless and endless field of intelligence available to every human being in the simplest state of human awareness.

ILLUMINATION KEY #2
reconnects your inner information highway.

Once you plug back into the quantum data stream held within your inner field, you can begin to consciously download all kinds of local and nonlocal information.

On an intuitive level, you have intrinsic access to data about everything that is happening in the world — past, present, and future. You live in a reality where it is now scientifically viable for you to gain awareness of information beyond your local position in both time and space, including awareness of happenings both in faraway places and in the future and the past. However, accessing nonlocal information is not as easy as typing into your browser's search bar. We are still developing our interface. As we continue to evolve and expand our consciousness into alignment with the field, its information will naturally become more accessible and abundant. Nonlocal information is built of codes that can be read by only your intuitive mind. To decipher these codes, we must learn its laws and its language.

Key #2 Activation: Making the Quantum Connection
Three Ways to Expand the Portal to Your Inner Dimension

The first step in accessing the inner knowledge field is to open your mind to its broadcast of quantum information. Every day, many transmissions are sent, yet few are received. We are constantly informed by the illuminating codes of subatomic reality, but until we train our mind with conscious attention, we can easily miss them. An insightful mindset is maintained by creating a habit of listening and a practice of open-mindedness.

Your conscious mind is a portal for superconscious information. For many people living in modern times, this portal is small — like a pinhole where isolated blips of data drip through from time to time. Our first task is to expand that portal so the code packets from our quantum intelligence can flow abundantly through it. Three factors are necessary for this to happen: receptivity, spaciousness, and awareness of your intuition:

1. **Receive more, share less.** Our culture has become addicted to sharing. When we experience something wonderful, we often feel a compulsion to share it before we even fully receive it — like the compulsion to share a photo of a sunset instead of watching it. When a magical moment arrives, practice receiving it as though it is just for you. When someone speaks, practice listening instead of thinking what you can share next. Set an intention that, at least for now, receiving is more important than sharing. This mindset shift opens up space for the magic to pour in.

2. **Soak up the space in the present.** Start a practice of fully receiving each moment. Immerse yourself in the beauty around you. Breathe in the natural splendor. Bathe in the silence. Absorb the life-giving energy that flows around and within you. Drawing in the vibrations of presence energizes the space where insight spontaneously arises.

3. **Look for insights that show up out of nowhere.** In the receptive, spacious state, your mind is fertile for inspirational guidance, epiphanies, and revelations. From the creative womb of silence, new ideas are born. Be alert

for those thoughts, feelings, and ideas that pop into your mind, seemingly from nowhere.

Living in a state of openness, presence, and attention to your intuitive impressions will help you cultivate a lifestyle of insightfulness and set you up to live by its guiding wisdom every day.

LAB #2
CATCHING THE CODE

The Information That Arrives from Nowhere

People are often surprised to learn that intuition follows a set of laws and has an implicit order. We are collectively so unfamiliar with processing insight that it feels like a miracle any time it happens. Until you get to know your intuition, it can feel unpredictable, random, and uncontrollable. But it's not. In truth, the field follows the natural laws of the quantum dimension that make interactions with it learnable, reliable, and repeatable.

Quantum intelligence manifests as *implanted knowledge*. It arises from the deep dimension of your nonlocal field, with no observable source in your deductive mind or the world around you. This information simply arrives out of nowhere. And since you are just beginning to learn its language, it will most likely arrive in small bits and bytes.

 A defining trait of quantum intelligence is that it arises from nowhere. It effortlessly arrives in your consciousness without any thinking process or outside stimulus.

Throughout history, we have given a label to people who are extraordinarily adept with their quantum intelligence: genius.

With this ability, Albert Einstein solved the world's hardest mathematical problems in a moment of epiphany, Steve Jobs came up with innovative technological ideas that changed the entire world, and the maverick scientist Nikola Tesla invented revolutionary feats of engineering. True genius is the result of opening the mind to the vast information flow of nonlocal consciousness. And you don't need to be anybody special to do it — you just need to learn how to start catching bits of its code.

Bits of information pop into your mind from the quantum field on a regular basis. Out of the blue, you might get the idea to call your mother only to find out that she was getting ready to call you. Or while you are taking a shower one day, a work solution might pop into your head. You might even think about a song, then hear it on the radio later that day. To get better at recognizing these quantum drop-ins, start paying attention to any thoughts that just *come to mind*. They can be new ideas, guiding thoughts, solutions to a problem, higher awareness, or any kind of information that can support you in that moment.

When a bit of quantum information drops into your mind, it feels like an instant download, as if your conscious mind catches a thought right out of the ethers. Processing quantum bits of intelligence involves two primary steps:

1. Recognizing the information
2. Connecting the information with meaning in your life

I created the framework below (also found in the Illuminator's Kit) to help you record and practice intuitive information processing. This process will not only help you understand what your downloads feel like but also help you build trust in the information they impart.

Here's how to get started with the second lab:

Step 1: To prepare, be sure you are practicing the activation steps from Key #2 regularly to cultivate a receptive headspace. Remember that a mind busy from stress, overwhelm, and overwork creates static that blocks the portal to your intuitive mind. Starting a relaxation or meditation routine can also be helpful.

Step 2: Take note of any insights you catch throughout the day — any thought, idea, or feeling that comes up without thinking. Keep your workbook nearby, or set up a notes file on your phone to record anything that downloads throughout the day. Some days you may have two or three drop-ins; other days you may have none. This is a normal part of your flow with the field; some days your mind is more in the insight zone than others.

Step 3: Every so often, reflect back on how these downloads connected to your life. Did you receive a helpful bit of guidance about something in particular? Were you moved to do something important? Did it lead you to any fun synchronicities? Try to find the meaningful application of your downloads. Sometimes just witnessing a coincidence or moment of serendipity is meaningful in itself.

Lab #2 Workbook: Instant Downloads
Recording Bits and Bytes from the Nonlocal Field

Record and apply the bits of information that you spontaneously receive from the field in your journal using the following framework. You can also find this table in your Illumination Workbook.

Date	Download (Dropped-in bits and bytes)	Meaningful Connection/ Validation (Evidence of the field)

Here are some examples:

Date	Download *(Dropped-in bits and bytes)*	Meaningful Connection/ Validation *(Evidence of the field)*
3/3	Had the idea to wear a shirt my grandmother gave me	Later I realized it was her birthday
3/4	Woke up with a song in my head	I heard it on the radio later that day
3/7	I thought I should call Dad	A couple minutes later, he called me
3/12	Was inspired to look up an old friend on Facebook but couldn't find them	A few days later they sent me a friend request
3/20	I had the thought that we should order pizza for dinner tonight	A moment later, my partner suggested we pick up a pizza on the way home from work

You can continue this activity for as long as you like. Often, it may take weeks or even months for the connections to become clear. Sometimes, too, you recognize the links in retrospect; you might not realize you had an intuitive hit until validation shows up. Be sure to record all your hits, no matter how they come about. This activity is the beginning of a personal evidence log that helps you to build trust in your intuitive process. Eventually, as you recognize how deeply intuition is interwoven into your daily life, there will be no way to doubt its existence or deny its helpful influence on your life.

CONCLUSION

Activating Key #2 of the illumination code opens a conscious line of communication with the nonlocal field.

The second key widens the portal of your mind so you can start intentionally receiving quantum insight from the boundless information highway of the universe.

Key Principles

- All the world is united by an ever-present, nonlocal, zero-point field.
- This field is the ground state of the universe, the source of all energy and information.
- Only your intuitive mind can read the illuminating codes from the field.
- The illusion of dislocation from this unifying field is the source of human suffering.
- A defining quality of quantum information is that it arrives out of nowhere; it is not manufactured by actively processing information or any outside stimulus.

Key Applications

- Observe the dynamics of the field when you are in stores or with groups of people.
- Practice doing nothing like it's your job.
- Record your daily insights and look for their meaning in your life.

When you catch and apply the codes of your quantum intelligence, you signal the universe that you are ready to engage on a deeper level. By acknowledging and working with your intuitive dimension, you activate a conscious connection with it. The intuitive hits that you are witnessing and recording are more than part of a simple validation exercise; they are the beginning of a beautiful relationship with the part of you that knows everything.

CHAPTER THREE

Metareality

Everything we call real is made of things that cannot be regarded as real. If quantum mechanics hasn't profoundly shocked you, you haven't understood it yet.

— NIELS BOHR

You and I aren't living in a material world. Despite appearances, the objects you see all around you — walls, chairs, and even living beings — are something quite different from what we once thought. Real, solid objects aren't so real or solid after all, and the universal laws that govern the reality those objects fill are far more interesting than anyone could have anticipated before the quantum revolution. The notion that we are physical beings populating a world of disconnected, lifeless matter no longer fits with our contemporary view of reality. You have may have personally witnessed evidence of this if you have ever experienced something that defies the known laws of physics. Maybe you or someone you know had a spiritual vision, a premonition, or even a meaningful coincidence. Every day, life gives us signs that the material world is part of something that goes beyond our understanding.

I received my first clues about this mystery while growing up in a haunted house. My young reality was full of bumps in the night, voices from nowhere, invisible childhood friends, musical instruments and toys that played themselves, and objects that moved around on their own. One night, every door in the house suddenly slammed shut, all on their own, in front of my whole family, like a scene right out of a Hollywood movie. Though it was scary at the time, in retrospect, those supernatural events did more than just frighten us — they gave us information about the true nature of reality and showed us that something deeper is at work beyond the material world. Regularly witnessing these "impossible" happenings made them undeniable. It instilled within me an unshakable curiosity to get to the bottom of their mysteries.

If you talk to enough people, you will hear all kinds of remarkable stories of things happening in the world that should not be able to happen. Though popular culture has made an art of capitalizing on our fears of the unseen dimensions, when you look at these occurrences as a function of the nonlocal field, they become a little less impossible and a little less scary. My paranormal experiences were always more startling than scary. They surprised and confused me. What made me most afraid was that I didn't understand what was happening. With time, it became clear that we need quantum physics to help us fully understand the supernatural.

The adoption of field-based thinking — an interconnected worldview where consciousness is interpenetrated with matter — offers a rational understanding of supernatural phenomena. In cases like my door-slamming house, we can't deny that something happened: multiple people witnessed it. It was not a mass hallucination. Something acted upon those doors to put them into motion — that's one thing we can all agree upon. Traditional scientific perspectives would tell us that a separate object or force would be necessary to move a material object, such as a human hand or the wind. But when we understand the door not as a separate piece of matter but instead as a coherent bundle of information existing in an ocean of invisible energy and manifested as material particles, an unseen catalyst is not so far-fetched. All evidence points to the fact that the atomic world of stuff and things is quite capable of being affected by subatomic dynamics. We go deeper into this concept in chapter 6.

To make sense of the interactions between the physical and metaphysical world, we need to be bold and look at the world in a whole new way. The material world is implicitly connected to the immaterial world, and the duality we perceive is an illusion. Supernatural phenomena are evidence that we don't have our world figured out yet. Until we understand these mysteries, we are missing something. Luckily, science is moving us closer to this understanding in its new, unified worldview. The book *First Intelligence* explained the importance of this cognitive shift: "The old ideas of science led us to believe that we were living in a universe made of inert and lifeless matter. But what we are now discovering is that the universe is instead alive, and that it is made up of the same stuff thoughts are made of. All this energetic, thoughtful stuff is a nonspecific and nonlocal field of pure subjectivity beyond time, space, and intellect."

The Old-School Worldview of Disconnection	*The New Quantum Worldview of Interconnection*
• The universe is machine-like, made of separate objects and minds.	• The universe is sea-like, made of interconnected matter and energy.
• Time flows in one direction.	• Everything is happening all at once.
• The space between objects is empty, and the world is disconnected.	• The space between objects is filled with an interpenetrating field that unites everything.

- Events are random or result from cause and effect.
- Events appear to be predictable, quantifiable, and systematic.
- Supernatural phenomena are not possible.
- Life is a rare find in a vast, mostly lifeless universe of inorganic matter.

- Events are meaningful and transcend cause and effect.
- Events appear to be unpredictable, impossible, and magical.
- Supernatural phenomena are a natural part of life.
- Life is everywhere in a universe that is itself is a cosmic living system.

To embrace the full reality of quantum mechanics in our lives, we need to throw away our fears of what we might discover in the invisible world around us. It is precisely there — in the void, the nothingness, the realm of the unseen — where you can find the real magic.

The World beyond the World

There is no such thing as the real world. We have been taught that "seeing is believing" — that our five senses are the be-all and end-all of reality. But today, we know that matter and the way we interact with it are both a lot more interesting than we previously realized. To begin with, matter itself isn't quite as ubiquitous as we thought it was; it makes up only about 5 percent of reality. The physical reality that you touch, see, and feel — all the things we label as *material* — appear to be a rarity in the universe at large. While matter, which are the particles that reflect light, take up space, and are subject to gravity, may seem abundant around us, most of the cosmos is made of other substances, many of which we don't yet fully understand, such as dark matter and energy.

What we do understand is that material particles are not what they appear to be. When you hold an object in your hand, it appears to be solid — hence the experience of touch when two material objects connect. But when we go down to the atomic level of the object, we discover that it is mostly composed of space. Both the object and your body may seem real and solid, but they are actually made of 99.999999999999 percent empty space. As cosmologist Carl Sagan so eloquently put it, "Atoms are mainly empty space. Matter is composed chiefly of nothing." You, me, our objects, the earth, the planets, and every *thing* in between is primarily made of immaterial space.

And what have we learned about this "empty" space? It's the location of the invisible, ever-present zero-point field of intrinsic awareness. If we removed all the space in our bodies, every one of the 7.6 billion people on earth could fit into your living room. This means that there is *a lot* of space in the universe — and inside you. There is spaciousness around us, and there is spaciousness inside us. Space is ubiquitous and interpenetrating. But, most interesting of all, *space is not actually empty* — it is a superdense sea of fluctuating energies and information. This means that every real thing around you, down to its fundamental particles, is interpenetrated with an energy- and information-filled spaciousness that holds all other things. Ervin László explained this clearly: "The world is not 'material'— it does not consist of anything we could call matter. Physicists have not found anything in space and time that would correspond to the idea of a material substance. What research on the universe discloses is information and energy. The entities of the physical world are clusters and configurations of informed energy."

 Space is not empty. It holds the information field that informs all things.

All the matter that forms your body — the atoms that make up your cells, organs, glands, muscles, and even your brain — is embedded in the boundless energy and information highway of the universe. All of you — your physical body and the consciousness that goes with it — is "in-formed" by this information-filled worldwide web called the nonlocal field. At a subatomic level, you interface with the energy-information source code of the cosmos. The concept of an intrinsic field of awareness — with an energy and information network that we can intuitively access at all times — suggests what is really going on in the seemingly empty space between us. Information is being shared; energy is being exchanged. Terms like *inner wisdom* and *inner guidance* have come to be associated with the field because its access point is only within you, where illuminating code packets rise out of your quantum dimension.

Here, at the touchpoint between the inner and the outer, between something and nothing, is where you enter into the beyond and the beyond enters into you. With this discovery, it becomes clear that true reality — the metareality that exists above, beyond, and within our reality — is the supreme reality. It is the one true reality behind all realities. We are conditioned to rule our lives by the external world, but everything we think, feel, sense, or do is intuitively informed from the inside. This "in-formation" shows up as experiences like intuition, insight, inspiration, and ingenuity — all words that start with *in* because they are born in the deep dimension within. Quantum experiences are not created by any cause-and-effect thinking process; they effortlessly fall into our mind as if from the heavens.

Nothingness and Somethingness

Some of the great questions in the human investigation of reality are, Where did the world come from? Where do *we* come from?

And what part do we play in this incomprehensible orchestra of existence? We do know one thing for certain: some kind of awesome, creative event gave birth to our universe about 13.8 billion years ago. From the big bang, all the things that we recognize in our reality — matter, time, and space — emerged out of an apparent formless, timeless spaciousness. From nothing came something — us — and the beautiful thing we call life.

Creation myths and traditions all around the world have their own way of telling the story of our emergence from the great no-thingness. This originating quantum vacuum can be equated with the formless void mentioned at the beginning of the Bible, Brahman from the Hindu religion, or the Tao of East Asian philosophies, among others. The quiet calm of space is the ground state of the universe itself — the deep dimension from which all things arise. This zero-point field of pure potentiality holds the seeds of genesis for all manifestations in our reality. Everything you are, do, or create today still rises out of this source state of zero energy that existed before creation began. According to László, at the moment of creation, the big bang somehow excited this primordial state of being, giving birth to our magnificent reality:

> According to quantum cosmology, we have evolved from the primordial "ground state" of the universe. In quantum cosmology, this state is best seen as a sea of coherent vibration. The manifest universe is the ensemble of the vibrations that emerged in this sea. The emergent vibrations "excited" the quantum sea: they brought it into what physicists describe as the excited state. The excited state is the basis for all possible vibrations in the quantum sea…. The vibration of the ground state is eternal and immutable, but it is capable of excitation. Its excitation produces the manifest universe. The cosmic ground state appears to have been last excited 13.8 billion years ago with the influx

of energies liberated by the singularity we know as the Big Bang. The cosmos entered the excited state where it is a universal field of vibration producing waves of diverse amplitude, phase and frequency. The interaction of the waves creates patterns of interference, of which the clusters and higher-order superclusters are the matter-like entities of the universe.

This act of excitation — of something arising from nothing — appears to be the cause of the duality that permeates the world we know. The unmoved mover *moved*. What was one then became another. Duality is so much a part of our perceived reality that it's hard to imagine what life would be like without it. We can't imagine day without knowing night, good without bad, positive without negative, up without down, in without out, cause without effect, nothing without something. Dualism appears to be an inherent attribute of the material world. The fact that a created reality exists at all gives it an implicitly dualistic role in the universe.

Metareality *(Unified quantum inner dimension)*	Reality *(Binary physical outer dimension)*
• Primary ground state	• Secondary excited state
• Nothingness	• Somethingness
• Nonbinary	• Binary
• Nonlocal	• Local
• Wave	• Particle
• Potentiality	• Manifestation
• Precreation	• Creation
• Known by intuition and insight	• Known by intellect and reason

- Right brain
- Collective experience
- Everything-all-at-once awareness
- Fundamental unity
- Source reality
- Zeros

- Left brain
- Personal experience
- Time-based linear awareness
- Illusion of duality
- Created reality
- Ones

You can see the implicit duality of the world reflected in the one we create around us, even in our technology. Binary code — a fundamental two-symbol data system — is the primary language of our computing systems. The computer sitting on your desk runs programs essentially built of ones and zeros, and complex codes are created with the dual patterns of *on* or *true* versus *off* or *false*. This structure is not so different from our own reality program, which is defined by contrasting opposites; to fully know anything, we define it by its opposite. How could you recognize peace if you have never known disruption? Do you appreciate happiness more after experiencing unhappiness? The same goes for pleasure and pain, love and hate, success, and failure, the list goes on. It's hard to escape our binary nature, but there is a good reason to do so.

Being the other to something is a state of separateness. Our binary nature gives us the experience of being an individual, a one; but it also gives us a sense of dislocation from our source zero. The great religions, philosophies, and spiritual traditions of the world point to the return to the nondual state as key to our conscious evolution. Finding the oneness behind the separation or the middle path between two extremes — like the Greek concept of the golden mean or the Buddhist Middle Way — allows us to transcend the trappings of a dualistic world. In the Hindu tradition, this opting out of the dual of opposites — and the pleasure-and-pain cycle that comes with it — is part of what gets us off the wheel of karma, which is the law of cause and effect, or action and reaction, that binds us to this reality. When we rise above this, we transcend the greatest duality of all: life and death.

What kind of information then exists beyond our binary reality? We can find clues to this answer in the emerging fields of quantum computing. The computers that you and I use run on binary code, much like our everyday reality does; they both operate on predictable, linear information patterns or algorithms. But quantum computers, just like the quantum realm, seem magical. They can process information in an instant — information that would take a classical computer days, months, or even years to compute. They are so fast that they can almost see the future. And they are poised to do many impossible things. Bernard Marr, author and well-known futurist, explained it well: "Quantum physics has defied logic since the atom was first studied in the early twentieth century. It turns out atoms do not follow the traditional rules of physics. Quantum particles can move forward or backward in time, exist in two places at once and even 'teleport.' It's these strange behaviours that quantum computers aim to use to their advantage."

Binary computers are the legacy of a binary world. Quantum computers may just be the legacy of our emerging relationship with the quantum world. Their code, which is made up of quantum bits, or "qubits," is not just a one or zero, on or off; it can also be both at once. Quantum computers transcend duality while also containing it, giving them extraordinary power. Some have even gone so far as to call them "psychic computers," as they have the potential to predict events — the weather, stock markets, and other unforeseeable outcomes. Their intelligence, just like the quantum intelligence within us, far exceeds the potential of binary information processing.

Some scientists propose that the most magnificent quantum computer is hiding in plain sight — the human brain. As theoretical physicist Michio Kaku once said, "Sitting on your shoulders is the most complicated object in the known universe." Bridging the gap between reality and metareality, the binary and the nonbinary, intelligence and intuition — the human mind exhibits many traits of a quantum system, including entanglement and the ability to instantaneously process information. Your brain powers your mind, like a magnificent local hard drive networked into the vast, omnipresent cloud of nonlocal data — the matrix of past, present, and future universal, microcosmic-accessible information. In the end, quantum supremacy may apply not only to our computers but to our minds as well.

Cosmic Consciousness

Could we be living in a localized, binary subreality of a nonlocal, nonbinary higher metareality? If so, is this evidence that we are, in fact, metaphysical beings contained in a physical reality? Could this prove that we are more than mere physical organisms that blink in and out of existence? If the universe itself is alive and eternal, so in some sense must we also be.

We are nonbinary beings living in a binary world. We exist in a hybrid state of being, with one foot firmly in each dimension of reality. We have a temporal physical body that interacts with the material world; and we have a quantum intelligence that interacts with the immaterial world. In the everyday world, we can't escape duality — it is even manifest in the dual hemispheres of the human brain. Our mind unites two very different forms of information processing: the left brain is logical, analytical, rational, and astute at problem-solving, reading, writing, and making linear calculations derived from our experience of everyday reality; the right brain, on the other hand, is the imaginative and creative visionary and genius fueled by an inner, intuitive connection to the deep dimension within us.

In the West, we have been living for decades in a left-brain-dominated world. Right-brainers, who are often artists, imaginative free spirits, rule-breakers, or creative types, are often seen as outliers. This ideology was so pervasive that past generations used to force left-handed (right-brained) children to switch dominant hands. We were so focused on getting left-brain smart that we gave up our right-brain genius. But we don't have to choose between one or the other; the real secret to success is using both sides of your brain, to become *whole*. Only when the intuitive mind and the rational mind are developed together, as complements, can we rise into the full potential of our human design.

THE HYBRID NATURE OF HUMAN CONSCIOUSNESS	
Right-Brain Mind	**Left-Brain Mind**
Metareality awareness	Reality awareness
Quantum thinking	Linear thinking
Intuitive insight	Intellect
Yin (receptive)	Yang (active)
Genius and inner wisdom	Intelligence and information processing

How do creatures like us, who are bound to the binary world, gain access to the unified dimension of universal consciousness? Are we locked out of this deeper dimension of existence? The veil between realities often feels impenetrable, and its magic eludes us. But that all changes when we learn to access the quantum intelligence that pervades the cosmos.

With your intuition, you can dive deep into an inner field that is alive with information and energy — a sea of signals and fluctuations that arise from the nothingness, or everythingness, depending on how you look at it. The empty space around and within you holds the seeds of all creation — energy that is encoded with the information that generates our reality. The quantum field is where the universe sparks life, how particles spontaneously arise out of nothing or exist in infinite potentiality. It is the true place of genesis, creation, and manifestation. And this ocean of fluctuating energy and information is more than a scientific phenomenon — it is the home of consciousness itself.

Information-filled consciousness is the fabric of the universe, its fundamental state. This cosmic intelligence is part of who you are and the fabric of your being. It guides you and connects you to all other intelligences and manifestations in the excited state of reality. As László put it, "The manifest world is a set of clusters of coordinated vibration in the excited state of the cosmos. The coordination of the clusters of vibration indicates nonrandomness at the heart of reality. The clusters are 'in-formed' by a factor we identify...as an underlying cosmic intelligence. The presence of intelligence at the heart of reality is a familiar tenet in religious and spiritual systems."

Could this be the point where science and spirituality finally come together, both recognizing intelligence as the source of the universe? The boundless information-filled space that holds the whole universe in its loving embrace is a cosmic consciousness that unites us all. László said, "Consciousness is fundamental. As far as we can tell, consciousness is as basic as energy, as information, and far more basic than matter and anything based on matter. This is a conscious universe. Consciousness is not something that you have, it's something that you are. The world itself is consciousness."

It is as if the universe is a great omnipresent thought composed of an ocean of individual thoughts. Thoughts are things, and things are thoughts. If this is true, thoughts and things have a much deeper connection than our experiences in material reality suggests; maybe thoughts can interact with things in ways once thought impossible. If the whole world is an interconnected matrix of thought, then maybe we are communicating with each other on levels deeper than we realize. Most importantly, if the whole universe is alive, then how can anything really die?

The separated reality of a physical world is only an illusion, a smokescreen that conceals a greater unified dimension of being and its supernatural phenomenon. According to László,

> We know that interactions between things in the physical world are mediated by energy. Energy can take many forms — kinetic, thermal, gravitational, electric, magnetic, nuclear, actual, or potential — but in all its forms energy conveys an effect from one thing to another, from one place and one time to another place and another time. Energy must, however, be conveyed by something; and if it is conveyed across space, science would consider that it is conveyed by a field. In that case, space is not empty — it is filled with an effectively acting field.... The field that fills it conveys light, gravity, electromagnetism, and energy in all its forms.

The unified field opens the door of possibility to all kinds of external supernatural phenomena, like synchronicity and psychokinesis — explaining how it is possible for the doors in my childhood home to be slammed shut by nothing. The ever-present, limitless, invisible quantum-thought field informs *and moves* the material world. A physical object (like a door) might not require another physical object to move it (like a hand or particles of moving air); it could be moved by an originating information-energy impetus in the field. We will look deeper into this in chapter 5 as we explore the idea of information as both thought (ground-state information) and motion (excited energy).

The quantum field of cosmic consciousness doesn't just intellectually inform us, it also energetically *moves us*. It inspires us, motivates us, and guides our way. It can move us intuitively and literally — putting the clusters of atomic particles we call matter into motion from the inside out. With its intrinsic power, the quantum field is the maker of miracles and the doer of impossible things.

INVESTIGATION: EVERYDAY MIRACLES

What kind of impossible things have you experienced in your own life? Let's pause to make an assessment of any extraordinary events that have given you glimpses of reality's deeper dimension. You don't have to be a saint or superhero to make miracles — the unified field offers them to us all. They can arrive in many ways: as a bit of serendipity, a healing, a vision or extrasensory perception, a dream come true.

To get started, relax and think back on something unexplainable that has happened to you or people close to you. This could be in the form of supernatural events, mysteries, or strange coincidences. Now that you know more about the quantum field, you can decode the true meaning of extraordinary experiences. Miracles and impossible moments, though they may appear to happen for no reason, usually have a meaningful purpose in your life. You can unpack and explore that meaning using the evidence log below or in your Illumination Workbook. This is also an excellent way to archive your experiences for future validation and reference.

Here is a sample evidence log from my life to give you a framework for your own.

Personal Evidence Log (Sample)

Date	Extraordinary Experience	Meaning, Connection, or Insight
1994	*A helper shows up in a moment of need* — One day I was stranded after my car was unexpectedly towed. I had no one to call or help me get home. Suddenly, out of nowhere, a friend that I had not seen in years pulled up and asked me if I needed a ride. They saved the day and drove me to retrieve my car from the impound lot.	This experience felt like a validation that we are living in an interconnected, supportive universe. Today, we can understand, through concepts like the zero-point field and quantum entanglement, that it is possible for someone with an energetic connection to me to intuitively pick up on my quantum distress call and end up in the right place at the right time to help me.
2006	*Mysterious orbs of light* — One night during a forest hike in Lilydale, New York, my friend and I started noticing small lights appearing and then disappearing around us. For nearly an hour, we caught orbs of light blinking in and around the darkness in the woods.	Many people have also reported seeing orbs at Inspiration Stump — rumored to be the lights of consciousness that guide the way for local seekers. The vital role of light in the quantum realm suggests the potentiality for such orbed packets of energy-light-information to travel through the field as individual points of consciousness. (More on this in chapter 7.)
2010	*Communication from beyond* — During the evening after we had to unexpectedly put our dog to sleep, my husband and I both heard his bark, loud and clear, echoing through the house as though he was right there with us.	Not only did this reinforce the continuous nature of life, but it felt like a goodbye — a bit of closure between beings who no longer are sharing the same dimension of reality. The multidimensional nature of quantum reality suggests the possibility of transdimensional communication and the ability to share information between worlds.

If we are all participating in a shared, cosmic consciousness, shouldn't it follow that we would have some kind of personal access to it? A part of you knows everything because a part of you has access to all the information the universe holds. The veil of illusion that separates your inner and outer worlds is just that — an illusion, one that can be transcended by bypassing the linear thinking mind. You need to go beyond it to see what exists beyond it.

ILLUMINATION KEY #3

THE REAL WORLD IS NOT THE REAL WORLD

*Man's dilemma — now and always — has been that
he misidentifies his own intellectual artifacts as reality.*

— DAVID R. HAWKINS

We are all unique individuals wired with our own unique connection to the deep dimension. The purpose of this section is to help you recognize how you personally interact with the quantum field, and what it feels like to download its bounty of data. You receive this information through natural energetic pathways that connect your local body and your consciousness to the nonlocal universal field. These pathways are built into your natural design and run through the three primary dimensions of your existence: your bodily sensations, your mental thoughts, and your emotive feelings.

Your body can be in-formed by quantum intelligence as both sensory and metasensory experiences — you might see, hear, feel, smell, or taste things that don't originate in physical reality. Your mind can be in-formed with insights, ideas, epiphanies, and knowingness — as you are often guided by information stored beyond your local reality. Your heart can be in-formed with feelings, callings, and passions that excite you and move you into transformational states of mind. The universal intelligence employs all these intuitive mechanisms to assist you in the shared unfolding of your consciousness.

When you activate your connection to the nonlocal dimension, you open up your faculties of sensing, thinking, and feeling as channels for expansive information sharing. In this way, the universe becomes a kind of guide, constantly course correcting your life toward its implicit truth. This happens in small ways most every day. For example, you could get a gut feeling that something isn't right, or you could make a choice to go to work a different way despite not knowing that there is a traffic jam ahead. You could even be moved by a sense within you to reach out to a friend, just when they need you. This is because a deeper part of your intelligence has access to nonlocal information such as a traffic jam that is happening far away or what people are doing when they are not with you. This information from your field of intrinsic awareness is constantly pinging your mind and can be picked up by your metasenses, thoughts, and feelings. The trick is to learn to recognize them when they come, so you can begin to trust the guiding code they share with you.

ILLUMINATION KEY #3
expands your awareness beyond the limits of reality.

Once you open your mind to the idea that material reality is made of, informed by, and moved by a greater metareality, you can bring the deep dimension to life within you.

How exciting to think that your life is so meaningful that it comes with a built-in guidance system designed to speak to you personally. And how comforting to realize that, at all times — even in your darkest moments or aloneness — you are intrinsically intertwined with people, places, and things that may seem a million miles away. This vast web of life force communication is always operating in the background, delivering inner wisdom to illuminate your path.

Key #3 Activation: Using Your Metasenses
How to Use Your Body as an Interface with the Quantum Field

The human body comes with a set of powerful sensors designed to help us navigate reality. Not unlike the sensors we build into robots, our five senses are the interface with our little slice of material reality. Other mammals, like dogs or cats, have slightly different sensory systems that enable them to perceive things we often cannot, reminding us of our limited range of physical perception. Your human sense of hearing might not pick up a dog whistle, but that doesn't mean the sound isn't there. Most humans would also have trouble navigating the darkness as adeptly as a feline. Human beings can see only about 0.0035 percent of reality. The entire rainbow of radiation observable to the human eye makes up only a tiny portion of the electromagnetic spectrum — about 0.0035 percent. This range of wavelengths is known as visible light.

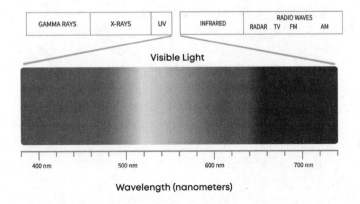

The electromagnetic spectrum with our perceivable area enlarged.

Knowing that we perceive only a minuscule portion of reality underscores the amount of invisible energy-information endlessly swirling within and around us. This extrasensory realm beyond our perceivable reality is the domain of your metasenses. The five senses of your physical body may not be able to interact with it, but the intuitive sensory systems of your deep dimension can. Your metasenses are the energetic equivalent of your physical senses. Instead of receiving sensory impressions from the material world outside us, your metasenses receive their input from the information field that touches you *on the inside*.

You experience the metasenses every night when you dream. How real our dreams are — with form, feeling, and all kinds of sensory experience. None of them are real in the material sense, but they are very real in terms of consciousness. But you don't need to be unconscious to use your metasensory system. Spontaneous dreams, visions, sounds, feelings — all of these can arrive in the waking state, appearing as so-called impossible or supernatural experiences. Chinese philosopher Lao-tzu eloquently expressed the metasensory experience in the Tao Te Ching, verse 14:

That which cannot be seen is called invisible.
That which cannot be heard is called inaudible.
That which cannot be held is called intangible.
These three cannot be defined;
therefore, they are merged as one.

Each of these three is subtle for description.
By intuition you can see it,
hear it,
and feel it.
Then the unseen,
unheard,
and untouched
are present as one.

The delicate and powerful oneness touches you through your metasenses. As László put it, "The fundamental reality is not matter but energy, and the laws of nature are not rules of mechanistic interaction but 'instructions' or 'algorithms,' coding patterns of energy." A metasensory impression can feel like any other sensation on your body, thought in your mind, or feeling in your heart — only it arrives not from a stimulus in the outside world but from the nothingness within you.

Impressions from the quantum field relay through your intuition and manifest as, for example, seeing something in your mind's eye, hearing a sound that isn't there, having a song playing over and over in your head, getting a gut feeling, or sensing a phantom taste or smell. The metasenses can feel like an imaginative version of your physical senses, but they are real. These psychic senses are often labeled as the *claires* — clairvoyance, clairaudience, clairsentience, and so on. You don't need to be born with any special gifts to use them; they are part of your nature. They give you the ability to dream and will remain with you even when you transcend this physical reality.

Your energetic sensory system is made up of five functions:

- Metavision sensors
- Metasound sensors
- Metatouch sensors
- Metascent sensors
- Metataste sensors

We call these faculties the *metasenses* because they are activated by information beyond our physical reality; they instead come from the metaphysical reality. As cosmologist Jude Currivan explained in her book *The Cosmic Hologram,* "Everything we call physical reality is literally made up of information." The same information source, then, informs both physical and metaphysical reality. As we will explore more deeply in the next chapter, your metasenses are the inner-impetus version of the outer-impetus senses you use each day. Both systems are designed to decode information that connects you with the interpenetrating reality fields — turning data into thoughts, feelings, and sensations that your mind can process. Both systems can influence our physical bodies, minds, and emotions. Below is an experiment to show how your internal, immaterial reality can create very real effects on matter.

EXPERIMENT:
TASTE VERSUS THE THOUGHT OF TASTE

Take a moment to daydream about your all-time favorite food. Whatever it is, imagine it on a plate in front of you. Maybe it's a hot, delicious pizza slice melting with cheese, or maybe it's your favorite flavor of ice cream, dripping with sweet goodness. Maybe you even remember a commercial you saw on television that made you hungry. Tune into that tastiness and pay attention to how you feel. Do you notice your stomach start to rumble? Your mouth might start watering, or you could even think that it's time to get something to eat.

Though there is no actual food in front of you, the *thought of the food* still affects your body and mind. This is one example of how something inside us affects reality outside us. It doesn't matter if you see a real pizza or an imaginary pizza, your mind can process them in the same way. Whether you're experiencing an insight, a conscious thought, or bit of sensory input, all of it is made of information.

In addition to manifesting as intuitive experiences, like the experiment with the pizza, a metasensory impression can have real effects on the physical body. It can make the hair stand up on your neck when danger is near — a warning sign. It can give you a tingle in your stomach when you get a gut feeling that something is off. It can make you crave a food that contains vitamins your body needs. In this way, the quantum realm consistently informs your body with guiding information.

LAB #3
USING YOUR METASENSES

Receiving Quantum Information through Your Body

Right now, you and I are living in a mirage where a material world of duality hangs like a veil over a vast, interconnected universe of oneness. Your intuition is the singular power that can pull back that veil — and bring you the life-guiding information that exists beyond it. You can touch this cosmic intelligence because you are a part of it. You embody it, as it embodies you. There is no reason for you to be denied access to it any longer.

When you are operating from your whole being, the dynamics of reality and metareality coalesce to create an intimate experience of cosmic consciousness — made just for you. The information that pervades all the world isn't a random, meaningless collection of ones and zeros; it is a richness of wisdom available for you to personally decode — information that will support, nurture, and guide you through all you do in this world. You are more than a computer receiving data from the internet. You are part of an active universe that shares wisdom through a living intuitive field. Cosmic intelligence isn't a relay through dead, empty space; it travels through the aliveness of your being.

Your metasenses are one of the most tangible receptors of quantum information, as they give the universe an opportunity to speak to you through physical impressions that you can easily recognize and interpret. One of my favorite ways to do this is with a simple metasensory exercise. Since we have been exploring the nature of our binary reality in this chapter, we will start with a binary exercise — tapping into the cosmic *yes* and *no*. Let's put the grand principle of duality to work in your own life and see what the universe has to say to you right now. *Should you do this, or should you do that? Should you go or not? Yes or no?* This lab is designed to connect you to the all-knowing quantum information field through the interface of your metasenses.

This lab is a practice for answering yes-or-no questions with your metasenses. To begin, think of a binary choice you are making in your life right now — anything that can be answered with a *yes* or a *no*. Since we live in a binary world, binary choices are a natural fit for your metasensory faculties. You can pose a question such as these:

- Would this new job be beneficial to me?
- Is Hawaii a good place for me to go on vacation?
- Is this new relationship supportive for my personal growth?

Try to keep your questions grounded in the present and based on situations you have the power to affect with your choice. (Save questions like *Is this relationship going to lead to marriage?* or *Will I stay at this for the rest of my career?* for our precognitive work in chapter 6.) This exercise is focused on guidance for this moment, so you are simply looking for information to help you make the best choice.

The Cosmic Yes and No Exercise

To begin, read the instructions below, then sit in a quiet place where you won't be disturbed. For best results, keep it simple, and ask yourself a clear-cut question about one situation in your life. You can record your experiences in your Illumination Workbook at the end.

1. Close your eyes. Set your intention on finding *yes* or *no* guidance for something in your life.

2. In your mind's eye, imagine a red light and a green light in your field of vision. Your lights could look like traffic lights, lightbulbs, or any other way you want to envision them.

3. With the two lights imagined before you, move your attention back to your question. Ask yourself if the answer is a *yes* or a *no* — with the green light symbolizing a *yes* answer and the red light symbolizing *no*.

4. Relax your mind and release any distracting thoughts. Move into the calm stillness, and hold your question in that quiet space.

5. As you sit quietly with your eyes still closed and imagining the two lights, notice how they begin to change in your mind's eye. With time, you will notice the images begin to take on a life of their own. At first it feels like your imagination, but it doesn't take long to see that the change is not being orchestrated by your own mind. They move and change on their own with no conscious effort from you.

6. Watch how the objects transform to metaphorically give you the answer you are looking for. Your intuition codes often are transmitted as symbols and metaphoric actions. How is the movement of your lights conveying yes-or-no information to you? Observe the two lights and their behavior until an answer resonates with you.

7. When you are finished, record your experiences in your Illumination Workbook, and reference the chart below to help you decode the information you received.

TRAITS OF *YES* ENERGY AND *NO* ENERGY	
Yes Energy	**No Energy**
• Expanding	• Contracting
• Growing brighter or larger	• Dimming or turning off
• Increasing in intensity	• Becoming smaller
• Moving closer	• Moving away
• Moving more quickly	• Retracting
• Radiating light or color	• Staying still or becoming stuck
• Multiplying	• Disappearing altogether

For example, let's say you asked the question *Is this a good car to buy?* A *yes* answer could be the green light bursting into a strobe light and taking over the scene, while the red light just faded into the background. On the other hand, if the answer was *no*, the red light could have been the one to flash in bursts. The dominant energy can manifest as any kind of activity that makes it the focal point of your attention. This is the real key: attention. Like a magnet, your intuition will resonantly draw your attention to the abiding truth that exists within your all-knowing dimension. Therefore, watch for whichever sign draws your attention so you can discern the message it is sending you.

Tips

- **Try not to be attached to the outcome:** Be sure to release any fears or desires connected to the outcome of the situation. We don't want to project our own thoughts onto our mental theater. Just relax and enjoy the show!

- **Try not to overthink:** Let go of any instinct to control the situation or expectation for the objects to behave in any certain way. Often, if nothing happens and the objects don't move, it is due to a mental tension within us. When you let the objects be on their own terms, the universe will bring them to life.

All kinds of metasensory experiences can arise when you search the inner field. Along with the transformations of your objects, you might have a phrase or song come to mind or feel physical sensations in your body. The scenario can even take on a life of its own. The last time I practiced this exercise, both the red and the green light did nothing — then a yellow light appeared in between them, and the phrase "Proceed with caution" fell into my mind. I understood that message to be about not taking the right or wrong action but making my choices carefully. Whatever happens, your intuitive mind uses this imaginative, metasensory scenario as a stage for cosmic intelligence to communicate to you. Like puppets moved by the forces of the deep dimension, the objects in your mind's eye act out a simple scene to convey the true information stored within you. In most cases, when you get an answer, it will *feel right* — because a part of you already knew it.

Lab #3 Workbook: The Cosmic Yes *and* No
Red-Light / Green-Light Practice

It is helpful to do this exercise multiple times and with different questions to compare experiences. You will likely notice that the red-light and green-light objects react differently to different questions. If you do this regularly and get the message right, you may notice themes developing — that a *yes* usually happens in a certain way, while a *no* happens in a different way. As you learn to decode the information you are receiving, you build your intuitive language, one that you will strengthen and become better at with time and practice. You can use the framework below to record your experiences in your journal or workbook.

Date: _____
Yes-or-no question: _____
_____
Intuitive response: _____
_____
Conclusion/answer: _____
_____

CONCLUSION

Activating Key #3 of the illumination code deepens
your conscious connection with the metareality.

The third key reveals your metasensory interface and creates an opportunity to consciously interact with the cosmic intelligence that guides the world. When you activate this key, you can see that a bigger version of reality is waiting for you — a reality that can be known only through your intuitive faculties.

Key Principles

- The universe is more like a great thought than a great machine.
- Duality is an illusory byproduct of living in a created world.

- Material reality appears to have a binary nature, while metareality is wholly unified.
- The universe is alive with consciousness — including yours.
- Cosmic intelligence is supremely personal, ready to inform you at all times.
- You have five metasenses to process metaphysical information.

Key Applications

- Observe and experiment with your metasenses in dreams and daydreams.
- Practice flexing your right-brain muscle with imaginative or creative activities.
- Try the Cosmic *Yes* and *No* Exercise to make a decision with your metasenses.

By opening your mind to the metareality, you can overcome the limits of the dualistic, material world. You live in both a local, personal, physical reality and a nonlocal, universal, metaphysical reality. Amazingly, we all live in the *something* that came from nothing. And maybe, just maybe, we all became something so we could know the *nothing*; maybe we became separate just to recognize our part in the eternal, unified whole — to ultimately rediscover the boundless beauty of everything.

CHAPTER FOUR

The Mind Matrix

Mind is the matrix of all matter.

— MAX PLANCK

Let's talk about *this* world. Once we recognize that the world we know and love emerged from a formless, timeless, primordial everythingness — an expanding metareality of unified consciousness — how does that change our relationship with the material world? How does the interplay between physical and metaphysical reality affect our daily lives? To answer these questions, we investigate the dynamics between the seen and unseen worlds and how they are woven together in the great matrix of existence — the co-creative, universal chronicle that unfolds your life story and holds all the stories of time.

Our personal and universal consciousness come together to create a mind matrix — the great theater of life — of the past, present, and future. Scientifically, we can understand this matrix as a coherent system of local and nonlocal realities created by the individual and collective mind of the universe. What that means for you and me is this: not only are our lives unfolding right now, in this specific moment, here on planet earth, but our lives are also simultaneously embedded — or stored — in the timeless memory of the ever-present universe via the nonlocal field. In this way, nothing can ever truly be lost. Everything is, in some sense, eternal.

Information in the universe cannot be canceled or obliterated; it can be transformed or saved. Though we live in our present reality, we are in constant connection to a cosmic archive of all other current, former, and future realities.

The mind matrix is the framework of all existence.

With the zero-point, nonlocal field as the ground state, the mind matrix is the data reserve of all individual somethingness that has ever or will ever come into being. The mind matrix is a record of the symphony of existence; it stores all the energy-information of all time and space that arises from the eternal cosmic void. As the song of the universe unfolds, each of us contributes our own note — playing out our lives from our unique point of consciousness. Your mind, my mind, and all the minds that have ever been create and share in this grand universal theater.

ALL THAT IS CONTAINED IN THE MIND MATRIX

- All manifest consciousness
- All space-time
- All the information of existence — past, present, and future
- Local and nonlocal interfaces

You may not realize it, but what you perceive as material reality is actually your local interface with the mind matrix. Though the inescapable realness of our world can trick us into thinking that's all there is, that perceived existence is only the surface of the metareality — a more expansive, inclusive dimension of existence that meets us at the touchpoint of the present moment. We are dreamers, awake in our personal reality, amid a deeper reality that feels like a waking dream; but it is all part of the same big dream — and the more we wake up, the more clearly we begin to see both worlds.

This kind of "awakening" is part of our return to wholeness — overcoming duality and embodying the core oneness of our being. This includes a unified experience of the local and nonlocal realities. We are all aware of the local world that we touch and see and interact with, but there is also a litany of nonlocal experiences that require us to integrate the nonlocal dimension into our accepted model of reality. We will go into this evidence in detail in chapter 7, but here are a few preliminary examples of how the unseen, nonlocal realm manifests itself in you in your daily existence:

- Knowing something before it happens
- Recognizing a place that you have never been
- Feeling like you have already known someone the first time you meet

- Remembering something from somebody else's life (past or parallel lives)
- Having a natural talent for something you never learned

In essence, you interact with your local reality via the thinking mind and five senses, but you interact with the nonlocal reality via the intuitive mind and five metasenses. Your physical body and mind read local reality as it happens, but the metaphysical, quantum dimension of your mind reads nonlocal reality as a kind of past, present, and future memory storage bank. This is how you can intuitively know things that should rationally be impossible to know or to intuitively feel things that you should empirically not be able to feel.

Local Reality Interfaces	*Nonlocal Reality Interfaces*
Thinking mind	Intuitive mind
Five senses	Five metasenses

I had a powerful experience of nonlocal awareness the first time I visited Los Angeles. I felt instantly in sync with the city, something I had never experienced in any place I had lived or traveled. One night after I visited Paramahansa Yogananda's gardens on Mount Washington, my phone — and the only GPS I had — ran out of battery. It was already dark out, and I somehow had to find my way back to Venice without a map. I can't fully describe what came over me that night, but it felt like I was in *alignment*. A part of me knew the way home. I didn't see it all planned out in linear steps — I felt it, every next move. *Turn right here. Go this way.* It felt like I was remembering which way to go, even though I had never been on any of those roads before. I didn't get lost once. I drove with the flow like I had lived there my whole life.

How is it possible to know our way around a place we have never been? Have we been there in another time or life? Or are we tapping into the collective nonlocal information field of the city? Did my resonance with Los Angeles somehow activate my intuitive GPS system? Whatever the case, we can look to the mind matrix for answers.

Everything All at Once

A primary feature of the mind matrix is that time, like matter, doesn't really exist. Time is a byproduct of the illusion in our container of local reality, making it both subjective and relative. The notion of a successive past, present, and future doesn't exist objectively anywhere out there — it exists from only the subjective perspective in our local point of consciousness. Einstein was one of the first scientists to come to this realization during the development of his theories of relativity, ultimately concluding that past and future are illusions; only the present moment exists.

Everything that has ever happened, is happening, or will happen is happening right now. The only real part of time is *the now*. Science and spirituality finally agree on that. The spaciousness of the present moment is a portal to the deep dimension and the information-energy held in both local and nonlocal realms of existence. In the words of Austrian physicist Erwin Schrödinger, "For eternally and always there is only now, one and the same now; the present is the only thing that has no end." The now is where we are alive in the eternal. All the rest is information in the form of potentiality, manifestation, or memory playing their parts in the theater of life.

Time is springing into existence with every firing of a neuron in your brain. Your consciousness is constantly generating time. For as long as a person is alive, they are creating time; we never run out. If time is a byproduct of our local consciousness weaving its way through everything that has ever happened or could happen, which in turn is navigated by our choices, then a whole wide world of information is out there right now, ready to be discovered by the part of you that knows everything.

Think about it: if the future already exists as information stored in the nonlocal field matrix, that explains why people throughout history have been able to gain knowledge about the future. The same goes for information about the distant past or about any other places in space and time. If all of space-time is contained in the mind matrix field, all the events of space-time are fair game for our individual minds to explore.

History is full of examples of nonlocal information transfers that are now verifiable in hindsight. People from all walks of life have provided evidence of this process, such as Saint Joan of Arc (who won multiple battles in the Hundred Years War with divinely inspired war strategies), Nikola Tesla (who predicted artificial intelligence, the internet, and cellphones), Nostradamus (who foretold calamities like the Great Fire of London, the Holocaust, and the atomic bombing of Japan), and even visionary authors like Jules Verne, Ray Bradbury, and Mark Twain (who forecasted his time of death). Today, a gold mine of nonlocal information also shows up in quite an unexpected place: Hollywood.

For example, a recent documentary called *Meltdown: Three Mile Island* exposed the story of the infamous nuclear power disaster in the late 1970s — one that actually threatened my hometown in eastern Pennsylvania. During the film, they talk about a strange similarity with a movie called *The China Syndrome*, starring Jane Fonda and Michael Douglas. The movie played out a nearly identical disaster scenario as Three Mile Island's, and it was released, in an act of pure synchronicity, *just twelve days before the incident*. The fictional story detailed the same chain of events and industry cover-ups as the real disaster and, hauntingly, predicted that the meltdown could render "an area the size of the state of Pennsylvania permanently uninhabitable." It even referenced the exact location where the future disaster took place! Michael Douglas said the whole thing gave him "an eerie feeling."

Before the Covid-19 pandemic, a surprising number of movies and television shows depicted a play-by-play similar global disaster, including *Contagion*, *The Dead Zone*, and even *The Simpsons*. Are these prophetic ventures evidence of the human ability to creatively draw information from the nonlocal field? Creativity is an intuitive process. Isn't it also then a quantum process? Writers, artists, and creators of all kinds work from inspiration and channel creativity from their inner dimension. Could the creatives behind prophetic media unknowingly tap into nonlocal information stored in the field? Could the stories we write sometimes be stories that are yet to be told?

The idea that we can, on some level, know the future does not mean that everything we do is predetermined or that we are just living out a prescribed drama. The future, and some even say the past, exists in waves of potentiality — which means that we still consciously choose our direction and cocreate our reality with the cosmic source. Therefore, it's quite possible that successfully predicted events are the ones most likely to happen. It also explains why some predicted events *don't* come true. It could be that you, me, or the world at large chose a different pathway of space-time — a different string of potentiality to travel onward.

The mind matrix also explains one of the most common phenomena associated with near-death experiences. Time and again, we hear that when a person is near death their whole life flashes before their eyes. Often finding it hard to articulate in words, they somehow experience all their life in a single moment. Is this the moment that they step out of time and witness the nonlocal wholeness of existence? Is this all-knowing, timeless awareness the final step on the step-by-step journey through their personal, local reality? Perhaps in this instant, they break through their bubble of space-time as their mind expands beyond the limits of this dream and awakens.

All Reality Is Virtual

Here is what we know about our local reality so far: We live in a secondary world that emerges from a primary source field. We participate in it as part of our space-time bubble — where we experience the illusion of time passing. This reality is binary and linear, operating on cause-and-effect principles. It is also full of immaterial things that appear to be material. Everything that happens in it is recorded in the eternal theater of existence. And, finally, the part of you that knows everything has access to both the information within your local reality and everything beyond it.

The Hindu concept of maya describes this concept beautifully: *maya* is a term that explains that this life is a kind of "magic show, an illusion where things appear to be present but are not what they seem." The world of maya is changeable, finite, and known through your five senses. It gives you time and space to grow, evolve, and expand your conscious awareness. Your existence in this local world is an opportunity to learn, discover, and become more than you are. This is where your intuition comes in. You carry your intuition with you throughout this world as your personal compass. Its primordial power guides your way home to our true reality, where life is eternal, whole, and in the realm of *being* as opposed to *becoming*.

Modern science offers an interesting expansion on this philosophy: simulation theory. Growing evidence shows that our local reality may, in fact, be a kind of simulated projection that emerges from the quantum field. Though we may not be living in a video game, the simulation metaphor is viable in theoretical physics. As Nobel laureate Sir John Eccles explained, "I want you to realize that there exists no color in the natural world, and no sound — nothing of this kind; no textures, no patterns, no beauty, no scent."

It is all just information — codes that come alive in the sensory and metasensory play of your individual consciousness.

To design such a magnificent world as ours would be an act of supreme intelligence, which some scientists speculate could be our own destiny: "An advanced civilization should reach a point where their technology is so sophisticated that simulations would be indistinguishable from reality, and the participants would not be aware that they were in a simulation. Physicist Seth Lloyd from the Massachusetts Institute of Technology in the US took the simulation hypothesis to the next level by suggesting that the entire Universe could be a giant quantum computer." Could our body and the world around us be a high-definition participatory holographic projection, one that we continuously create in the present moment?

Jude Currivan suggests that our reality is far more than a simulation. She explains in her book *The Cosmic Hologram* that "light can embed vast amounts of information — one of the holograms most important attributes." If this is true, then we are living in a universe made of light. Everything — not just the stars and galaxies but every bit of matter they contain — is built of information-energy codes stored as light. If everything is made of light, that means you and I are, fundamentally, made of light too. With the ability to dismantle molecules, particles, and atoms, we have discovered what's really behind it all: tiny quanta of light. Pixels, if you will.

At the deepest level, nothing is solid, and all things are made of concentrations of information, energy, and light. Currivan goes on to explain that "pixels...are the single points or smallest programmable components in a graphic image. Nowadays, the development of high-definition media has increased the number of pixels enormously, and the image appears as a continuous visual no matter how close you approach. Cosmologists are beginning to view space-time itself...as being pixelated." But the manifestation of our light-projected material reality adds up to something far more magnificent than a simulation; instead of being players in a great cosmic game, we are microcosmic cocreators in a living, loving, nonlocally unified, innately informed, and holographically manifested universe.

You and everything in the world around you are made of tiny pixels of information-infused light energy. It's not a coincidence that words like *enlightenment, brilliance,* and *illumination* are associated with an increase in awareness or intelligence. If our core, true self is light — and all the wisdom embedded into it — then growing into that light is surely part of our self-actualization. Perhaps some scientific truth lies within the Old Testament, which states that light was the first thing created in the world: "Let there be light" (Gen. 1:3). We can also explain it in terms of physics as László did: "The phenomena we encounter in the world are projections of holographic codes from the deep dimension." In either case, the beautiful, exciting, painful, glorious pageant we call life — and the many, intricate, interwoven lives within it — is like a motion picture of our universe. Only, instead of watching it, we are participating in it.

How, then, do these tiny pixels of light make the world go around? How can they carry all the information in the universe — including the wisdom that informs and guides your life? According to László, "All the information that codes the system is present in each of its parts, and this information does not vanish. The information that makes the universe what it is, is both spatially and temporally nonlocal. And it is present in every particle and in every atom — and in every organism, including you and me." Holograms, like fractals, contain repeating patterns, and each individual piece of reality contains all the information of reality within it. This is why you don't have to *go* anywhere to find your inner truth.

All the guiding wisdom and information in the whole wide world is present in the holographic light source within you.

When something is holographic, it means that the whole is present in all the parts. To live in a holographic universe means to live as a part that contains the whole. You and I both contain the whole world within us. *The whole world is contained at every point in the whole world.* This means that everything everywhere at every time is interconnected — as all points in space and time are connected. And this implicit oneness links and informs all the light-built beings and things in the world you see around you. Your intuition is built to decode this information — a secret hack to break through the simulation — to bypass the illusion of the real world and access the truth of the metareality.

Intuition is the hack that gets you through the seemingly impenetrable barrier to the deep dimension. According to Michael Talbot, author of *The Holographic Universe*, extrasensory perception, telepathy, and other paranormal phenomena are a product of this holographic model of reality. You have inner access to the world's holographically interconnected web of information and energy. Since this network is everywhere all at once, you have access to information from all times and all places. It is as though everything that has happened or will happen in your life, in some dimension, is still happening. All events are held in the great universal hologram, and so too in all things accessible to all minds.

In the illusory world, we have secrets, and we can tell lies. The mind you use to process everyday reality is easily deceived. Things are often not as they seem. The information we receive here doesn't always tell us the whole story. We misunderstand situations because we have only a limited understanding of them. With your intuitive mind, however, the part of you that is at home in the field of metareality has access to all information — hence, the truth. There is no code for deceptions or illusions in a unified, connected reality. This higher part of your mind can see all sides of a situation; it knows all the dynamics that occur around you, near and far; it knows the past and future. Reality may be our playground, but metareality is our home. Where we are whole again, there is no deception and no need to deceive. When the cosmic veil drops, there is only truth.

The Universe Remembers Everything

Once upon a time, there existed a mystical realm called the *akashic records*. This illustrious library of deeds was said to stretch to eternity and back — holding within it all the events, thoughts, feelings, acts, and stories of everything and everyone in the world. Recordings of all the loves, all the lives, and all the adventures that anyone has ever known could be found there. In this great hall of records, mystics like Rudolf Steiner and Edgar Cayce are said to have intuitively retrieved deep knowledge of the past, present, and future. But could this mysterious place actually be real? Could an ethereal plane of existence truly hold the whole story of humanity and beyond?

You may have already noticed that the description of the akashic, information-filled realm sounds a lot like your field of intrinsic awareness — the unified, zero-point field that holds all information and connects all things. László suggested that the nonlocal field is modern science's answer to the age-old concept of akasha. He also gave it a new name: the akashic field: "The Akashic Records might seem to be some heavenly office room filled with file cabinets. Akasha, however, means 'space.' The 'records' implied are intrinsic to the oneness of infinite consciousness." As such we can reimagine the akashic records not so much as a library of books but as a compendium of quantum data stored in the ethers of the universe. In the late 1800s, when the idea of the akashic records was popularized in the West, no one knew anything about quantum physics, computers, or electronic data; those who accessed the akashic field intuitively described it in the only way they knew how — as books, the primary source of information in their time.

Today, with this modernized understanding of the akashic tradition, we are discovering more about its vital role in the ecosystem of universal consciousness and the part we play in it. According to László, "The unified field is a space-filling medium that underlies the manifest things and processes of the universe....*It's also the element of the cosmos that records, conserves, and conveys information.* In the latter guise it's the Akashic field, the rediscovered ancient concept of Akasha." The akasha — which is, interestingly, translated as *ether* or *space* — is the basis of all things, the cosmic source that stores all the data of creation.

The existence of a personally accessible, collective cosmic memory bank has been proposed not just by scientists and mystics but also by philosophers, biologists, and psychologists around the world. In 1896, French philosopher Henri Bergson published a book called *Matter and Memory*, which suggested that memories are not materially embedded in the brain but are instead an integral part of our consciousness. English parapsychologist and biochemist Rupert Sheldrake expanded on this concept with the idea of *morphic resonance*, claiming that memory is implicit in nature and accounts for the "telepathy-like interconnections between organisms." He specifically compared morphic resonance to the akashic records. Another idea rose to popularity with Swiss psychoanalyst Carl Jung, who suggested that human beings are connected to each other — and even their ancestors — through a "collective unconscious."

Not only does the cosmic memory field act as a database of everything that is, was, or ever will be, it also creates, records, and stores all the events of our individuated consciousness. Everything we observe, do, feel, think, make, or intend is imprinted and forever saved in the timeless annals of existence. Furthermore, since all knowledge is stored as mind-accessible information in the quantum field, all of it is intuitively retrievable. Thus, we can explain phenomena such as past-life recall, remote viewing, and various other intriguing psychic abilities. All the information is out there; we just need to train our minds to receive it.

Interconnected with the nothingness of metareality and the somethingness of our material reality, the akashic realm is the thought matrix of all creation. Unlike the material world, which is part of our local matrix of reality, the akashic realm is the dreamlike world of our collective consciousness, where all things can be known. It echoes in the space between eternity and the present moment, an ineffable somewhereness that holds the deep wisdom of the universe. It feels like a memory you never had, a story that feels familiar, or even an invisible touch.

Unlike the local reality you explore with your thinking mind and five senses, you explore the akashic, nonlocal dimension with your intuition and your metasenses. This is the in-between realm where the eternal and temporal meet — where all local manifestations in time and space are stored nonlocally and eternally. It is where your childhood memories are stored, where your future destiny is held, and where everything you do lives on. All this information can be read by your intuitive mind, revealing experiences from the distant past or future, even events happening in faraway places. Here, you can regain forgotten moments of your past (like a memory retrieved through hypnosis), potential details about your future (like a premonition), or elements going on behind the scenes in your life (like other people's actions that you are unaware of).

Years ago in IntuitionLab, I began to explore the possibility that the nonlocal field is the storage facility for other lives, something that would explain the countless reports of past-life experiences. Once a year, I challenge a new intuition development group to dip into the inner field and see what information they can extract about my past lives. In the beginning, some students didn't even believe in past lives but were curious to see what was possible. Almost everyone doubted they could actually do it, but in the end, nearly everyone did. And they were surprised at how easy the process was. Here is what happened:

- Each year for seven years, numerous participants (who had never met each other) shared overlapping information about one of three primary other-life scenarios.
- Multiple people picked up on the same information, including location description, specific objects, vocations, gender, and overarching life themes.
- Most interestingly, all three other-life scenarios have elements that relate to my current life: they occur in places I have lived or visited in this life, they include talents or interests that I have in this life, and they have similar life challenges and evolutionary themes as in this life. Though none of the participants knew any of these things about me personally, they were able to pick up on correlating hidden information in the quantum field.

While this may not prove that past lives exist, it certainly affirms that we do, in fact, live in a shared information field. Whatever the origin story, people were able to tap into the same information. The students described their experience as feeling like a personal memory, as though they were living the other life themselves. Sometimes the connection was so intense that, when information was sad, it would bring them to tears, or, conversely, happy experiences would fill them with joy. Reading the information was not like reading a book from a detached perspective; it was as though they were reliving a memory.

Nonlocal information feels like memory because the quantum field is the cosmic memory bank. *Memory is the saving of information.* It is as if your personal consciousness is a local hard drive of memory that backs up to the universal storage cloud — available to be read by other people with the right connection. David R. Hawkins presented this idea in *Power vs. Force*: "The individual human mind is like a computer terminal connected to a giant database. The database is human consciousness itself, of which our own consciousness is merely an individual expression, but with its roots in the common consciousness of all mankind." All the information that you process, in every moment of the day, is recorded and saved in the eternal information bank of the nonlocal field. These memories fill the timeless dimension of the mind matrix and form what has been called the akashic record.

The universal field contains everything that ever happens in the world. This means that your inner "universal *information-and-memory* field conserves the information that creates and maintains the universe. Nothing that has ever taken place in space and time fails to enter the universal information field and be conserved in it." All your life experiences are conserved in the memory of the universe. The common practice of hypnosis validates this idea. How is it possible to retrieve long-lost memories from our childhood or from events our mind has repressed? They are stored somewhere. Hypnosis, like intuition, works only when the thinking mind is out of the way. Mindlessness is the common denominator for accessing nonlocal information. By loosening our grip on this reality, as László prescribed, we allow ourselves to receive information from beyond it:

> There is empirical evidence supporting the assertion that the totality of human experience is conserved. The evidence is that our experiences are lasting "memories"; they are not subject to erosion and attrition. Our experiences

are permanent memories present in the deep dimension of the universe, and in principle they are always available for conscious recall. Experimental psychologists find that under suitable conditions people can recall practically all experiences they have ever had — for example, in so-called spiritual emergencies, in altered states of consciousness, and under hypnosis.

If this is true, then nothing is ever really lost; all our fond memories, all the people we have known and the places we have been, all the beautiful moments of love and joyful existence are still alive in the nonlocal field.

"We don't have to do anything to access the field," explained Peter Smith, author of *Quantum Consciousness.* "We simply have to remember." When I first started working with my intuition, I was astounded at how much it felt like memory. So often, when I was working with my intuition, it felt like I was grasping for a memory — like when you are trying to remember someone's name but can't quite put your finger on it. *Maybe it was Charlie or Cheri or Chelsea?* Bits and bytes of the code would drop in — a set of letters or maybe a rhyming sound — but I couldn't catch the whole code. Could this be because in both cases — in memory and intuition — we are pulling information from the same storage field? Perhaps we store our short-term memory on the local hard drive that is our brain — and everything else gets synced with the universal cloud? In that case, some memories — like intuitive insights — may be retrieved nonlocally.

Could the difference between an intuition and a memory simply be one of relative time? Is intuition simply nonlocal memory? Memories in future tense? Today, I have an intuition about tomorrow; tomorrow, it becomes a memory. Through intuition, I sense the future; through memory, I sense the past. But since there is no real future or past, both are relative to my place in local reality.

In the end, both — in their own way — simply connect us to the eternal now.

EXPERIMENT: YOUR INFORMATION HIGHWAY

How is it possible for your brain to access, whether through intuition or memory, the information-infused matrix of the nonlocal field? Growing up, you were probably taught that memories are stored in the brain, but what is the brain? Your brain is composed of matter and nerve tissue, which are both made of cells; cells are made of molecules, which are made of atoms. Atoms are composed of subatomic particles that form the link between the macrocosmic and microcosmic worlds. These particles of energy, including the pixels of light that form the holographic universe, are made of the information and consciousness held in the zero-point field. This is the pathway to and from cosmic intelligence — from matter to mind and from mind to matter.

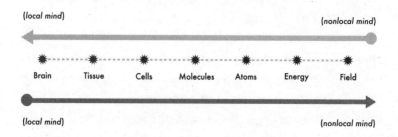

Your information highway runs both ways.

Your information highway is a two-way street — running from local consciousness to nonlocal consciousness, from the material reality around you to the immaterial reality within you, and vice versa. The relay from your local mind begins with an active intention, such as remembering or intuitively thinking. Conversely, you receive the relay from the nonlocal field of mind as a passive download, such as a moment of insight or genius, gut feeling, knowingness, or revelation.

Knowing this, you can start paying attention to the active and passive relays of inner information. If a thought arrives out of nowhere and for no apparent reason, it most likely arrived from the field. If you are using your memory, you are using the same process as intuition; the difference is that, with memory, you are accessing information from your local past — information you have already run through. Theoretically, you can remember the future, too, since your local experience of time runs in both directions.

 Your mind is a recording device that saves your story into the eternal memory of the universe.

Past, present, and the future are interwoven in a matrix of timeless existence. Your mind — and every other mind — records reality as you live through it and saves it for all time in the akashic, nonlocal, zero-point field. *Your mind is more than a point of consciousness, it is a recording device.* Our minds record our personal stories and conserve them in the field so that they may live on eternally.

Universal memories can be retrieved through the practice of intuitive insight. We receive them as a lived, personal experience, even though they are not either our own life or experience. Through the field, we have the ability to see nonlocally through another's eyes in a process that conveys very real information to the mind and senses. We see this process at work not only through creative visualization or insight (as we see in Hollywood movies that seem to predict the future) but also through a vast array of personal experience, including past-life recollection, remote viewing, premonition, psychometry, and other kinds of nonlocal awareness. Your consciousness is ready and able to pull from this matrix of timeless mind-recorded existence a compendium of both individual and unified consciousness since we are all able to intuitively access this record of all that is, was, and ever will be.

Vibration: Your Inner Access Code

If all the information in the whole universe exists in our intuition-accessible quantum field, how do we access more of it? How can we receive its messages with more clarity? Though universal information appears to be hidden to us, we can overcome its invisible barrier — the veil of separation — when we develop our innate intuitive ability.

Why can't we access the inner field?

- Human intuition is collectively underdeveloped. To access nonlocal data, we need to use our intuitive minds. After so many generations of overreliance on logic and reason, with our intuition, we are like children exploring a new world. Intuitively speaking, we can barely walk, let alone run. As we accept the reality of our quantum intelligence, we can grow into it and discover what we are truly capable of.

- Our consciousness is vibrating at the wrong frequency. Downloading data from the field is not as easy as typing a command into a search bar. We need to be on the same wavelength as the information we want to receive. Quantum intelligence is not just informational; it is stored at different energetic vibrations and frequencies, most of which are at a higher level than our everyday consciousness. To reach high-vibration information, we must be in a high-vibration state of mind.

Awakening to our quantum dimension not only activates our intuitive ability, but it also lifts our consciousness to a naturally higher vibration. As such, we can begin to resonate with the ephemeral codes of the field that are impervious to lower or semiconscious states of mind. This is what the early stage of enlightenment looks like, as the life-changing expansion of the mind opens us up to higher realities. We are all participating in a magnificent evolution of thought, where, with each insight caught and each intuition followed, we fuel our personal transformation.

Joining the Cosmic Dance

To better understand the quantum field, envision the universe as a cosmic symphony of information vibrating at different levels. Like in any song, there are high notes and low notes — with codes of interplay that create the melodies and harmonies we so love. In this scenario, the deep dimension vibrates at the highest of high — the ethereal, high notes on the scale — while our material world vibrates as the low notes — the denser and heavier ones — as our base reality. As beings living in this base reality, we are naturally wired to perceive our range of low notes; the higher, subtler energies of the upper notes elude our perception. In our ordinary state of mind, we can hear only our local part of the cosmic symphony.

On some level, we all long to hear the higher notes of this universal song — to complete it and know it in its wholeness. To merge with the divine melody of the deep dimension, we must rise to its level. We must elevate our minds and hearts into alignment with its high-vibration codes of information. As such, your ability to go deep into your inner dimension is largely determined by your state of physical, mental, emotional, and spiritual well-being. The higher your personal vibration is, the deeper into truth you can go.

Nikola Tesla instructed that "to find the secrets of the universe, think in terms of energy, frequency, and vibration." Like attracts like. Therefore, the best way to gain entrance into the enlightening wisdom of the deep dimension is to become like it — become a high note — illuminated, filled with light, and uplifted. The energy-information that you have access to in the field is a direct reflection of the emotions and thoughts you carry within you. A high-minded, compassionate, loving, selfless state of being will naturally align with the high-vibration notes in your field of truth; and on the contrary, they remain out of reach to any low-minded, self-centered, unconscious state of being. You access information in coherence with the wavelength it is stored on. This is why the most important first step in working with the field is moving into a state of calm, clear-minded lightness of being. Simone Wright explained this in *First Intelligence*:

> When our mind is calibrated for the intuitive information we are looking for, it vibrates at a specific frequency; we literally become a biological antenna. The information within the unified field that matches our intuitive request vibrates at that same frequency. And when the two frequencies metaphorically bump into each other, they form an interference pattern that shows up in the field as a new pattern or frequency. *This new vibration is the energetic footprint, or source code, of the intuitive hit, the precognition, or the inner vision.* As long as we are able to maintain our initial mind frequency, we can recognize this new interference pattern and use the information held within it to guide us to solutions we seek.

In terms of information retrieval, it all comes down to vibration. You can feel it when you get that intuitive hit — something aligns. The code clicks together. *It feels right.* Feeling, the long-underrated faculty of the left brain, is how we navigate the quantum field of vibration. The insightful, creative part of our mind doesn't just process emotional feeling, it processes energy as well. It guides us through the recognition of resonance and dissonance as we play our part in the great cosmic dance of life. Intuitively, we move to the music of the universe. String theory, a contemporary quantum field theory, also envisions the universe as a great cosmic symphony — a world of strings vibrating to create the song of life. According to string theory, everything vibrates. The universe is composed, at a fundamental level, of infinitesimal vibrating strings of information — even smaller than subatomic particles like electrons or quarks. We are all vibrating. It is this vibration that creates energetic relationships between and among objects and people — between you and me.

Quantum vibrations are excitations of the zero-point field. They create the manifest world and the energy codes that are stored in the field as universal memory. As they interact and their waves interfere with each other, they create the informational messages that form the illuminating codes of the universe. These vibrational information codes touch you locally and nonlocally; you can know them and feel them. The dual nature of intuition — sometimes experienced as a knowing and other times experienced as a feeling — is a result of the unified energetic and informational nature of the inner field.

In essence, a sea of vibrating, interfering information waves creates the code packets that program the realities of the mind matrix. In a participatory universe like ours, you create wave patterns with every choice you make, every thought you have, and every feeling you experience. Every mind in the universe adds their code to the akashic repository of the quantum field. These wave interference patterns are a highly efficient memory storage function, holding incredible amounts of data — more than a full lifespan of accumulated human memory, estimated to be over 28 quintillion bits of information. The repository of information-energy abides;

it exists for everyone to access when the time is right — when you are in alignment with the code it holds and when certain conditions are met:

- Your wavelength is vibrating in line with the wavelength of the code.
- You are tuned in to the same frequency of the code.
- The code exists in the same medium as you (local reality).

It is much easier for your mind to access the codes of everyday reality because your point of consciousness is in the same environment where they are activated. Being in a singular moment of space-time may make accessing nonlocal data appear to be impossible, but we can transcend that illusion when we shift our point of consciousness beyond local parameters. The key to making that shift is changing your vibration.

Shifting Your State of Mind

Vibrational shifts give us passage into the field. Both upshifts and downshifts have been known to create awakenings and open the floodgates of illumination. The first time this happened to me, I was nineteen years old on summer holiday with some friends in Toronto. After a fun night and a bonfire at the beach, we went back to a friend's house, and I went to bed in their sister's room. I remember noticing that she had a beautiful Monet poster hung so high up at the top of the wall that it touched the ceiling. I wondered why she would hang it up so high where it was hard to see. I fell asleep that night feeling so happy and carefree. The next thing I remember is being awake and looking at that Monet painting — but I was looking at it at eye level. I didn't feel like I was dreaming; I felt wide awake. A thought immediately came to mind: *How can I see this at eye level? It's at the ceiling!* With that one thought, as soon as I began to consciously think, I broke the spell. I woke up in bed, my body tingling and heart racing. It took me many years to fully understand what happened that night, but it revealed to me three very important clues about the universe:

- It is possible to experience awareness in a location apart from your body or brain.
- Changing your vibrational state can induce a field experience. (For me, this happens during times of intense *upshift*, when I am ecstatic or joyful; but for others, like Eckhart Tolle, awakenings can also be induced by suffering or intense pain.)
- The act of conscious thinking, observation, or mental focus often ends the experience.

You may have had your own experiences with alternate frequency perception at night. Have you ever heard random, dreamlike voices just as you are falling asleep? These could be words or phrases that sound like a conversation, almost as though you are changing the station on a radio. Maybe you heard a man or woman's voice — someone you don't recognize — who seems to be talking to someone else? This phenomenon is quite common and often is so clear that it wakes people up. It occurs when the brain shifts its frequency into a relaxed state. In the past, you may have told yourself it was part of a dream, but now, in light of your awareness of the quantum field, you can see that your intuitive mind is receiving metasensory information transmissions from the field around you.

As you fall asleep, your inner antenna picks up otherwise imperceptible information from the field. This could come in the form of a local conversation resonating through the ethers around you or even nonlocal audial ghosts imprinted from another moment in time. Either way, your relaxed, intuitive state of mind shifts into the right frequency to pick up signals coded into the quantum field. This is why so many metaphysical experiences happen while falling asleep or waking up, just on the cusp of sleep. In this state of relaxed attention, your critical mind is out of the way. And, as always, the moment you think, *What just happened?* you break the spell and wake up.

Different vibrational levels of consciousness can open us up to different levels of awareness and metasensory experience. How is this possible? Lynne McTaggart explained it in her book *The Field* like this:

> In ordinary perception, the capacity of the dendritic networks in our brains to receive information from the Zero Point Field is strictly limited.... We are tuned in to only a limited range of frequencies. However, any state of altered consciousness — meditation, relaxation...dreams — relaxes this constraint. According to systems theorist László, it is as though we are a radio and our "bandwidth" expands. The receptive patches in our brains become more receptive to a larger number of wavelengths in the Zero Point Field.

While high-vibration states create resonance and alignment with the field, low-vibration states create dissonance — a kind of mental and/or emotional static that prevents harmonization with the field's expansive energy. Low-vibration states make us feel smaller, disempowered, confused, or egocentric. Peter Smith, the author of *Quantum Consciousness*, called these lower vibration states a "request for resonance," which is an empowering way to understand the dissonant state. On some level, we all crave resonance; at times, the challenges of life can make that difficult. When we experience loss, disappointment, or disillusionment, we can fall out of alignment with life; the ensuing states of mind are symptoms of a lack of resonance and are a cry for its return.

Vibrational States of Mind

Field-Resonant High Vibrations	Field-Dissonant Low Vibrations
Love	Fear
Joy	Anxiety
Peace	Anger
Self-love	Grief
Well-being	Depression
Compassion	Personal ambition
Intuitive state of mind	Overthinking mind

Ultraresonant, highest-vibration awareness (also called *super-consciousness*) is the destination point of the great spiritual masters. In Eastern religions, this state is called *samadhi* — the profound, joyful, absorptive state of contemplation that unites one with the raptures and beatitudes of the highest order, with full mental acuity. On this frequency, human beings have the ability to perceive beyond the limits of space-time and recognize the deep dimension within.

The Vibration of Consciousness

SUPERCONSCIOUSNESS
High-Vibration State of Expanded Bandwidth
The nonlocal and nonbinary experience of the quantum field

CONSCIOUSNESS
Earth-Vibration State of Everyday Bandwidth
The local and binary experience of the quantum field

UNCONSCIOUSNESS
Low-Vibration State of Diminished Bandwidth
A barrier to the quantum field created by emotional blocks or overthinking

Your entire life is an interplay between these states of consciousness: The field itself is pure superconsciousness — your intuition guides you to it for a higher perspective on reality. In the conscious state, you have access to a local pocket of the field defined by your everyday, binary reality. And finally, the unconscious state is not one of physical unconsciousness but instead the mental unconsciousness that comes with ignorance, unresolved feelings, or toxic thinking. Most humans spend most of their time in unconscious and conscious states, only touching the superconscious in extraordinary moments. But that is starting to change as more people embrace their quantum nature. Like sea creatures in an ocean of vibration, we all rise together. The whole universe is a single resonating field that we navigate according to our vibration.

 Your vibration is your personal access code to the information of the deep dimension.

Matching the universe's frequency is the key to unlocking information embedded in the quantum field. You get access to the data you resonate with. Through this resonance, you can rise above the barriers created by the thinking mind. When you flow with the energy of life, you are in sync with your inner field. This coherent state aligns you with truth so you can act from a place of truth. When you create your life from a place of truth — and the peace and power it holds — you can see, at last, that there are no real boundaries; there is only *the way*.

ILLUMINATION KEY #4

My Intuitive Mind Is Limitless

We are here to find that dimension within ourselves
which is deeper than thought.

— Eckhart Tolle

Once you recognize that you are part of a timeless, interconnected universe of conscious light, you can tap into its eternal memory field to inform and guide your life. Wisdom from the deep dimension is your true north — the one and only guidance system you can fully trust because *it is truth itself*. The deeper you go into the field, the more you align with the way of truth, including both your personal truth and the truth of all existence. The goal of our work in the field is to move past the illusions of local reality and our personal, relative experience of awareness to draw closer to our source — the zero-point, nonlocal unified field of *all awareness*.

ILLUMINATION KEY #4
opens your mind to the timeless wisdom
stored in the cosmos.

Knowing that everything that has ever happened, is happening, or will happen is stored in the ever-present information and memory field of the universe, you can attune your mind to explore its nonlocal illuminating codes.

In the key practices ahead, you will begin to explore how your local, personal consciousness connects with illuminating information codes from the nonlocal, akashic field. You will learn how to attune your body, mind, heart, and spirit to receive the best and brightest guiding light from your inner wisdom.

Key #4 Activation: Attuning to the Quantum Field
Expand Your Bandwidth of Awareness

To access the most powerful information stored in the field, our goal is to both expand our intuitive bandwidth and elevate the vibration of our consciousness. It's not just about receiving more information — it's about receiving *more of the right kind of information*. Your personal consciousness is a local access point, continuously connected and communicating with the universal field; when you uplift and open your heart and mind, your inner information highway flows abundantly to the purest, abiding truths of existence. "Yogis and spiritual masters decode a wider-than-ordinary range of frequencies," explained László. "Prophets and visionaries are not necessarily delusionary dreamers: they may be accessing a wider band of frequencies in the world than people in ordinary states of consciousness."

Lighting Up Your Inner Space

To live in harmony with your inner dimension, it essential to tune your mind into the illuminating rays of cosmic consciousness — the wisdom that is traveling in the high-vibration waves of light. Our various states of frequency affect our ability to connect to this wisdom in different ways:

- When you are filled with radiant, empowering thoughts, loving feelings, and physical well-being, you naturally resonate with radiant, empowering, loving energy that guides you from the field as your true north. You can easily read the intuitive information codes that offer you hope, confidence, self-love, creativity, and reassurance.

- At other times, when you aren't feeling well, are stressed out, or are down in the dumps, you may find it harder to hear the guiding codes of your inner voice. The inner field has many voices, and when we are low, we are more likely to doomscroll the field — to be attracted to the codes that manifest as self-doubt, fear, insecurity, or anxiety. The low notes of the field connect us to the information that brings us down and tells us we aren't good enough or are unable to ascend higher.

Most likely, you have experienced both situations during the ups and downs of your life. We all do. There are times when you feel great, your heart is full, and your mind is at peace; in these moments, you can feel the intuitive connection all around you. Ideas flow, passions call, solutions are found, and doors open wherever you need them. Your being is in an expansive state of uplifted consciousness. Synchronicities abound because you are in sync with the deeper dimension of life.

But then, there are other times when things are not so great. Think back to a time when you were sick or not feeling well. Was your energy so low that you didn't feel like your usual happy self? Were you tempted to sink into sadness or depression? Did intrusive thoughts get the best of you? No matter how consciously evolved we are, physical illness can zap our energy, making us feel heavy, deflated, and unable to reach the high notes of the field — the enlightened places that reassure us and guide us forward. But, if we can ride these moments out, we see that these highs and lows are the natural rhythm of a dualistic world; they are the waves that create change, growth, and the expansion of our consciousness. Without the lows, we would have no momentum for the highs.

To ride the waves that expand your consciousness deeper into the field, relax and go with the flow. The more you live in a state of calm acceptance and trust in life, the more your life unfolds with ease. Integrating mindful practices — like meditation, yoga, qi-gong, or even a quiet walk in the park — gives you the clarity to navigate your life as you get into a state of flow with your inner dimension. Whatever you do to relax your mind and find your peace, do more of it so you can attune your intuition to the highest guiding light of the field.

The great cosmic symphony is playing, and we don't want to hear just one or two of its high notes — we want to hear it all. Like tuning into a song on the radio, a slightly attuned intuition gets bits and pieces along with a lot of static interference. A more attuned intuition with an expanded bandwidth plays more of the song more clearly and with less interference.

Your mind is a kind of living antenna that gives you the power to tune in to information that flows invisibly all around you. The field, like our cosmic symphony, is imperceptibly broadcasting its universal memory field, which is filled with a range of energy-infused nonlocal data — high notes and low notes from our individual and collective stories, the akashic records of all life. As we know, these stories include the beautiful, rapturous, empowering highs and also the painful lows of sadness and suffering.

The Highs and Lows of Your Inner Connection

Your inner connection will have natural ups and downs. This dynamic rhythm creates the upshifts and downshifts that fuel your personal growth:

- **Upshifted state:** When we are in the high places, we naturally align with high thoughts. We are on top of the world, and we think nothing can bring us down. How could it? We feel so good inside; we are living in resonance with the unfolding of life. In this state, the field corresponds with uplifting energy that we naturally attract and draw from it.

When we think about our lives or look back over our past, we may feel so blessed — like we have had the best life ever, even with all the challenges. We see the high points and are proud of ourselves for all that we overcame. Through the eyes of this illuminated state, we see the light in our lives, and we effortlessly pull light from the field.

- **Downshifted state:** No matter how perfect life seems, inevitably something happens — we get sick, we lose something we love, we fail, we are hurt by the world, or a dream dies. Our energy plummets with our struggling heart, body, and/or mind. Where is the guiding light from our inner field now? This state is often the most frustrating because we need the light during this time the most. Instead of connecting to its wellspring of inspiring, empowering energy, we seem to be able to muster up only diminishing thoughts and disempowering feelings.

  When we look back on our life and pull up memories from our cosmic scrapbook, we find our mind going to the lows — the painful memories, the mistakes we made, the moments of heartache or disappointment. The future and the past can seem bleak when we are disconnected from the high energy and power of the field. It is important to remember that when we find ourselves in the low point of a wave, life will inevitably lift us back up. We just need to keep riding the wave with our hearts and minds set on getting back up. The gift of the downshift is the opportunity to rise into a new beginning.

Your state of mind directly correlates to the information you receive from the field, either as intuition or memory. In our high points, we can connect to expansive power; in our low points, we often cling to the past or old memories that no longer serve us. If you are holding on to anything that prevents you from receiving and living by your truth, now is the time to let it go. The higher you rise into yourself, the deeper you can go in the field. You can't get fully into the high zones of the field by taking a pill or through scientific procedures; the deep dimension is a part of you — one that you can only access by becoming it.

EXPERIMENT: LIGHTEN UP

Even the slightest upshift can make a big difference in the amount and quality of insight you receive. Living in a low-vibration state, without intuitive access to your inner field, is like living without your internet, cut off from the system that connects you to the world, shares your stories, and immortalizes them in history. Try this quick practice — either now or the next time you are in meditation — as a simple way to raise your vibration and expand your access to the inner field.

1. Close your eyes and relax into the moment.
2. Take a few deep, cleansing breathes.
3. Smile. Keeping your eyes closed, put a big, happy, beautiful, ear-to-ear smile on your face.
4. Notice how that smile lifts you up and raises your spirit. Let it take you higher into a sense of inner radiance and peace.
5. Feel this state of resonance bring you into alignment with the wholeness of your being and the flow of the field as you open heart and mind to its guiding insight.

Your smile is one of the most powerful tools for uplifting your energy, especially during meditation or intuition practice. Have you ever wondered why the Buddha is so often represented with a smile on his face? The smile is a tool to embody the light and its higher vibration wavelengths. With a smile, you light yourself up and instantaneously raise your vibration. Buddhist monks often teach the practice of smiling as a meditation ritual. The smile elevates your mind and opens your heart. Whenever you need a boost or are seeking to cultivate inner resonance, you can lift yourself up with a smile.

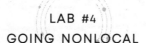

LAB #4
GOING NONLOCAL

Your Intuition and Memory Codes

Now that we have a basic understanding of the mind matrix — its timeless nature, local and nonlocal realities, and primary state of vibration — it's time to start exploring. Are you curious about what its field of wisdom holds for you? In this lab, you will have the chance to see for yourself how the quantum field touches your life personally. To begin, let's go over the four primary ways that you naturally receive downloads from the quantum field and how it is naturally at work in your life, whether you are aware of it or not — nudging you, prompting you, and dropping in those bits and bytes of guiding information.

Four Types of Intuitive Downloads

To recognize how quantum intelligence naturally and passively drops into your mind, pay attention to any thoughts, ideas, feelings, or impressions — anything that arrives in your consciousness with no apparent effort. Pause for anything that comes to you out of the blue or in a flash of insight. The act of attention engages the field and invites its energy flow. Creating a simple habit of observation expands your own energy and hones your receptive powers.

Restful Downloads: Semiconscious Downloads from the Field

Sleep is often a backdoor portal to intuitive insight. In unconsciousness, we are still connected to the field with one advantage: our critical mind is out of the way. For this reason, we often wake up with big ideas or revelations in our heads. Some of the most valuable breakthroughs, solutions, and creative ideas arrive in the semiconscious state of mind.

Here are some examples of restful downloads:

- You wake up in the middle of the night with the solution to a problem.
- A brilliant idea pops in your head after you wake up in the morning.

Aimless Downloads: Relaxing into the Insight Zone

The time we spend awake and alone with ourselves is a gold mine for insight. The moments when we are zoning out — such as having a cup of tea, listening to music, or sitting on a rocking chair on the porch — activate our inner receiver as our mind wanders off.

Here are some examples of aimless downloads:

- When strolling through the mall, you get the idea to go a specific store, where you find exactly what you were looking for.
- During your morning shower, you think of a friend, then find a text message from them on your phone when you get out.

Inspirational Downloads: Getting into the Creative Energy Flow

The creative process is a state of union with our inner field. Inspiration and all that flows from it are part of the manifestation process of life itself. Being in the creative flow revitalizes our being as we participate in the process of growth and expansion. Watch for anything that moves you or inspires you to do something: this is the outpouring of the field's energy flow carrying you forward.

Here are some examples of inspirational downloads:

- You are inspired to rearrange the furniture in your house. After you do, the energy feels so much better.
- You have an unexplainable calling to start your own business and share your gifts with the world.

Intentional Downloads: Consciously Accessing the Field

The fourth type of download comes as we consciously open space to receive insight. We can do this through various means, including conscious intuition "field work" and practices that we will go over in depth in part 2 of this book.

Here are some examples of intentional downloads:

- During meditation, you receive a powerful revelation about your life.
- You pull an insight card that gives you a higher perspective on a situation.

Tip: Remember, genuine insights come from a place of peace and power. Since insights arrive from the highest frequencies, they are never scary, negative, or fear-based. Genuine intuition is always empowering. Its whole purpose is to support your life journey, so it will never diminish you or share anything that holds you back from your highest path. You can explore your personal relationship with intuition — and how to deepen it — in my book *Radical Intuition: A Revolutionary Guide to Using Your Inner Power.*

How the Information Field Works

As you raise your vibration and expand your bandwidth deeper into the quantum field, you naturally connect with the information it carries via your intention. Remember these two defining factors of your inner wisdom:

- Quantum intelligence is instantly available and downloadable in seconds.
- Quantum intelligence is available at any time and from any place.

Embracing the deep dimension allows you to replenish your insight-starved unconsciousness and gradually rise into the illumination of the higher realities. Regular practice with the field amplifies the signal from your inner antenna and aligns your frequency so that you get clearer intuitive signals.

Downloading Past, Present, and Future Information from the Field

This lab explores the nonlocal nature of the quantum field. It includes practices to take you beyond time into the confluence of memory and intuition; it also includes practices to take you beyond place to recognize the ever-present nature of your inner dimension. As you work through the activities ahead, it's helpful to remember:

- There is no such thing as past and future; you are always in the present — past and future are only relative to your point of consciousness in this moment.

- You hold all the information in the universe within you, so you don't have to do anything or go anywhere to access it.

All the information of time and space is available to you through the holographic nature of your inner dimension.

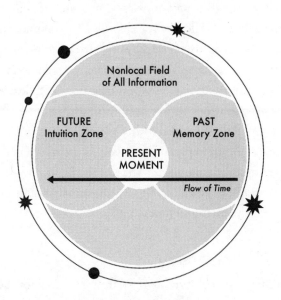

You access the inner field through both intuition and memory.

A Local Memory Exercise

Let's warm up with something easy — calling up a memory from the past. In your journal or Illumination Workbook, take a moment to recall and write down your earliest childhood memory. Describe the situation, the place around you, and how your felt. Include as much detail as possible.

As you are recording this memory, notice how the information comes to you. Are your memories in the form of mental pictures? Do they come with feelings? Thoughts? Sensations? Remember how these memory impressions feel. Soon, you will begin to see that they are quite similar to the intuitive impressions you receive from the field.

Finally, go back to your memory. Can you remember the day before it? The day, week, or even year after it? Probably not. Most likely, there is wide blank space around it. It is almost as though this memory has taken on a timeless dimension. It stands alone, outside the day-to-day flow of your life. Of all the moments, hours, days, weeks, and months of each day of your early life, you remember this one experience because it made an impression on you. You are still connected with it. All the rest falls away from locality into nonlocality. The further you go away from this moment, the less information you are entangled with. Only select memories — ones that made significant impressions on you — are stored in the local hard drive of your memory field. The rest is offloaded to the cloud, to a folder in the nonlocal field that you can still access but only with the intuitive, nonlocal function of your mind.

A Nonlocal Memory Exercise

Next, let's try digging up a memory from the nonlocal field. To begin, take a moment to get into your intuitive zone. Consider doing an uplifting meditation, perhaps using the smile technique to raise your vibration and get into the same wavelength as your inner field. When you feel good and are ready, read through the steps below, then begin:

1. Set your intention to pull down a forgotten memory from the nonlocal storage field. Be open to any memory from any time in your experience. Receive whatever comes to you.
2. Relax and clear your mind. Don't think too hard or force anything. Just be open to whatever comes.

3. Imagine yourself in another place and time. Where are you? What are you doing? Notice the first impressions that drop into your conscious awareness — any seemingly random images, words, situations, feelings, even physical sensations. Does a scenario begin to form?

4. Go deeper. What is going on in this place and time? Let your imagination flow. Follow it wherever it goes. *Important: Do not try to place the memory yet or make sense of the impressions; just let them fall into your mind and accept whatever comes, even if it seems wild or nonsensical.*

5. Once the download stops or the impressions begin to repeat, take a moment to contemplate what you received. Do you recognize this memory? Can you relate it to this life or maybe even another life? Allow the impressions to resonate in your mind and see if you get a feeling for its source.

6. Finally, place your memory:

   o If you recognize and remember this situation in your life, feel into the memory. How does it feel to have it come back to you now? Does this memory ignite other forgotten memories? Are you surprised that you had forgotten this memory? Is there a meaningful lesson or something important you are going through in this memory? In this way, hypnosis and other psychological exploration practices can help us to reconnect with all kinds of lost memories.

   o If you don't recognize or remember this situation in this life, feel into your intuition. What is it showing you? Is this another life? The past? The future? Feel into as many details as possible to get a sense of the location, time, and other surrounding details. Do you feel any connection to your life in this moment? In this way, we can explore other lives and what parts of them remain entangled with us today. (We will talk more about other lives in chapter 6.)

Tip: Sometimes memories hold sensitive information. If anything you receive makes you uncomfortable, you can simply stop the process, release it, then start over when your mind is clear again. To keep things upbeat, set your intention on accessing a happy or joyful memory; this will steer your energy to a high-vibrational place in the field.

Field work like this is both a valuable self-discovery and intuition development practice. You can experiment with this process by setting your intention on specific nonlocal scenarios, like recalling a past life, sensing future potentialities, or even getting perspective on life events and relationships. The process is most effective when practiced in service to your personal growth; the universe cares about your awakening and will lead you to information that supports it. By consciously tapping into meaningful parts of the field — ones that deliver memories with learning lessons or life-altering experiences you may have forgotten — you discover the higher perspectives that can reframe your past and inform your future.

With these two simple exercises, you can start to feel how intuition and memory share a common function: pulling information out of the quantum field. You experience them as similar functions because they are two facets of the same process. A memory is simply a past-tense intuition. Both intuitive insight and memory recall give you the ability to explore the high and low notes of the great cosmic song of life.

Lab #4 Workbook: Intuiting the Past, Present, and Future
Streaming Nonlocal Data

Becoming aware of your stream of intuitive impressions as they arrive from nowhere is a key step in living by your inner code. As you begin your intentional field work, it's a good idea to start keeping a daily record of your intuitive hits. Doing so helps you to build trust in yourself and understand which of your inner pathways are naturally open to the field. You have your own unique way of processing quantum information; this practice makes you consciously aware of how intuitive and memory impressions feel. You can record your experiences using the frameworks below or using the log provided in the Illumination Workbook.

Daily Insight Log: My Intuitive Downloads

1. **Restful downloads:** _____
2. **How they support your life:** _____
3. **Aimless downloads:** _____
4. **How they support your life:** _____
5. **Inspirational downloads:** _____
6. **How they support your life:** _____
7. **Intentional downloads:** _____
8. **How they support your life:** _____

Local Memory Exercise

1. **Intention:** Recall your earliest childhood memory.
2. **Download:** Record all the information that flows in to help you relive it.
3. **Reflection:** Can you recognize how your memory impressions are similar to your intuitive impressions? Is there a reason why you are still entangled with this particular memory?

Nonlocal Memory Exercise

1. **Intention:** Connect with a nonlocal memory.
2. **Download:** Record all the information that flows in to show you a nonlocal scenario.
3. **Reflection:** Where do you place this memory: in this life or another? Could it be the past or the future? Why do you think this intuition or memory relates to this present moment? Can you now recognize how similar your intuitive impressions are to memories?

CONCLUSION

Activating Key #4 of the illumination code opens
your mind to its limitless nature.

The fourth key reveals the dynamics of the local and nonlocal realties that permeate our lives. When we understand our world in terms of the mind matrix, which acts as an interplay between the vibrational fields of a local and nonlocal reality that coexist everywhere all at once, we can see how experiences that we once called impossible or supernatural are a natural part of the fabric of existence.

Key Principles

- The world around us appears to be a local, holographic container in an interpenetrating nonlocal metareality.
- We and everything in the world are made of tiny pixels of light.
- There is no past and future: everything in the world is happening everywhere all at once.

- The quantum field stores the memory of the universe
- Your access to the field is determined by your vibrational state.
- Mental focus interferes with the intuitive flow from the field.
- We can access the field with both intuition and memory.

Key Applications

- Start recognizing the four types of intuitive downloads as they show up in your life.
- Try new ways to raise your vibration and attune your energy to quantum information.
- Notice how your vibrational level affects your intuitive abilities.
- Practice exploring the local and nonlocal memory fields.

In the first part of this book, we have explored the true nature of reality and how it is inextricably related to our intuitive faculty. We have learned that a part of us knows everything and that through communion with our inner dimension, we can cultivate the ability to expand our awareness beyond the local confines of our reality. Next, we venture inward to understand and develop our quantum intelligence.

PART 2

FIELD WORK

CHAPTER FIVE

Quantum Intelligence

What intellect is to the physics of yesterday,
intuition is to the physics of tomorrow.

— RADICAL INTUITION

In the space between your thoughts lies a silent wisdom — an illuminating code that is part of a computing system that exceeds the grasp of ordinary intelligence. This deep knowledge, which is more powerful and true than any other, can be known through only your intuitive nature — your quantum intelligence. To master the art of quantum thinking, you must let go of your attachment to the illusory limitations of local reality and the idea that time or space is a barrier to what you can know. You can no longer think that your five senses show you all of reality or that intelligence is something you achieve only through hard work.

The highest form of intelligence takes no work at all; it is something that you effortlessly receive. It is not bound by time, space, or the walls of your physical reality but rather is omnipresent and available to us always. The purpose of this emerging faculty of metacognition is to enlighten you, to keep you safe from harm, to guide your life's path, and to expand your mind along with the universe. As a bona fide cognitive system, it draws nonlocal information from the quantum dimension to inform you according to the purest abiding truths of the universe. When you live in a state of alignment and trust it, you cannot go wrong.

Metacognition: A Zero-Point State of Mind

Intuitive insight arrives from the everythingness-and-nothingness void — *the source* of all things. Returning to this universal source is the secret to harnessing our great quantum intelligence. How do we personally access the womb of everythingness where all the information in the world exists? All truth is accessed through the eternal now. We find the magic of the zero-point field in presence with this moment. The gateway to your quantum reality is open only in *the now*, where the spaciousness of being invites the overthinking mind to surrender to the sovereign flow of universal insight.

Before you can enter into harmony with your inner dimension, you must rise above the quagmire of compulsive thinking, judgment, confusion, and uncertainty that locks you out of it. The mental dissonance we live with every day is not our natural state. We have become desensitized to it, as if it is normal to live with fear, anxiety, and chronic suffering of all kinds. These states are not intrinsic to human nature; they are symptoms of the loss of our connection to the unified field and our own wholeness.

To become whole again, we must go back to the start. It is time to step back from the mind and its circus to reenter the magic of the primordial stillness. The silence of being is a portal that unites our local consciousness with its nonlocal source and opens the pathways of intuitive insight. Here, we commune with our inner field and receive its gifts of awareness. Out of the cosmic source arises truth and the answers to everything we seek. The silence, the stillness, the nothingness — this is where the deep magic is born.

The great masters of life have known this. The Buddha sat

in stillness under the bodhi tree to reach enlightenment, Jesus retreated to the quiet of the wilderness to pray, and even Einstein's best ideas came when he was aimless. To step into the mystery, we must first step back from this world and the overthinking minds that trap us here. In the stillness, there is an invitation to truth. According to Joe Dispenza, author of *Becoming Supernatural*, "If you want to experience the supernatural in your own life — by healing your body, creating new opportunities you could never have imagined before, and having transcendent, mystical experiences — you first need to master the concept of the present moment: the eternal now." Deepak Chopra also eloquently described our relationship with time: "In truth, the present moment never ends and eternity is in the moment."

Your quantum intelligence flows through the empty space between your thoughts and shows you the magic held in the eternal now. Your mind might trick you into thinking that the stillness is boring and empty — that it has nothing interesting to offer. But nothing could be further from the truth. In stillness, you can discover the whole world. Your thinking mind rejects stillness because it has no power there. The linear mind runs on a binary operating system based on action and reaction, cause and effect — in essence, *time*. But, in the dimension where your quantum intelligence reigns, there is no time, hence there can be no cause and effect, no train of thought. In the inner dimension, *thinking* is replaced with *knowing*.

Intuition is instantaneous because all things in the field are simultaneous. This is why intuitive insight shares information in a flash, while your logical mind takes time to process the data and figure it all out. W. Brugh Joy explained how conditioned patterns of time-based thinking have come to dominate both our consciousness and communication:

The present necessity of communicating by means of words underlies the major entraining of consciousness into sequential linear patterns. Language is indispensable to most human beings — not because it is innate but simply because it is usually the only developed means of communication....When simultaneous states of awareness begin to appear, there is an even better alternative to sequentiality — through symbols or through telepathy. Telepathy is capable of impressing in a single moment the *totality* of what is to be communicated....As I have said before, telepathy is our natural form of communication.

Quantum intelligence, with all its mystery and magnificence, is your natural state of being. It is your natural form of communication. It is how you innately learn from the universe and connect with other beings.

INVESTIGATION: YOUR NO-MIND PORTALS

You can access your quantum intelligence only from a place of no-mind. Your intuition flows only when you are not thinking. A no-mind portal is any state of being that turns off the thinking mind and opens a connection to your quantum field. In this relaxed state of consciousness, you can intuitively explore the field and download its instant revelations.

Peter Smith described this process in his book *The Transcendence of Celeste Kelly* as the main character, Celeste, discovers what Einstein, who was known for his appreciation of intuitive genius, was actually doing while sitting in his favorite no-mind portal, his rocking chair: "You mean to say that you think he was going into the quantum field to find the ideas? That would've made him a conduit, and his thought process wouldn't just have been the development of ideas but, rather, him moving through the field to find the piece he needed. He thought he was exploring his brain; perhaps he was exploring the universe instead!" In the mindless, aimless act of rocking in his chair, Einstein mused through the vast expanses of his inner field.

Everyone has their own personal favorite no-mind portals. Here are some examples of states that are known to deliver new ideas, intuitive insight, solutions to problems, or even reminders (since intuition is also memory). You can experiment with these activities and pay renewed attention to any information that you receive during them.

Check your favorite no-mind portals below.

- ❏ Having your morning tea or coffee
- ❏ Driving in your car
- ❏ Taking a bath or shower
- ❏ Waking up from sleep or half-sleep
- ❏ Meditating
- ❏ Listening to music
- ❏ Practicing yoga, qigong, or tai chi
- ❏ Walking in nature
- ❏ Exercising, running, or riding bike
- ❏ Daydreaming
- ❏ Being creative
- ❏ Journaling

What other no-mind portals do you enjoy?

As you are cultivating your intuitive nature, try to get into your no-mind portals on a regular basis.

> ### FIELD WORK STORY: A VOICE IN THE SILENCE
> #### by Maria, entrepreneur
>
> *Maria's story is an example of the power of no-mind portals — how guiding information arrives effortlessly into an open mind. In this case, she received valuable guidance from the quantum field through her metasense of hearing while driving in the car.*
>
> My father always had an intuitive connection and encouraged me to feel it too. He explained that there is a voice inside us that we can trust and that we should not be afraid of — that we should always listen to this voice, even if we don't know the meaning or purpose, because it is there to keep us safe. One night when I was a teenager, as I was driving alone on a dark and winding road, I heard a voice shout out of nowhere: "Pull over!" Without thinking, I immediately pulled over into a nearby parking lot, my heart pounding, as I watched a speeding vehicle swerve toward me and into my lane. *If I had not stopped, it would have hit me head-on.* I was in shock. At the time, I wasn't exactly sure what that voice was, but I was so thankful that I listened to it. Since that day, I have honored the intuitive voice that my father helped me to understand, and I work to strengthen it every day. This voice can speak to us all — we just need to learn how to listen.

The Knowing Feeling

To help reactivate your natural quantum intelligence, let's explore how information rises out of the cosmic stillness and becomes the guiding codes that are deciphered by your intuition. As the universe's ever-present ground-state, information-infused consciousness moves into a state of excited energy, wave interference patterns create packets of code that build our reality and intuitively inform your mind. Your intuition translates this cosmic code into two primary forms of impressions: *intuitive thoughts* and *intuitive feelings*.

When you think intuitively, your mind receives bits and bytes of intuitive information. When you feel intuitively, your heart receives waves of energy that put life into motion. In a moment of insight or knowingness, you instantly receive cosmic truth; with a gut feeling or inner calling, you are pulled forward by its guiding energy. You are both informed and guided by your quantum dimension. The bits and bytes of thought information, also known as your inner wisdom, impart awareness, while the flow of resonant energy from the field moves you in the right direction. In the following sections, we will go over in detail how the universe uses the dual functions of heart and mind to naturally inform your life.

PARTICLES AND WAVES OF INFORMATION

Quantum intelligence is dual-faceted: it operates through both intuitive thinking and feeling. We see this idea reflected in the concept of particle-wave duality, which states that every quantum entity may be described paradoxically as either a particle, which is a small, localized object, or a wave, which is a dynamic disturbance that propagates from equilibrium. This duality specifically applies to quanta — those tiny pixels of information-infused light energy that fill the quantum field and inform your consciousness. The dual and complementary nature of quantum information reaches us through the dual and complementary nature of our quantum intelligence: intuitive *thought* is a means to interface with bits of *nonlocal information*, while intuitive *feeling* is a means to interface with excited waves of *energy and potentiality*.

Quantum Thinking: Using Your Inner Wisdom

Have you ever had an experience where you *just knew* something, but you didn't know why? An unexplainable awareness is one of the hallmarks of quantum intelligence. You know you are in contact with your inner field when you are privy to information that has not been generated in response to your local reality yet. In many cases, no evidence from your life validates this awareness, yet somehow you are confident it is true. When you are using your intuitive mind, it can feel like any of the scenarios below — and it often defies reason:

- A sense of knowingness
- An insightful understanding
- An inner certainty
- An awareness of something extraordinary

When you have an intuitive awareness, you often can't shake it. Other people may doubt you, but in many cases, a sense of conviction accompanies your insights — a byproduct of your connection to the quantum field, which is the home of all truth. When your mind is united with the field, it is united with the undeniable truth of existence, and no amount of rational thinking can persuade you otherwise.

For example, one evening when I was a young artist, years before cellphones, I stayed up late working. I fell asleep around midnight only to wake up a short time later with a strange knowingness. For some unexplainable reason, I knew that an out-of-town friend of mine was on their way to visit me — that they were coming to my house and would arrive any moment. Rationally, this made no sense since it was so late at night, and I didn't even know my friend was in town. I got up, went to the front door, and peered out into the darkness. Sure enough, a few minutes later I saw two headlights heading down the road to my house. When they arrived to surprise me with a late-night visit, they were shocked to see me standing at the front door — and even more shocked when they asked me what I was doing outside, and I answered, "Waiting for you." It turns out they had been in town visiting friends and stopped by to see if I was still awake.

 Quantum intelligence: When you know, even if you don't know how or why you know, *you just know.*

The part of me that knows everything knew my friend was on their way, and through the no-mind portal of sleep, bits and bytes of information that shared their whereabouts dropped into my intuitive mind. In this case, my conscious mind was informed by an impetus within me instead of from the outside world. I didn't need a phone call or text message to alert me to their arrival; I downloaded the information from the field. Since the person was someone close to me, I had a natural field connection with them that enabled this extraordinary information transfer. We are going to talk more about this kind of entanglement — the magical way people stay connected despite distances in both time and space — in chapter 6.

Quantum Feeling: Guided by the Energy Flow

Have you ever been inspired to do something or felt a deep calling to take your life in a particular direction? These gut feelings, creative ideas, and inner nudges are signs that quantum intelligence is moving within you. Intuition is often associated with living from the heart; when you follow your true heart, you follow the part of you that guides you from beyond. When your intuitive heart comes alive, it can feel like this:

- An inspiration to do or create something
- A new idea to change something

- A passionate sense of purpose
- A gut feeling that moves or guides you in a certain direction

When energy from the deep dimension pours into your life, you can feel like you are on fire with passion and energy. You feel alive. Your heart sings. You have an abiding sense of alignment with your path and your purpose — with the way forward. This is how communion with the quantum field feels when you are living and acting in the expansive flow of life. *Quantum feeling* is how the universe puts you into motion, excites you from the ground state of complacency or even stagnation, and draws you to any transformation your life requires.

By moving you from within, the universe magnetically draws you toward the best version of your life. You have the free will to choose to follow it or not, but living in flow with your inner dimension allows you to align with your highest potentiality from the ethers. I learned that the hard way many years ago when I was getting ready to leave my career in arts and technology to transition full time into my intuition work. I was called to this new vocation, but the change was scary. I kept procrastinating, thinking of reasons why I should wait another year or why I shouldn't leave a job that I loved where I was doing good work. But no matter what I did, the call remained; the universe persisted. Finally, while on a call with my boss one day, I got the message — my dog knocked me down the steps, and my house caught on fire. That's what it took to get me to take the quantum leap into the unknown — and I am so glad I did.

The energy from your inner field is constantly guiding you to your truth. You are naturally moved toward it, whether you are conscious of it or not. No amount of logic or reason can change its abiding direction. The more you resist it, the stronger it moves to correct you — like in the case of my quantum leap. If I had listened to the whispers gently calling me toward my true vocation,

I would not have had to endure the shouts or, finally, the roar that forced me into action. As you grow in sensitivity to your quantum dimension, you will be able to notice the gentle nudges and act on them with conviction — the process that ultimately leads you into communion with the unfolding of the universe.

EXPERIMENT: INTUITIVE KNOWING AND FEELING

When our intuition is operating at its full potential, we experience the complementary nature of thought and feeling as one. With your heart and mind both in coherence with your inner dimension, you simultaneously know and feel the truth. The result is a *knowing feeling*. With your intuition, sometimes you may *know* things, and other times you may *feel* things. When feeling and knowing come together, you are experiencing the purest form of intuition. Watch for this; it is the telltale sign that your quantum intelligence has spoken.

The knowing feeling clearly distinguishes your intuition from your ordinary thoughts. For example, let's say you got a new job offer. You may be confused if you *think* it's the right choice but don't really *feel* like it's the right choice, or vice versa. But when you *both know and feel* that the job is right, you can act with confidence. The next time you are making a choice, put it to the *knowing feeling* test:

- Does a part of you know that it is the right decision? Is there an abiding sense of assurance that comes with this choice?
- Does a part of you feel that it is the right decision? Are you assuredly moved, inspired, or called to this action?
- Does this *knowing feeling* abide? Revisit your decision again in a few hours: does it hold fast and steady in the same message?

Guiding information from the field is the ground-state truth, so its signals are consistent. This is how the universe imparts a sense of conviction into our intuitions. The knowing feeling is a manifestation of alignment between the mind and the heart, information and energy. When you both *know it* and *feel it*, you are being informed with the same information through your mind and your emotions. Recognizing this unified state of mind is the key to successfully navigating the challenges of life and living by the truth within you.

Resonance: Harmony with the Field

Once we understand that the quantum field is rich with guiding information and energy, the next step is to attune to a vibration that makes both more accessible. As we know, intuitive thoughts and feelings can be hard to reach or catch, especially while we're in low-vibration or dissonant states of mind. When you raise your vibration and align with the flow of energy in the deep dimension, you experience one of the most important states of connection with the quantum field: resonance.

We have already learned the foundational role of vibration in the great song of our universe — how all things exist and relate to each other according to their vibrational states. Resonance is a state of harmony with the field; it draws us into deeper communion and calls us forth in alignment with the way of the universal unfolding. Resonance moves us to participate in higher states of awareness and expanded consciousness. With resonance, *you feel the way*. Resonance is the byproduct of a world in motion, magnetically pulling you into alignment with the expanding universe and attuning your being to its cosmic song.

EXPERIMENT: ECSTATIC MOTION

Have you ever fallen in love with a song? Have you ever been so moved by music that you felt one with it or it transported your mind to another state of being? Whatever kind of music resonates with you, the vibration of song can take you into instant states of coherence — the rapture of communion with your inner dimension.

To feel the ecstatic motion of the universe through music, find a quiet place where you have some privacy. Then, turn on a song that moves, uplifts, or empowers you. Amp up the volume, or surround yourself in deep soundwaves from your headphones. Let the music carry you on its journey. Dance if you are moved to dance. Smile if you are moved to smile. Feel the vibrations penetrate your body, and shift your mental state as you connect with the music. At moments it may feel so intense that you get chills or feel totally consumed in your alignment with its energy. Feel it revitalize and recharge you from within. Even in small moments like this, you can feel the energy of the cosmos move within you and carry you away.

Resonance is a call forward. It draws you into coherence with the energy that radiates from our expanding universe — all ships rise together on the waves of the quantum field. Resonance is a guiding force and a valuable tool for all the wayfinding in your life. It helps you to self-actualize and make choices from the highest energetic state. When you are following your inner resonance, life *feels right*. You come alive. Resonance leads you to truth, new experiences, and personal growth. If you find yourself in a state of stagnation or living in a rut, this is often because you aren't following the resonant callings within you. Resonance leads to expansion and new life; its absence leads to the path of contraction or the sensation of dying on the vine.

Change creates energy. Movement creates power. This is one of the gifts of living in a dualistic world. The friction between opposing forces ignites transformation — empowering us to adapt and *become*. This transformation generates energy and fuels the expansion of life itself. Every one of us is an active energy generator, contributing our own part to the collective growth of existence. We live in a participatory universe. We are part of an ever-changing, dynamic system of life that we cocreate through our thoughts, choices, and actions. Resonance guides you through it all.

The counterpoint of resonance is resistance. While resonance calls you forward, resistance holds you back. You might feel an inner resistance when you are faced with an opportunity or choice that is not in your best interest. You might catch yourself trying to rationalize something despite what your gut is telling you. One of the keys to successfully living by your quantum intelligence is recognizing the difference between resonant and nonresonant energy. When you learn to tell the difference between resonant feelings of expansion and feelings of nonresonant resistance, you have a powerful wayfinding practice that applies to all areas of your life.

Next time you make a choice, pay attention to how each choice feels. Does the decision expand your being, as though it is pulling you toward something good for you? Does it make you feel alive, renewed, or excited? Does it feel like it is opening up your experience of life? Or, conversely, do you sense resistance? Are you rationalizing a course of action that somehow doesn't feel right? Are you trying to talk yourself into it? Most importantly, if it makes you feel smaller or in any way diminished, you can be sure it is not your inner wisdom leading the way. Your true path will always be one that empowers you and opens you up to the truth you hold within.

EXPERIMENT:
WAYFINDING WITH EXPANSION AND RESISTANCE

Next time you are making a choice about something in your life, put away the pros-and-cons list, and try this instead. Instead of thinking in terms of right and wrong, think in terms of resonant expansion and nonresonant resistance.

Your best path — the one supported by your intuition — feels expansive; it draws you into alignment with the unified field and uplifts you with potentiality. Dissonant paths — ways that feel confusing or misaligned — do not feel expansive; when you are headed in the wrong direction, you feel an intuitive resistance as you get out of sync with the field. You feel dissonance when you go against yourself. Your true, whole self exists in union with the inner truth of the field. Resonant expansion aligns you with that truth, while feelings of dissonance or resistance indicate you are moving away from it. Here is a quick way to identify how expansion and resistance feel to you so you can recognize them when they show up in your life:

1. **Expansion:** Think of a time when you met someone who expanded your life — a teacher, friend, family member, or loved one. Remember how they made you feel. When you were with them, did you feel inspired? Full of life, safe, aligned, excited, at peace, or growing? Like you were fully yourself?

2. **Resistance:** Next, think of a person who set you back in life — someone who worked against you or did not support your path. How did they make you feel? Uninspired, stuck, small, unworthy, or less than? Like you couldn't be your true self?

You can apply this process to any area of your life. Next time an opportunity comes along, ask yourself, *Does it feel expansive or is there some inner resistance?* If you are unsure about any decision, you can use the feeling of resonant expansion as a litmus test: If it excites you, opens you up to new energy, or feels aligned, you are likely moving in harmony with your inner dimension. If you have to talk yourself into something, make justifications, or overcome intuitive reservations, it may be a good idea to pause. When you are guided by resonance, you are happier and more fulfilled, and you are living your purpose. The goal of resonant expansion is to bring you fully into yourself; any action not taken in that spirit takes you away from yourself, your truth, and your highest path.

Regardless of how much we rationalize, at the end of the day, on some level, we want a decision to *feel right*. A recent study at Yale showed that "decisions made on the basis of feelings hold up longer in the face of new information than decisions made deliberately and rationally." As though a deep part of us recognizes the resonant call back into coherence with our deep dimension, we are better off when we choose the path that authentically feels right over the path that logically makes sense.

FIELD WORK STORY: GUIDED BY RESISTANCE
by Chantal, real estate agent

Chantal's story is an example of how uncomfortable feelings of resistance can be a valuable guiding force in your life. In her case, she learned through hindsight how her guiding intuition was working for her all along.

One morning, I was planning to take a hike with my husband after my son came home from school, but he suggested we go at lunchtime. I had an uncomfortable feeling about going earlier, but I dismissed it, and we went anyway. At the park, I went to put my purse in the trunk, but my husband insisted it was fine and told me to stick it under the seat. Again, I had this uncomfortable feeling, but I dismissed it, thinking I was being paranoid, and left my purse in the back seat. After our hike, when we returned to the car, the back window was broken, and my purse had been stolen, which was something out of the ordinary for my small town. This was so eye-opening to me as my intuition was right there the entire time, trying to steer me away from a negative experience. It tried to keep me safe repeatedly, but I didn't listen. But even so, this experience anchored me in my intuition; it revealed, in hindsight, how to better recognize my inner guidance and trust myself.

The Secret Power of Attention

Late one night many years ago, I came home from work to find my two roommates deep into a chess match. After saying hello, I went to my room to get settled and change clothes. My room was on the third floor of an old Victorian building with a beautiful view of the city and a fire-escape door overlooking a park behind our house. As I took off my coat, I happened to notice that the sheer curtains on the fire-escape door window were slightly disheveled; for some reason they caught my eye, so I walked across the room to straighten them. Just as I reached out to fix the curtain, I was startled by a loud knock on the other side of the door. My heart leapt. My mind raced: *Who would be knocking at my fire-escape door at eleven at night?* Confused, I cautiously opened the door, with the screen door still locked between us. A young man was standing there in a baseball hat. As he was silhouetted against the streetlights, I couldn't see his face, but I could tell he was smiling at me. He casually said, "Hey!" like he knew me. He was so friendly, but something felt *off*.

I looked at him while my brain tried to process what was happening. Then he said, "Is Matt here?"

No, Matt did not live here. I didn't know any Matt. I said, "Who?"

"Matt Miller. Doesn't he live here?" My spidey senses tingled. I had lived there for over a year. Nobody in the building was named Matt. Plus, why would anyone risk their life walking up three flights of a rusty old fire escape instead of knocking on the front door? As his face came into the light, I saw something in his eyes that I didn't like. The inner alarm bells started to officially go off.

Thank goodness, at that moment my roommate overheard what was going on and came into the room. "There's nobody here named Matt, dude," he told the guy abruptly. The man seemed surprised to see him, and his demeanor instantly changed.

"Sorry, man," he said, nervously retreating down the fire escape. "Must've had the wrong place," he mumbled as I closed the door. Adrenaline pumping, we instantly reported him to the police.

We learned that ours was the third report of a Peeping Tom in our neighborhood that week. When we went back out to check the fire escape, we realized that from the small stoop at my bedroom door, he could see into the apartments of three different young single women. He had likely been out there before, watching us all. Who knows what might have happened if *something hadn't drawn my attention* to the fire escape at that moment.

My intuition came to the rescue. It *drew my attention* to those curtains to make me aware of a situation I would not have otherwise perceived. Though it felt like I *just happened to notice* what was going on at that fire-escape door, the guiding energy of the field was relaying vital information on a deeper level. Then, when faced with a nonresonant situation, my state of confusion gradually shifted into conviction as my intuition continued to inform me of a potentially dangerous situation — discerning that a person who acted friendly and well intentioned was, in fact, neither.

Intuitive impressions from the field catch your attention in all kinds of ways every day. Have you ever randomly noticed serendipitous messages or synchronistic numbers? Maybe you noticed a guiding message on a billboard just when you needed it or happen to glance at the clock at 11:11 (or some other meaningful number pattern) on a regular basis? Somehow, your attention is magically drawn to look at something at just the right moment. These meaningful coincidences are not random; they are the byproduct of intuitive relays sending information from your guiding inner field.

One of the big revelations of quantum physics is the important role of *observation*. Concepts like wave-particle duality and the intelligent observer effect have revealed the powerful impact of attention. The popularity of the law of attraction and manifestation is rooted in the notion that your intention and attention create your world — that your focused mind collapses the quantum field's waves of potentiality into the particles of reality that form your life.

Attention is deeply linked to intuition. Through attention, you connect to the field — and the field connects to you. It is the intuitive dance that allows us to both actively and passively interact with the inner dimension. Intention is *active attention*, how you purposefully create and expand with the quantum field; conversely, with *receptive attention*, you are subtly touched, moved, or informed by energy directly from the field. With receptive attention, your inner guidance speaks to you through details that you unintentionally notice. You may not realize it, but the universe is attentive to you. It knows you because it is part of you. You have a pull to connect to it, and it has a pull to connect to you. And just like any relationship, attention fuels the dynamics of your interaction. We explore ways to consciously work with this intuitive phenomenon in the signs and synchronicities section of chapter 7.

Whether we are participating in it actively or passively, attention is energy. Observation appears to be a kind of force field that invisibly influences the interplay between reality and metareality. W. Brugh Joy famously demonstrated this principle by showing how the growth of yeast-filled petri dishes increased with direct observation. The yeast that was observed flourished more than yeast that was not observed. Other studies showed that microscopic crystal solutions could be influenced by looking at them under a microscope. Even our houseplants are said to thrive when we talk to them. As the saying goes, energy flows where the attention goes. When you are attentive to something, you send energy to it.

On that fateful night at my fire-escape door, the quantum-connected part of me *noticed that man noticing me.* Perhaps his observation of me pinged me to observe him. Maybe it wasn't the curtain I was noticing at all; maybe the curtain was the only thing standing between our mutual observation. On the other hand, maybe the part of me that knows everything, my quantum guardian angel, simply drew my attention to danger. Whatever the driving force may be, the message is clear: your intuition guides you through what you notice. The subtle details that catch your eye might just be intuitive nudges that could save your life.

INVESTIGATION: OBSERVING THE OBSERVER

Have you ever looked at someone only to have them unexpectedly look back at you? Have you ever looked at someone as you passed them in a car only to get a jolt when — for no apparent reason — they turn and look at you? This could have even happened in school or a public place when you are looking at someone from a safe distance, and then they spontaneously return your gaze.

On the other hand, have you even been on the other side of that awkward moment? Have you ever glanced over at someone only to see them looking at you? Or have you ever been woken up from sleep to find a parent or partner watching you sleep? It's like a part of you knows you are being watched before you even realize it.

This phenomenon is very common and even works with animals. Many times, when I have been watching a squirrel or chipmunk in my backyard, they turn and look at me just as I start looking at them, even if they can't see me inside the house. Moving forward, you can start to recognize these serendipitous moments not as random coincidences but as evidence of our interconnectedness in the quantum field. Next time this happens, whether you are the observer or the observed, make a note of it in your journal, notes, or workbook. How did the connection make you feel? Was there a little bit of magic in that moment of shared intuitive connection?

Once we become aware that attention is a force of the field — one that can impact us both locally and nonlocally — we can work with it to make deeper connections on all levels and align with the flow of life. As physicist and expert remote viewer Russell Targ said, "The choice of where we put our attention is ultimately our most powerful freedom. Our choice of attitude and focus affects not only our own perceptions and experiences, but also the experiences and behaviors of others." Not only does the quantum field enable us to download nonlocal data from our inner realm, it also gives us the ability to send and receive information with other living beings. The secret to doing both is becoming conscious of how we use our attention.

The Focus Trap

With your inner dimension, the magic often happens when you aren't looking for it or when you least expect it. Since the intelligent observer effect works on the quantum level, it operates in a state of no-mind. Only in the aimless moments, like when we are driving in the car or getting settled after a long day, can intuition catch our attention. When we are problem-solving or hyperfocused on something, we close our mind to our quantum intelligence. The act of focus then becomes a trap for your thoughts: the more you think, the less you can intuit.

The reason for this phenomenon: when you are focused on one thing, you are open only to that one thing. When you focus too intently, try too hard, or overthink, you are no longer in a state of receptivity — you are trapped in your mind. For your quantum intelligence to thrive, you must approach it in a *relaxed state of attention*. Be attentive but open. A great example of the focus trap is beginner's luck. We often naturally or intuitively do something better the first time we try it than in all the times after that. The first time I went bowling, I scored over one hundred; I never came close to scoring that again. My daughter's friend sank three balls in a row the first time she played pool only to struggle after that. When we have no idea what we are doing, we are likely to rely on our inner guidance system. Once we think we have it figured out, we rely on our critical mind, which often can't create the same results. We get stuck in a focus trap.

Focus traps are everywhere. Did you ever push someone away by trying too hard to win their affection — or vice versa? The more someone tries to make you like them, the less you often like them. Have you ever known someone who worked so hard that they failed to succeed? Maybe they overthought a project, overworked a creative idea, or were so overly ambitious that other people did not want to work with them. Focusing too much, grasping, or *trying* to do something can make us rigid, intuitively blocked, and unable to put our energy in the right place. The act of striving, as well intentioned as it may be, can do us more harm than good if we don't remain open to the intuitive flow of life.

The key to success is balancing our intention (our personal focus) with our intuition (our universal guidance). Instead of manifesting what we think we should have, we should trust our quantum intelligence to help us manifest what is truly best for us in a universal sense. Mental focus is the catalyst to actualizing the quantum world into reality, a process reflected in the wave-particle duality of quantum mechanics. Through conscious intention, you manifest from the field. According to quantum theory, as long as a photon or electron isn't being observed, it acts like a wave. It exists in a state of pure potentiality as part of the quantum field. As soon as the photon or electron is observed, it behaves like a particle, displaying a specific location along with other features, such as charge and momentum. The wave collapses into a particle in the process of manifestation — all of which is incited by the simple act of attention.

When you use your thinking mind to focus a wave into definitive reality, you create a limited state of being; you draw the finite out of the infinite. As Lynne McTaggart explained in her book *The Field*, "In the act of observation, we are transforming the timeless, spaceless world of interference patterns into the concrete and discrete world of space and time." The focused, thinking mind, then, is a *limiter* by nature. It acts as a kind of reduction valve that draws specific information from the cosmic field. Physician Larry Dossey wrote about this in his book *The Power of Premonitions*: "A key feature of this view is that the brain restricts consciousness by acting as a 'reducing valve,' as Aldous Huxley put it. The brain is like a dirty prism that cannot collect all the light to which it is exposed. It is like a tourniquet on consciousness, choking our perceptions down to a trickle. Thus physicist David Darling suggests that we are conscious not because of the brain, but in spite of it."

Your thinking mind is a reduction valve that limits the information you receive from the world within and around you. It is also a reduction valve for your intuition. This is also why, no matter how intuitive you are, you don't have access to *all* the information in the field. To be a conscious individual is, in itself, a reduction of awareness. With the reduction valve principle as an innate feature of our brain design, it would be impossible to download a universe of data through our focused — limited — mental bandwidth.

Nevertheless, the reducing power of the mind is a necessary part of individuated consciousness. Without it, we could not know the singular. We could not experience the relativity of time and space. If your mind consciously contained all the information in the universe, you would have no journey of life; there would be an unfolding of time, no becoming. There would be no privacy or individuality since everyone would know all things. The power of attention and focus allows us to create our story and participate in the beautiful dance of life while remaining intuitively connected to the great oneness.

When we balance our limited mind with our limitless mind, we can create and participate in the journey while still remaining open to the flow of life. In the ideal state of *relaxed attention* — where concentration relaxes into intuitive receptivity — you can have both clear-minded intention and open-minded insight. In the ease of relaxed attention, your thoughts magnetically attract and catch the high-vibration waves of the field, while your feelings align with and surrender to the movement of its resonant vibration. You are open to receiving truth regardless of your personal needs, aims, or ambitions. This is the true spirit of cocreation, of living your life in tandem with the universe.

FIELD WORK STORY: LOST AND FOUND
by Melissa, yoga teacher

Melissa's story is an example of how easily you can solve problems and receive information from the field when you shift your overthinking mind into a state of relaxed attention.

One day, my husband lost the key to his truck. He spent the whole afternoon looking for it and nearly gave up. We didn't have a spare, so we were in a real bind. At that point, I decided to try my intuition. I went into my closet, the only quiet space I could find with a house full of kids, and tuned in. I took a breath and relaxed my attention, opening up my mind to where the key could be. Suddenly, I had an urge to look in the truck. On my way, he even said to me, "It's not in the truck!" He had looked there a thousand times already. But I trusted my gut. It was pitch-black outside in our driveway, so I couldn't really see what I was doing. I opened the passenger door and felt around behind the seat. There it was! Right under my fingertips. My husband is now a believer in intuition!

ILLUMINATION KEY #5

INTUITION IS MY UNIVERSAL LANGUAGE

The real knowledge is free; it's encoded in your DNA. All you need is within you. Great teachers have said that from the beginning. Find your heart and you will find your way.

— CARLOS BARRIOS, MAYAN ELDER AND
AJQ'IJ OF THE EAGLE CLAN

Though the universe has many languages — verbal, mathematical, even musical — there is no language as fundamental as intuition. All of life intuitively connects with the unified field of everything-ness. Animals, plants, and beings of all kinds share information with this field. Through intuition we can know one another without a common language. Intuition is the universal language of life; the illumination code is a vocabulary that all consciousness shares.

In our fifth lab, we are going to explore ways to develop our intuition and start cracking our mind's intuition code. As every person is unique, so each intuitive language is unique. Your powers of quantum intelligence are uniquely developed from your personal journey through life and the inner field — from your personal relationship with the universe. Intuition uses whatever language you understand. The universe knows you even better than you know yourself and speaks to you personally.

There are no external set of rules or formulas needed to understand the illuminating cosmic code; it is both universal and personal, often speaking to you as though you are speaking to yourself. You experience messages from the inner field as insightful thoughts and resonant feelings, which often feel like your own thoughts and feelings. But with time and practice, it becomes easier to distinguish the thoughts of your personal mind from that of the universal mind. Since you live within the boundaries of a local environment immersed in space-time, your individual thinking mind runs on limited, local information; but the unlimited nature of your inner dimension — the part of you that knows everything — uses your intuitive faculty to share as much of its wisdom with you as possible.

Quantum intelligence is thinking with the universal mind. Your intuition has one singular purpose: to guide you into an expanded state of oneness with the universe. It is on a mission to help you rise above the dissonant energies of confusion, fear,

and suffering so that you, and all beings, can live in full communion with all that is. Since the universe is built of information *and*
energy, it speaks to you through both thought (zero-point information) and feeling (excited information). Your thinking mind
processes codes of information that arrive from the quantum field.
Your feeling heart is moved by its flow of energy.

Here are some ways that we receive guiding codes from the
quantum field.

Information
(Guiding awareness from the field)

- Arrives as insightful thoughts
- Codes of data that present as:
  o Metasensory impressions
  o Instantaneous knowledge
  o Sudden insight
  o Epiphany
  o Revelation
  o Knowingness

Energy
(Guiding expansion into the field)

- Arrives as resonant feelings
- Flows of energy that move you with:
  o Inspiration
  o New ideas
  o Gut feelings
  o Callings
  o Ingenuity
  o Empathy
  o Passions
  o Creativity

Whenever you respond to an experience in the outer world, your
inner world is also responding at the same time. For example, when
you run into a stranger on the street, your outward-thinking mind
receives information through local, personal observations and sensory input, while your inward, field-connected mind receives nonlocal information that goes beyond your local perceptions. Your
thinking mind might tell you someone is cool because they wear

nice clothes or say the right words, but your intuitive mind can see right through any deceptions of the material world. The intuitive mind knows only the truth — a truth that is inwardly encoded into your thoughts and feelings. Your quantum mind is the perfect guiding force because it runs on the truth.

ILLUMINATION KEY #5
teaches you the secrets of quantum intelligence.

As you learn to recognize how quantum information and energy flows through your intuitive faculties, you deepen your relationship with the mind of the universe and gain access to its all-knowing wisdom.

With the fifth illumination key, you can explore the different ways the universe speaks to you. With time and practice, you will become more adept at decoding the messages the universe is sending your way.

Key #5 Activation: Entering the Inner Truth Circle
Get into Your Intuitive Zone

As you begin your field work, the first step will be to create a centering practice to shift your energy into a high-vibration quantum-access mindset. Before practicing Lab #5, allocate ten to fifteen minutes in advance to get into your intuitive zone — your inner truth circle — using any of your favorite meditative practices or no-mind portals.

The inner truth circle is a sanctuary for your intuitive thoughts and feelings. Only the highest-vibration information and energy can penetrate it. While in your personal *happy place* in the quantum field, you are open to receiving only life-affirming wisdom and guiding energy. When you live from this circle of inner truth, you live with clarity, higher awareness, and understanding. You align with the coherent vibrations of love, trust, and fearlessness. You move into a state of presence and oneness with the unified field, where it shares information and energy easily. You will know you are in your intuitive zone when:

- you have left behind your worries, stress, or fears.
- you are not focusing on the past or the future.
- you aren't actively thinking about outcomes or problem-solving.
- you have an abiding sense of peace.
- you feel empowered and alive.

In this mindset, you have access to true peace and power. Here, you can tune into your inner wisdom and let it flow using any intuitive practices you enjoy.

Step 1: Get into the Zero-Point State of Mind

Slow down, breathe, and release any stress from the day, using a no-mind portal activity like:

- meditating in a related state
- playing music
- going for a walk or run
- practicing yoga, qigong, or gentle movement
- journaling or doing another creative activity

Step 2: Raise Your Vibration

With a quiet mind, expand your awareness into a high-vibration state with upshifting practices like:

- being in the now, fully alive in the moment
- smiling
- visualizing becoming one with your inner field
- radiating light, truth, and unity out into the world

Step 3: Engage the Quantum Field

From your high-vibration state, you are now ready to intentionally tune into the field — downloading bits and bytes of its guiding information or moving deeper into its resonant flow. If you don't take time to get into the high-vibration zone before starting intuitive work, you are more likely to receive lower quality information — impressions that are confusing or incomplete, junk thoughts that feel meaningless, or energetic static that interrupts high-quality information transmissions.

Think of the inner truth circle as your warm-up for field work. Just like when you work out or go to the gym, you do the best when you warm up and gently ease yourself into the activity. Though you might not hurt yourself by skipping your warm-up when you work with your intuition, you run the risk of getting a bad connection. The more centered you stay in the field and its truth, the more expansive your intuitive awareness becomes.

LAB #5
SACRED SEEING

Learning to Use Your Inner Vision

Since the dawn of civilization, people have been using oracles to gain extraordinary insight into the ways of the world. Whether it was tea leaves, cards, coins, sticks, or stones, these ancient practices have been known as messengers of secret knowledge that guide our way forward. To the twentieth-century thinker, these practices may have seemed primitive or even fraudulent. But, today, with our understanding of the quantum field and a fresh scientific perspective, we are returning to the ancient wisdom that guided our ancestors.

Wise ones from nearly every culture on earth have practiced intuitive rituals to interact with the deep dimension — almost as though they have had a conscious relationship with the quantum field, one that most of us today still lack. For over five thousand years, the Chinese have used the I Ching, also known as the "Book of Changes." This text is one of the oldest oracles in human history and is used in tandem with coins that divine the future and bring enlightenment. The Tibetan Buddhist tradition teaches Mo, a divination tool based on the throwing of dice. The Norse popularized the casting of rune stones to learn one's destiny. The Druids read wind, smoke, and water to reveal the fates. In the 1400s, medieval Europe took oracles to the next level with the creation of the tarot card deck, which is still one of the most popular intuitive tools in our culture today.

Though many religious organizations have feared intuition — labeling it as dangerous to avert people from wielding its full power — even traditional religious institutions, such as the Catholic Church, have had their own brand of intuitive communication with the universe. Visio Divina, or "divine vision," is a contemplative practice of sacred seeing, an ancient form of communication with the higher realms. Originating in the Benedictine community, this practice involves opening up your heart and imagination to a sacred image. In the silence and through the dynamics of the image, God — the universe — speaks to you. For the practice of Visio Divina, all that is required is an open, receptive state of stillness. Sound familiar? This beautiful ritual, created by monks hundreds of years ago, echoes the same process we use today to commune with our inner wisdom. No matter what methodology you use to tap into the eternal, omnipresent cosmic consciousness that we call the universe, God, the supreme self, spirit, or life itself — we all use our intuition to do it.

Visio Divina: A Picture Is Worth a Thousand Words

The practice of sacred seeing is the act of reflection on a picture or image as you intuitively see with your higher mind and heart. The universe — the part of you that knows everything — guides your attention, speaking to you through images instead of words. As you gaze at the image, you naturally receive revelatory insights and feelings from your inner field of wisdom.

The sacred seeing practice works via the symbolic nature of our visual language. As we learned earlier in chapter 3, your inner dimension doesn't communicate in sequential time-based language like we do. Field communication is all at once — instantaneous — arriving in a flash. Images are one of the most effective forms of communication because a singular symbol can represent a much larger packet of data. As metaphors, symbols and pictures do not fully collapse the waves of potentiality — they are open for personal interpretation. Images are a simple yet powerful medium for intuitive communication. In this lab, we are going to learn how to use pictures to decode important messages from the universe.

Creating a Sacred Seeing Practice

The sacred seeing process brings you into connection with the universal guiding presence within you. Begin with the following steps:

1. **Find a quiet space for reflection.**
2. **Get into your inner truth circle.** Raise your vibration and get into a state of resonance with your inner field.

3. **Set your intention.** Close your eyes and open up to receive a message of guidance, clarity, or understanding for your life. Relax your attention.

4. **Open your eyes, and look at a sacred seeing image, like the one on the next page.**

5. **Notice the first thing your attention is drawn to.** You may initially notice a section of the image or a specific object that becomes a focal point. Your attention will naturally align with the first bit of information, a point of departure, of an intuitive message. This first impression initiates the sacred seeing journey.

   Note: Do not try to interpret the whole image; just follow your intuition through the image and allow it to unwind a symbolic message.

6. **Let the image speak to you.** How does this first impression relate to your life? The answer may become clearer as you go deeper into the image. Use your sense of inner resonance to explore the image, like a visual language telling a story. Simply follow where your attention leads you, and notice the message that begins to reveal itself.

   Note: You might end up focusing in on a small section of the image, or you might bounce around to different areas. There is no right and wrong way to observe as long as you are following your intuition.

7. **Decode the message.** Take a moment to reflect on how the image is personally speaking to you. Did the image offer guidance or a new understanding for you? Hold space with the image until the connection is made. Try to resist overthinking, and allow the information in the picture to illuminate you.

Use this sample sacred seeing board for your practice. You can also practice with more sacred seeing images in your Illumination Workbook or at KimChestney.com/sacred-seeing.

You can use your workbook to record your experience or write in your journal. Often, information from the field continues to flow, so writing is a great way to let it all out. Ask yourself, *What message has this image brought for my life?* Notice how this experience invites you to see something in a new light, offers a pathway forward, or validates your life decisions in some way.

Here is an example of a sacred seeing practice using the image above:

After getting into your intuition zone, you calmly open your eyes and notice the person standing in the center square in the middle of the labyrinth. The thought *I finally made it* comes to mind. This is your first impression and point of departure. You sense that this image symbolizes that you have at last found your center, a home on your journey. Next, you notice the person is walking away from the center. You feel like this is showing you that it may be time to walk on, perhaps to a new path or venture. Next, you notice the candle sitting on a book. Interestingly, you have been considering writing a book. You wonder if this is guidance that you should share your light through your writing. Then, your eyes follow the little orbs of glowing light upward to the photo of the woman sheltering under an umbrella. Something clicks inside you as you recognize that your book is planned to be about helping women. This final image lights you up inside as a validation of your intention to shift your career to helping women. The meaning feels right and aligned with your personal growth.

Though you might be tempted to think that you are only seeing what you want to see, this is not the case. To prove this to yourself, try this process on another person. You will be amazed at how profoundly you can tune in to scenarios in other people's lives, particularly situations you know nothing about. When you use this process, your intuition uses the imagery to send you a coded message from the deep dimension. If you keep your mind out of the way and trust yourself, the truth will arrive.

If you would like to practice with different types of sacred seeing imagery, you can use my online Illuminate! Interactive Insight Card Deck at KimChestney.com/insight-cards.

Lab #5 Workbook: Decoding a Message from the Universe
The Art of Sacred Seeing

You can practice sacred seeing as part of your daily routine. Use the framework below with an insight card or one of the sacred seeing boards in your Illumination Workbook to receive a message of guidance whenever you need it.

Selecting Your Sacred Image

1.   Set your intention to receive a guiding message for your life.
2.   Select a sacred seeing image.
3.   Relax your mind, take a deep breath, and gaze at the image.

Information

Notice the first bit of information in the image that draws your attention. Ask yourself: *How does this first impression symbolically relate to my life?*

Energy

Let the card speak to you as you follow your intuition through the information in the image, allowing it to gently move your attention with resonant energy. Ask yourself: *How is the card leading me into deeper understanding of my life situation?*

Message

Continue to observe the image until its full meaning is revealed. Ask yourself: *What is the overall message the image is sharing with me?*

Record as much information as possible for future validation and insight.

CONCLUSION

Activating Key #5 of the illumination code teaches
you to use your quantum intelligence.

This key shows you how to interact with the quantum field and
learn to speak its language. You can intuitively channel its information and energy as part of your inner guidance system to intentionally gain insight into any part of your life.

Key Principles

- Stillness is the gateway to your quantum intelligence.
- The quantum field's guiding code arrives in the form of
  both information and energy.
- Your brain processes universal codes as intuitive thoughts
  and resonant feelings.
- Quantum intelligence thrives in the state of relaxed
  attention.
- Overthinking is a trap that creates a barrier to intuitive
  receptivity.

Key Applications

- Notice the intuitive thoughts that drop into your mind to
  inform your everyday life.
- Notice the resonant feelings that guide you through expansion or resistance.
- Create a regular sacred seeing practice to develop your intuitive language and start an ongoing conversation with
  the part of you that knows everything.

The secret to true wisdom is found in the union of opposites —
creating complementary relationships instead of oppositional
ones. Intelligence and intuition are designed to work together; you

don't have to choose one over the other. The two hemispheres of your brain — one geared for thought, the other for feeling — are part of a greater union of mind and heart. The mind knows truth; the heart recognizes it in the beauty of resonance. We do not have to choose the mind or the heart because they are, in the end, one and the same. As the poet John Keats famously expressed many years ago: "Beauty is truth, truth beauty — that is all Ye know on earth, and all ye need to know."

CHAPTER SIX

Impossible Things

Quantum behavior forces us to be even more
tolerant of impossible things.

— DEEPAK CHOPRA AND MENAS C. KAFATOS,
YOU ARE THE UNIVERSE

If you ask someone how they know that intuition is real, the answer is often the same: because it led them to experience something that they thought was impossible. Once you have experienced *an impossible thing*, you can no longer take the dictates of science on blind faith. You realize something magical is going on in this world. Impossible things happen every day to millions of people all over the planet. Finally, in this age of global communication, we can share our extraordinary stories and join forces with scientific leaders who are coaxing a revolutionary view of reality out of the fringes of quantum theory. At last, the possibilities are overshadowing the impossibilities.

In this emerging era of postmaterialism, leading-edge scientists around the world are attesting to the scientific reality of so-called impossible things. People know the future. They can naturally communicate across vast distances. They know things that should be impossible for them to know. This worldwide paradigm shift is being fueled by one simple revelation: *consciousness, not matter, is the fundamental building block of reality.* "The materialistic focus that has dominated science in the modern era cannot account for an ever-increasing body of empirical findings in the domain of consciousness and spirituality," stated the authors of the *Manifesto for a Post-Materialist Science*, explaining that scientific materialism has "brought a severely distorted and impoverished conception of ourselves and of our place in nature.... The shift from materialist science to post-materialist science may be of vital importance to the evolution of the human civilization. It may be even more pivotal than the transition from geocentrism to heliocentrism."

The acceptance of a consciousness-centered universe — and the psi phenomenon that accompanies it — puts us at the threshold of an exciting new era of potentiality. "What the future holds remains to be seen, but one argument is the development of psychic abilities is going to be the next step of human evolution, that unlocking these abilities, that perhaps lie dormant within all of us, is going to be key to upgrading humanity to the next level," explained British journalist Nick Pope on the television show *Ancient Aliens*. Author and psychologist Ira Israel envisioned the possibilities:

> Much that was considered normal three hundred to four hundred years ago is now considered absurd and unscientific. In three hundred to four hundred years, historians will look back on gasoline-fueled cars the way we look back on horse-drawn carriages; they will look back on our cement cities the same way we look back on cavemen. In 2400, people might say things like "Those imbeciles.... They had to use those silly devices called iPhones — they did not realize they could communicate telepathically" or "Hard to believe they had to use those silly things called airplanes — they did not realize they could teleport themselves."

We Are Entangled: Soulmates,
Synchronicity, and Telepathy

Quantum entanglement is one of the most beautiful and observable phenomena of contemporary physics. Einstein called it "spooky action at a distance" because it demonstrates how two particles can be linked together no matter how far apart they are in space or time. As Paul Levy explained,

> When two quantum entities interact, they become intermingled in such a way as to remain forever linked together....Exhibiting a form of contagious magic, each seems to telepathically "know" what the other is doing.... Their quantum telepathy is due to the fact that they are not, and never have been, separate. Seeing quantum entities as separate is a delusion, an artifact of our limited, classically conditioned perspective. In actuality, there is just the underlying, unified, information-filled quantum field giving rise to transitory patterns...the expressions of a singular and indivisible field.

If we accept that the fundamental core of all things — particles, atoms, quanta — is consciousness, shouldn't we expect to witness entanglement between human beings like those particles studied in the laboratory? The mind is a quantum entity. Our bodies are connected to all things through the unified field. Electrical engineer and psi researcher Dean Radin is one of many scientists who believe that "at very deep levels, the separations that we see between ordinary, isolated objects are, in a sense, illusions created by our limited perceptions. The bottom line is that physical reality is connected in ways we're just beginning to understand." He goes on to say:

> Today we know that entanglement is not just an abstract theoretical concept....It has been repeatedly demonstrated as fact in physics laboratories around the world

since 1972. As research accelerates on this surprising characteristic of nature, entangled connections are proving to be more pervasive and robust than anyone had previously imagined. A review of developments on entanglement research in March 2004 by *New Scientist* writer Michael Brooks concluded that "physicists now believe that entanglement between particles exists everywhere, all the time, and have recently found shocking evidence that it affects the wider, 'macroscopic' world that we inhabit."

But you and I don't need any advanced technology to experience entanglement; it is part of our natural state — a function of the inner technology we are built with. This magical connection reveals itself through intuitive awareness and synchronistic behavior of all kinds, showing up in a multitude of everyday instances:

- Simultaneous thought or action between you and another person when you are apart
- Thinking of someone, then having them show up unexpectedly in your life
- Noticing repetitions in multiple different situations in a short amount of time
- People showing up to see each other dressed in similar colors or styles
- Love at first sight or a feeling of instant connection with someone
- Ideas or trends that emerge collectively by individuals in separate world cultures

Entanglement is why you pick up the phone just as someone you know is about to call you. It is what wakes you up at the same time as your partner, even when you are sleeping apart or traveling in separate time zones. It explains why you think of an old friend only to have them reach out to you soon after. It is the reason you discover something new, then suddenly see it everywhere you look. Your whole world is a web of entanglement, facilitated by conscious energetic connections. You are entangled with the books you read, the thoughts you think, the places you go, the memories you make, the people you meet. While you are subtly entangled with general interactions and acquaintances, you are deeply entangled with what you love and those you care about. The more you care, both consciously and unconsciously, the more you are entangled.

Soulmates and Loved Ones

Love itself is a powerful form of entanglement. When we truly love another person, we enter into a relationship that defies both time and space. No matter where you go or how much time passes, the deepest love abides. As centuries of literature, poetry, and love songs attest, an invisible force connects entangled minds so that they forever follow one another. Through this entangled love, we create lifelong emotional and karmic connections with people who are important to our personal evolution — whether we are conscious of it or not.

Love entanglement can be present with people you have known your whole life or people you have yet to meet. Have you ever felt love at first sight? Or met someone and instantly felt a connection with them? Entanglement, as a function of the nonlocal quantum realm, is not bound by time; you may be entangled with all kinds of people you have yet to meet. When I met my husband for the first time, a part of me recognized him before I was aware how he would change my life — so much so that I took a picture of him as a stranger randomly driving in front of me on the parkway — a whole year before we officially met. *He caught my attention.* And the synchronicity that brought us together on the road that day was an expression of the alignment that was to come. When love at first sight arrives, it may not feel like love as much as a magnetic force pulling you toward one who is about to change your life for the better.

"When particles are entangled, the actions of one will always influence the other, no matter how far they are separated," explained Lynne McTaggart in her foreword to Michael Talbot's *The Holographic Universe*. "They act like a pair of star-crossed lovers... who continue to not only know each other's moves, but also to imitate the other's every activity for the rest of their days." Entanglement offers a scientific explanation of how the dynamics of love work — how you connect with and relate to one another on a quantum level. When our hearts and minds are in a coherent state with another human being — even for an instant — the bond is formed. This is why falling in love for the first time is such a momentous occasion: it is our first experience of conscious coherence, as two energetically become one. The resonant hearts and minds of soulmates and lovers imprint upon each other and interconnect in ways that can fuel entanglement for lifetimes.

We entangle with our soulmates through love — the abiding, eternal quantum connection. Though some say we have only one soulmate, we can be entangled with many people throughout the course of our lives. Wherever there is genuine caring, affection, friendship, or selfless love, entanglement is at work. Entanglement exists beyond sex or gender as our true being is beyond both; it exists between lovers, friends, parents, children, teachers, and fellow travelers on the path of life. This entanglement is not a function of our reality and the cause-and-effect world; it does not end when relationships end or when individuals move apart in space or time.

Entanglement is undaunted by the changing forces of the material world; it holds fast in the changeless deep dimension of the quantum world. Have you ever seen an old friend after many years apart only to feel like no time has passed at all? When you are entangled, your connection is the same as it ever was. The quantum field has held it timelessly in its truth, awaiting the moment the two of you reactivate the connection.

EXPERIMENT: WHO ARE YOU ENTANGLED WITH?

Take a moment to look back on your life and the relationships that have transformed it. Do you have any soulmates — one person or a group of people — who have supported you, guided you, or facilitated your growth? Are there any people you can always count on or who seem to show up right when you need them? Think about the people who have really touched your soul.

Then, let's put entanglement to the test. In your journal, write down the names of any people in your life who mean something to you but who you are not regularly in contact with. These could be old friends, family members, lovers, or even coworkers. Spend some time thinking about the people on your list — reconnecting with any memories and feelings about them, especially ones who are not currently an active part of your life. Maybe even look them up on social media, but don't make any contact. Spend some time giving these relationships your attention — even sending them gratitude or loving thoughts.

On the quantum level, your friends are receiving your communication. Though they may or may not act upon it, they are pinged by your thoughts. Likely, they are returning thoughts of you, even if they aren't motivated enough to reach out. You have probably felt the same type of communication coming from them in the past when you thought of them, again out of the blue. This could be the case any time that you spontaneously think of someone or old feelings resurface.

It could take days or even weeks to get a sign of entanglement, depending on how far apart you have grown. People could also be shy or reluctant to reconnect, even if they are also thinking about you. It took months for my long-lost friend Robert to reach out to me after I started writing about him in this book; but, after thirty years, a few months is quite a validation! Don't be surprised when your old friends start showing up out of the blue.

Entanglement keeps people in sync. Research now shows that people who feel love or affection for each other also *physically entangle* — through synchronized heart rates and various activities throughout the day. Through an often-unconscious synchronized connection, you might still get glimpses of your continued energy exchange from time to time with experiences like:

- catching up with an old friend to discover that you both have developed similar interests or done similar things in life.
- randomly running into an old friend in an unexpected place.
- two people saying the same thing at the same time — a "jinx."
- dreaming about someone who shows up in your life soon after.

Jung called these experiences "synchronicities" and explored their quantum origins in his work with physicist Wolfgang Pauli in *Naturerklärung und Psyche*. Understanding this synchronicity as an acausal phenomenon — one that links events without causes — he wrote, "We often dream about people from whom we receive a letter by the next post. I have ascertained on several occasions that at the moment when the dream occurred the letter was already lying in the post-office of the addressee."

Your entanglement is fed by any attention you give the relationship. The deeper your entanglement, the more you witness its synchronicities. If you put an entangled relationship behind you, its noticeable effects may appear to go dormant, and the synchronicities may slowly fade. Still, on the timeless level, your connection remains. The original bond always exists. It is up to us to decide whether we carry our entanglement into the present moment or simply let it live in the eternal memory field of the universe.

Telepathy

In the 1960s *National Geographic* writer, photographer, and explorer Loren McIntyre got lost on assignment in Brazil, where he ended up spending two months with an uncontacted Amazon rainforest tribe called the Mayoruna. "Although they shared no common language, he discovered he could communicate with the chief via telepathy, in a manner he began to call *beaming*. This skill, he later learned, was known to the tribe as the *other language*, a way of communicating possessed only by the elders." It turns out that there was a language that McIntyre and the tribe members shared: the language of intuition.

Intuition is quite likely our original language. It is the only language that transcends cultures, lives, and worlds. As the purest form of communication, telepathy is the direct mind-to-mind connection — consciousness to consciousness. As a function of the quantum field, it is instantaneous and, unlike our verbal and written languages, loses nothing in translation. It is pure, simple knowing. It can be argued that telepathy is our native intuitive language, one that fell into disuse as we began to chronically rely too much on the linear language of the time-based thinking mind. The more we became estranged from our inner dimension, the more we were forced to rely on other languages to communicate. Nevertheless, we have never fully lost access to this first language.

Rupert Sheldrake talked about experiences of telepathy in his book *The Sense of Being Stared At*:

> Many people claim that they have had telepathic or other psychic experiences. In one national survey in the United States, 58 percent of those questioned claimed personal experience of telepathy. In another national survey, in 1990, 75 percent said they had had at least one kind of paranormal experience, and 25 percent had had telepathic experiences. In recent random household surveys in Britain and the United States, 45 percent of the respondents said they had had telepathic experiences. In a large newspaper survey in Britain, 95 percent of the responders said they were believers in ESP.

Have you ever known what someone was going to say right before the words came out of their mouth? Or have you and a friend ever come up with the same idea at the same time? Our original telepathic language is at work throughout our everyday life. The language is so universal that we can even communicate telepathically with our pets. My dog sits at the door every time my husband is about ten minutes away from home; a part of him always knows when a family member is nearly home. This everyday occurrence is the telepathic connection of the nonlocal field in action.

"Telepathy is real; it does happen," explained pioneering journalist Upton Sinclair. "Whatever may be the nature of the force, it has nothing to do with distance, for it works exactly as well over forty miles as over thirty feet…it can be cultivated and used deliberately, as any other object of study, in physics and chemistry." Your own telepathic ability increases as you begin to rely more upon your quantum intelligence in day-to-day life. You will begin to notice more telepathic experiences when:

- you spend more time in no-mind zones.
- you are strongly entangled with someone close to you.
- you live in deeper connection with your inner dimension.

Telepathy is a natural byproduct of a deepened relationship with the quantum field. You can't force it or learn it; you grow into it with openness and receptivity. Whether it's entanglement, synchronicity, or telepathy, all these functions underscore the fact that the whole world is consciously connected and that all forms of separation are an illusion. When you understand these principles, one thing is for certain: *The world itself appears as a nonlocally whole macroscopic quantum system.*

Mind over Matter: Moving beyond Miracles

We hear a lot of talk about miracles in modern spirituality — how we can create them and attract more of them. But what if the real secret is that there are no miracles at all. It's not that impossible things don't happen; they are simply a natural function of our reality. Quantum physics gives us back the magic of the universe and provides a framework to understand the impossible things we once called miracles.

Buddhist scholar Alan Wallace brought miracles into a modern context:

> In Buddhism, these are not miracles in the sense of being supernatural events, any more than the discovery and amazing uses of lasers are miraculous — however they may appear to those ignorant of the nature and potentials of light. Such contemplatives claim to have realized the nature and potentials of consciousness far beyond

anything known in contemporary science. What may appear supernatural to a scientist or a layperson may seem perfectly natural to an advanced contemplative, much as certain technological advances may appear miraculous to a contemplative.

Throughout history, miracles have been associated with elevated minds, expanded states of consciousness, and even holiness. Millions of people around the world accept that Jesus healed the sick, walked on water, and turned water into wine — or that the Buddha had psychic abilities, saw past lives, and could be in two places at once. Ancient yoga masters were reputed to have the power to defy gravity through levitation and defy space through teleportation. Saints have reportedly performed miracles of all kinds: the warrior Joan of Arc foretold the future and heard God's voice; the mystic Teresa of Ávila ascended to a higher dimension through the rapture of divine communion; and Franciscan priest Anthony of Padua spoke in tongues that people of all languages could understand. The bodies of gurus and holy people from all traditions, including Paramahansa Yogananda in recent times, are known to have demonstrated incorruptibility after death.

There is a fascinating story about Mary of Jesus of Ágreda, remembered as the *bilocating, flying nun*:

> Between 1621 and 1631, when she was aged nineteen to twenty-nine years of age, Sister Mary of Agreda bilocated over five hundred times. It would happen while she was praying. Her body remained in the cloistered convent, but at the same time, she would find herself in the continent of North America, in an area of land stretching across East Texas, New Mexico and Western Arizona. She appeared to the Jumano Indians and other tribes by flying

through the sky and proceeded to teach them about the Catholic faith. This resulted in many occasions of being tortured and left for dead, but she would return to her body in Spain, unharmed. Later, she would reappear to the same Indians who were completely dumbfounded as to how she was still alive.

Eastern yogic traditions call these extraordinary abilities *siddhis*, a term for the seemingly magical or spiritual powers exhibited by highly evolved human beings. The word *siddhi* means "perfection" in Sanskrit as their presence represents the achievement of ultimate spiritual practice. Siddhis include shape-shifting, levitation, invisibility, teleportation, and other forms of radical self-mastery. Though some may call them supernatural, we can understand them as demonstrations of human potential.

The existence of an information-based quantum field sheds light on many of the world's greatest mysteries of the mind. But the real question is not, *How do miracles happen?* but *Why do the miracles happen?* Why are they so rare? Why don't they happen all the time? And why do they seem to happen to extraordinary people? The answers can be found in the way we live our lives. I have never heard a story of someone bilocating while watching television and eating pizza. I have also never heard of anyone gaining miraculous spiritual powers by becoming rich or successful. These extraordinary experiences are not about the world at all; they are about our relationship with ourselves and the depth of our union with the inner dimension. They show us what we can one day be capable of if we dedicate ourselves to the inward-facing reality of existence. Many saints, gurus, and enlightened teachers were also regular people like you and me. The potential is there, we just have to aspire to it.

Perceiving beyond Time

In the early 2000s, I was in an intuition development group. During a partner exchange, one of my highly gifted classmates gave me a message: "Get ready. This year you are going to be writing a book." This came as a surprise to me since, at the time, I was a working artist, and the thought of writing a book had literally never crossed my mind. I was actually disappointed in the message, wondering how my insightful friend could get it so wrong. I even remember driving home and feeling a bit miffed. I wasn't going to write a book.

Yet, lo and behold, through a series of surprise opportunities, a little over a year later, my first book, *The Psychic Workshop*, was published around the world and translated into multiple languages. At that time, I had no idea my friend was actually seeing the future. I still didn't understand how it was possible — just like I still didn't understand how it was possible for a palm reader to predict a future date I was going to be in court. I had no idea how intuition was a part of the quantum field or how easy it was to break the illusion of time. Massachusetts Institute of Technology physicist Max Tegmark offered an analogy to help us understand how we experience both time and the timeless nature of reality:

> Life is like a movie, and space-time is like the DVD. There's nothing about the DVD itself that is changing in any way, even though there's all this drama unfolding in the movie. We have the illusion, at any given moment, that the past already happened and the future doesn't yet exist, and that things are changing. But all I'm ever aware of is my brain state right now. The only reason I feel like I have a past is that my brain contains memories.

And, perhaps, the only reason we don't see the future is because we don't have access to our *future memories*. The forward flow of time holds them at bay to give us the experience of free will, choice, and personal evolution. In true reality, all time exists simultaneously with the present. There is really no such thing as the past or the future; it's all happening now. As Schrödinger explained, "There is really no before and after for the mind." Even Einstein referred to the distinction between past, present, and future as "a stubbornly persistent illusion."

A person who is in touch with the nonlocal dimension can easily navigate the probability waves of the future or past using their quantum intelligence. This subatomic information transfer from the unified field occurs in the present moment and navigates the future in terms of potentiality. This means that the future is not predetermined or set in stone. We have many paths ahead based on many potential choices. When my intuition partner predicted my first book, she tapped into a high-probability wave of information, one that ultimately manifested. I also suspect this explains why inklings about the future sometimes don't pan out; it is quite possible that we took another path or made a choice that prevented the collapse of that expected wave of experience.

 The information in the quantum field does not dictate our fate; it holds all possibilities.

The concept of field potentiality stems from one of the key concepts in quantum mechanics, Werner Heisenberg's uncertainty principle:

> According to this venerable rule, it is impossible to determine both the position and momentum of a subatomic particle at the same time. Our knowledge of the attributes of a particle is fundamentally limited. When we focus on a particle's position, we distort its momentum, and when we focus on momentum, we cannot fix its position. Our

knowledge is partial, and there is apparently no way around this barrier. This situation bears a striking resemblance to premonitions. In one example after another, people may be stunningly accurate about the "what" of the event, but they can't come up with the "where" and the "when" of it. So when people report detailed images of impending disasters, as they did before the terrible events of Aberfan and September 11, but fail to specify the location and date of the happening, they may be demonstrating not flawed talents but a principle that penetrates much foreknowledge just as uncertainty permeates the world of atoms.

EXPERIMENT: PREDICTION AND POTENTIALITY

Part of the excitement of life is that we *don't* know the future. We never know for sure what could happen next. The dynamics of life offer an opportunity to grow and go on adventures through the great journey of life. However, the awareness of potential outcomes can help us find peace with our way and remain open to the possibilities. Every situation has its own dynamic of potentiality based on our thoughts and feelings about our life.

Building upon our lab in chapter 3, you can use the "Cosmic *Yes* and *No* Exercise" technique to explore some of those future potentialities in your life. This practice works great with questions like:

- Will I stay at this job or get a new one?
- Am I going to move to a new place in the future?
- Is this relationship going to work out long term?

Whatever questions you have about the future, write them down in your workbook or journal. To begin, read the instructions below, then sit in a quiet place where you won't be disturbed:

1. Close your eyes. In your mind's eye, imagine a red light and a green light in your field of vision — one to the left side and one to the right, just like we did in Lab #3.
2. With the two lights imagined before you, set your intention back on your question. Ask yourself if the answer is *yes* or *no* — with the green light symbolizing a *yes* answer and the red light symbolizing *no*.
3. As you sit quietly with your eyes still closed while imagining the two objects, notice how they begin to change in your mind's eye. Relax and let your imagination give you the answer you are looking for.

Resonant, expansive, or green-light activity is indicative of a stronger *yes* potential, whereas dissonant, motionless, reductive, or red-light activity is indicative of a *no* potential. No outcome is ever set in stone. Some situations have a stronger potentiality than others, which may also be reflected by the level of intensity of your imaginative response.

Note: Your answers reflect the potentiality of this moment. The direction can change anytime you change your own perception, thoughts, or feelings. If you received the answer that you hoped for, then staying the course will keep you aligned with it; on the other hand, changing your outlook and attitude toward life can also steer you away from any undesirable potentiality.

You might think that having a premonition is rare, but we are often more aware of the future than we realize. Year after year, during IntuitionLab group workshops, students report things like knowing who their partner is before they are assigned to them, receiving intuitive information about a person before they ask for it, and finding predictions in their personal evidence logs written long before they occurred. Premonitions can be big or small; we can be conscious of them or unconscious of them. For example, only one-third of the people working at the World Trade Center showed up for work on September 11, 2001. Though they had no conscious awareness of the impeding tragedy, the part of them that knows everything guided them to stay home, for one reason or another.

Whether it is a monumental event, like animals instinctively moving to high ground before the Indian Ocean earthquake and tsunami in 2004, or a simple act, like thinking to bring an umbrella to work before a surprise rainstorm, time-transcending events such as premonitions, precognition, and foresight no longer contradict the known laws of nature. I witnessed it in my own backyard this year. Everyday for the past three years, we have had the same family of five to ten squirrels visiting our feeder. Then, one late summer morning, nobody showed up for breakfast. The feeder sat abandoned. Days passed, no squirrels. Then, we realized it wasn't just our squirrels — all the squirrels were gone. You couldn't find a single one in our neighborhood, in the town nearby, or the large community park that was typically crawling with squirrels. I joked that it was the squirrel rapture, but it turns out that those squirrels didn't disappear — they telepathically communicated a mass migration. We had a late frost, and the acorn yield was low, so somehow, all at once, thousands of squirrels, over a span of many miles, left town together to find a better food source. They didn't have a conversation to figure out if they were going to have enough food for the winter, they just knew it — and they new it *together*.

FIELD WORK STORY: DESTINED FOR LOVE
by Stephanie, harpist

Stephanie's story is a beautiful example of how foresight can weave into our life in simple yet powerful ways — if we are paying attention.

Prior to college, as I was touring the West Chester University campus, I had a sudden thought that I would meet "someone very special" there. The words just kind of came to me, with a calm sense of knowing. Months later, during the first semester of my freshman year, a friend introduced me to a fellow student saying, "I'd like you to meet *someone very special.*" I instantly made the connection to the words that came to me when I first toured the place where I was destined to meet my future husband. We have been married now for fourteen years!

EXPERIMENT: FORESIGHT CODES

To build trust in your quantum intelligence and see it in action, try this daily foresight practice. Intuition activities like this are a fun way to play with the nonlocal field — especially when you get a hit and witness the magic of the illumination code in action:

- In the morning when you wake up or at night before you go to bed, take a quiet moment to contemplate the day ahead, ideally through one of your no-mind portals, such as while meditating or sitting in stillness.
- Keeping your journal handy, set an intention to connect with a piece of information about the day ahead. This can be any chunk of random information that you could potentially come across in the day ahead — usually as simple packets of code like:

- o   an object, like a red shirt or black SUV
- o   an occurrence, like a rainstorm or getting a package in the mail
- o   a word or a phrase, like a name or song lyrics
- o   the name of a person in your life
- Next, write down the first bits of information that drop into your mind. Make a mental note of any impressions of specific information, then put it on your radar for the day ahead.
- These foresight codes usually show up when you least expect it, so remember not to look too hard. Remain in a state of relaxed attention, allowing the information to find its way to you.

In the days ahead, the codes you listed could manifest in many ways. For example, in the cases listed above: a coworker could show up wearing a red shirt; a surprise gift could arrive in the mail; you could hear the same song lyrics on the radio; or you could run into the friend whose name you intuited. If you don't recognize anything at first, don't worry. Try going back over your notes from the morning or night before to see if you missed something. Oftentimes, when we read back over our list, we realize connections we missed throughout the day. There is also the possibility that the code packet was actually there, but you failed to notice it.

Note: You can also get more specific results by setting a particular intention. Try asking something specific, such as *What color will my friends at work be wearing today?* Notice the first answer that drops into your mind and abides. Then, when you get to work, be on the lookout for your color to show up in the color themes of your entangled coworkers.

Perceiving beyond Space

Now that we have explored the idea of knowing the future — the ability to perceive beyond time — let's shift gears to explore our ability to perceive beyond space. With the quantum field, not only are you able to access quantum information outside your present moment in time, you are also able to access information beyond your spatial location.

This means that, even if you are sitting at a desk in New York City, a part of you still knows what is happening at other locations all around the world. You are more likely to have intuitive awareness of these happenings based on the people, places, or other things you are entangled with. You are not likely to be consciously affected by happenings with people you have never known or places you have never visited unless you have some form of entanglement.

Have you ever known or felt something about someone in your life from a distance? Have you heard stories of parents knowing when a child is hurt or in trouble, even when they are separated by miles? Or tales of people knowing when loved ones have passed on, even if they haven't seen them in years? When my grandmother passed, I was overcome with an unexplainable feeling that something was wrong. I had no idea where the feeling was coming from, but the sense of foreboding was so strong that I had chills all over my body and couldn't shake it for hours. I felt a disturbance in the force. Though my rational mind could not put together the pieces of information I was receiving, I intuitively felt their message.

Dr. Helané Wahbeh, the director of research at the Institute of Noetic Sciences, explained the force in her book *The Science of Channeling*: "The Force is 'an energy field created by all living things. It surrounds us, penetrates us, and binds the galaxy together.' This is how Jedi teacher Obi-Wan Kenobi explained it to

Luke Skywalker in *A New Hope*. Jedis move objects with their minds (psychokinesis) and hear their master's voices in their minds (telepathy). They are essentially 'channeling' the Force."

Nonlocal intelligence can arrive in a variety of ways that often don't make logical sense at first. It naturally arises in your meta-senses via physical sensations, gut feelings, emotions, visions, voices, smells, or even yearnings. One of the most accessible and well-researched practices of location-transcendent intuition is remote viewing. Remote viewing is the practice of seeking impressions about a distant or unseen subject with the intuitive mind. A remote viewer goes into the quantum field and retrieves information about an object, event, person, or location that is hidden from physical view and separated at some distance. While remote viewing may at first seem impossible, it is one of the easiest and most verifiable practices of quantum intelligence.

How does remote viewing work? Lynne McTaggart wrote in *The Field*:

> If we could see remote places instantaneously, it argued strongly that it was a quantum, nonlocal effect. With practice, people could enlarge their brain's receiving mechanisms to gain access to information stored in the Zero Point Field. This giant cryptogram, continually encoded with every atom in the universe, held all the information of the world — every sight and sound and smell. When remote viewers were "seeing" a particular scene, their minds weren't actually somehow transported to the scene. What they were seeing was the information...encoded in quantum fluctuation. They were picking up information contained in The Field. In a sense, The Field allowed us to hold the whole of the universe inside us. Those good at remote viewing weren't seeing anything invisible to all the rest of us.

Remote-viewing experiments have been so successful and measurable that the United States government spent over $20 million between 1975 and 1995 on a psychic research program in collaboration with the Defense Intelligence Agency and the Stanford Research Institute. Its code name, the Stargate Project, was part of a trend in remote-viewing spy programs enlisted by world governments in the late twentieth century and included work with artists, civilians, and military personnel. For example, United States Army veteran Joseph McMoneagle participated in over four hundred remote-viewing missions during the Stargate Project; his colleague, artist Ingo Swann, along with Hal Puthoff and Russell Targ, developed the practice of *controlled remote viewing* — viewing locations with nothing but geographical coordinates, with government funding.

The fact that such programs exist validates the potential held in nonlocal field exploration. "The idea that extrasensory abilities are going to take on enormous importance in the near future is not just another empty prediction," explained Ingo Swann. "The world's three most important powers — the Soviet Union, the United States, and the People's Republic of China — have mounted increasingly large programs to research extrasensory potentials."

If you have ever wondered if there is any evidence that quantum intelligence, intuition, or psychic ability is real, you can point them to the massive expenditure of time, energy, and money that the United States government itself invested in it — over the course of two decades. Failed projects don't last that long or get renewed for funding. Remote viewing works. The government knows it, the research scientists know it, and the remote viewers know it. And during the lab at the end of this chapter, you will get to know it too.

EXPERIMENT: REMOTE PREVIEWING

To experiment with your own remote-viewing skills, here is an easy practice you can use anytime you are going to a new place, such as a business meeting in a new office, a gathering at a new house, dinner at a new restaurant, or any other place that you have never been to. Before heading out, take a moment to get into your intuitive zone, as you usually do. Then, follow these steps:

1. Set your intention on receiving any information on the space you are about to visit. Specifically, set it for the time in the future when you will be present there. (This way you can personally receive validation of your impressions.) These could include but are not limited to:
   o objects in the space
   o color themes
   o room layout or design
   o energy or feeling of the place
   o music or songs playing
   o people present when you arrive
2. Quiet your mind, tune in, and let any intuitive impressions drop in from the field. Go with the flow, and be sure to write or draw anything you receive. Sketch out room layouts or any visual information.
3. Bring them with you to your destination.
4. After you arrive, observe the space. Record any obvious intuitive hits. Then, dig deeper — remembering that not all intuitive information arrives literally. For example, if you get the impression of a gingerbread cookie, you may not see that exact same cookie. If there are cookies there at all, it's a hit. Remember, your intuition often uses personal experience and memory to convey messages. It is much

harder to translate a code packet of an exact cookie that you have never seen than it is to recognize the code of an archetypal cookie.

In most cases, unless you are extremely tuned into the field, you will recognize information *adjacent* to your actual impressions. What you discover in the space will be similar but not exactly as you imagined it. If you see someone wearing a red shirt, it may not be the same style as the red shirt you envisioned. If you got the layout of the room generally correct, the scaling could be entirely different from what you imagined. Give yourself some room for interpretation in the beginning as you begin to fine-tune your intuition. With time and practice, you may get more and clearer remote-viewing information.

FIELD WORK STORY: SEEING THE FUTURE
by Arlene, visual artist

Artists are often very attuned to the nonlocal field through the process of creative flow. Arlene's story demonstrates how easily we can literally see beyond time and space.

As I was envisioning my future home, I sketched an image of my ideal artist's studio/residence. A few days later, someone on Facebook shared a potential space with me and, when I looked at it, I realized it had the exact same floor plan as my sketch! Not long after, I moved into the apartment and still can't get over how much it looks like the original sketch I made!

The Invisible Energy of Biofields

The discovery of the nonlocal field is not only revolutionizing the way we think and experience reality, but it completely changes the way we understand our bodies, our life force, and the way we physically interact with the world. Since the material world can no longer be understood as a collection of separate objects and things, many forward-thinking scientists are moving toward a new model of understanding the quantum dimension of our physical reality: biofields.

We now know that matter, at its core, is not composed of solid particles but is instead formed by interactions of energetic fields. Something you hold in your hand seems to be separated from you as a function of matter, but actually you and it are separated by electromagnetic energy. Your body is an electrical generator that emits signals and creates your own personal force field. Physicist Jack Fraser explained, "Virtually every single process which is keeping you alive can be traced back to an electric field that some component of your body is creating. You are an electric field — a giant electric field which holds your atoms together, and which uses other electric fields to talk to other bits of yourself." Your biofield is what enables you to exist as a coherent, individualized entity.

A biofield is a set of interpenetrating fields of information and energy — big and small — and a cell, a plant, a person, and even the earth has a biofield. When we encounter, or entangle with, another biofield, the interactions are coded on the quantum level. They inform us — and potentially heal us — from the deep dimension. Dr. Shamini Jain, a psychologist and researcher at the forefront of biofield study, called the biofield "electromagnetic fields of energy and information that guide our health." Biofields are an essential part of alternative medicine, including acupuncture, Reiki healing, qigong, and other forms of energy medicine.

You are made of fields of energy and information manifesting as a physical body. Recognizing that you are a bioelectromagnetic entity — both biological and electromagnetic — is the key to a holistic understanding of both your body and life force. One cannot exist in this reality without the other because they are energetic manifestations of the same thing. Our vitalizing biofield energy, also known in Eastern spirituality as *prana* or *qi*, is our source of energy — the invisible power source that fuels our existence.

The quantum nature of the biofield, however, transfers more than just energy — it transfers information. Remember, energy is just information in motion. Through your biofield, you have the capacity to pick up signals and codes from other biofields, both locally and nonlocally. You can sense other biofields physically and emotionally. You can also download information from specific biofields that are stored as part of the greater quantum field at large. This never-ending microcosmic energy and information exchange makes extraordinary experiences like empathy, psychometry, and even quantum healing possible.

EXPERIMENT: FEELING THE LIFE FORCE

If you pay close attention, you can feel your energetic body — or biofield — as the life force flowing through you. Often experienced in a relaxed state as energy waves, tingling feelings, or vibrations, you can physically sense nonlocal energy and information interpenetrating and vitalizing your local body. Here are some interesting ways you may notice your biofield activating:

- **Inner wisdom tingle:** When you are tuned in to your quantum intelligence, don't be surprised to notice a tingling feeling on your forehead or a tickle on your nose. This often happens during inspired information sharing or in moments when you are downloading from the field. As nonlocal energy connects to your local awareness, it produces an energetic charge that can excite the energy around your third eye area of intuitive knowing, which extends from your forehead to your eyes and nose.

- **Healing hands:** If you have ever practiced Reiki or felt the healing power in your hands, you have most likely felt the biofield held in your palms — an area of the body where you can intentionally release and share your life force energy. When these fields are activated by an intention to heal or share energy with others, you often feel a tingling in your palms. Try holding your hands together, just an inch or two from touching. As you focus on the energy there, can you feel it build with warmth or tingling between your hands? The more you put your attention on it, the stronger the sensation becomes.

- **Body buzz:** When you enter a deep state of relaxation or meditation, you can feel the subtle energies of the field interpenetrating your physical body. You can try this at night when you are lying in bed. As you relax, do you ever feel waves of energy flowing through your body? Sometimes you might even notice areas of your body buzzing or feeling electrified. You may even sense this in the middle of the night while half-asleep, reminding you of your quantum connection.

There are countless ways to sense the life force as it vitalizes your being. Be on the lookout for any strange or electric-feeling sensations as they can be indications of a biofield activating.

Sensing the Energy of Persons, Places, and Things

Life with an energy-based body, not unlike life with a physical body, comes with *sensitivity*. Being physically or energetically sensitive — or both — enables our extrasensory perception. When your body is attuned to the quantum dimension, you may pick up on subtle energies that others do not — and be affected by energies that others are impervious to. This happens naturally whenever your biofield entangles with another biofield, expressing itself as a person, place, or thing.

One of the most prevalent byproducts of colliding biofields is the experience of intuitive empathy. Due to our field's constant energetic information exchange, we have the capacity to pick up on thoughts and feelings stored in the personal fields of people we encounter. People who are deeply in tune with their quantum nature are naturally more open to this energetic exchange and able to easily pick up data from other fields. Like the legendary Deanna Troi on *Star Trek: The Next Generation*, empathic people have a heightened ability to sense emotions and mindsets because they naturally move into connection — physically, emotionally, and intuitively — with other biofields. You may have noticed your intuitive empathy kick in if you have felt overwhelmed in large groups of people or if you prefer to be in open spaces or to live in the countryside rather than the city. An oversensitivity to other people's biofields can leave you feeling drained or unbalanced as you are bombarded by other people's energy fluctuations.

Biofields store energy and information that often present as intense intuitive feelings or states of mind. Simone Wright explained how a personal experience of the universal field comes about:

> We operate and exist in an entirely electromagnetic environment…our organs, bones, tissue, glands, and nerves each possess their own electromagnetic field of

consciousness, operating in another, larger electromagnetic field of consciousness. Each cell expresses its energetic idea of self as a mathematical equation, or code, or what we might simply call an energetic fingerprint. In the language of intuition, we call it vibration or resonance.... Every car, rock, tree, horse, piece of jewelry, building, amoeba, or idea has its own unique electromagnetic fingerprint that is part of the unified field. And because the field operates like a recording medium, the energetic fingerprint of everything, past, present, or future, living or dead, is held in the field forever.

This means that you are affected not only by other people's biofields in your vicinity but also by the biofields of places and things — along with the history that has been recorded in their fields.

In terms of location energy, imagine that every physical place in the world has an imprint of everything that has happened in its field of existence. If you could see the energy as something visible, some areas — such as sacred sites or loving homes — might be light, bright, and full of uplifting energy, while other areas where discord or traumatic events occurred may feel heavier or less illuminated. It is almost as though we can imagine the field as an interplay of high and low energy pockets based on the data that has been recorded in local material fields. Homes, towns, and even areas in nature all hold their unique energetic imprint. Here are some ways you may have sensed energy in a particular location:

- Feeling a heavy energy after entering a house only to realize the people living there had just had an argument.
- Experiencing an instant, joyful connection to a city the first time you visit, and later meeting the love of your life there. (Remember the field holds the past and the future!)

- Having nightmares during a sleepover at a friend's house, then finding out that their house had once been the scene of a crime.
- Feeling anxious on a walk by the ruins of an old factory, then learning that a worker's strike had happened there once, and several people were injured.
- Being overwhelmed by a blissful connection to nature or a natural wonder that was a sacred site for ancient peoples.

Impressions from biofields can show up as feelings — like joy, sadness, love, or anxiety — that, like all information from the field, arrive from apparently nowhere. With biofield empathy, you often have a strong feeling and have no idea why. Suddenly, you may feel great, or maybe not so great, and there may be no apparent reason why. Real understanding of the situation might arise only when hidden information in the field comes to light.

Place-based biofields can have practical applications as well. Our ancestors found a way to work with the subtle vibrational intelligence of earth energies when they created dowsing rods to locate underground water sources, oil, gemstones, and other hidden treasures. This practice has been a source of controversy in agriculture and industry for years since, without the understanding of the quantum field, it seems impossible. Here's how it works: dowsers hold a forked stick, rod, or pendulum in their hands and wait for a motion signal that directs them to the location of what they are seeking. Somehow, magically, at just the right time, the dowsing rods begin to move seemingly on their own. Or, rather, some might say that *the part of the dowser that knows everything* activated the rods at just the right moment. Samuel Hamilton, the insightful patriarch and water wizard of John Steinbeck's *East of Eden*, calls his dowsing rod his "magic wand" and explains our all-knowing nature: "Maybe I know where the water is, feel it in my skin. Some people have a gift in this direction or that. Suppose — well, call it humility, or a deep disbelief in myself, forced me to do a magic to bring up to the surface the thing I know anyway."

 The part of you that knows everything is aware of the past, present, *and future* energy stored in each place you go.

Being aware of the subtle energies of place can also be useful when moving into a new house, buying a previously owned car, or deciding what area to live in. When you are touring a potential house or apartment, pay attention to how you feel: Do you feel good in the space? Does the energy feel light and expansive? Vibrant and alive? Or is there any heaviness in the air? The same process applies to buying a car or visiting a new town or location you might like to live in. Cities, towns, and regions carry their own collective energy imprint. You probably have noticed how some cities feel different from others, and some natural areas feel different from others. If you tune in, you can sense how your backyard feels different from other places in nature — like the Himalayas or the Gettysburg battlefield. Ask yourself, *What has happened here over the years?* All places carry their history in their little piece of the quantum field.

Psychometry

Physical objects carry a wealth of intuitively accessible quantum energy and information in their local quantum field. Psychometry, the act of intuitively sensing the history of a place or object via touch or localized contact, is a great way to sense biofields. This practice is one of my favorite IntuitionLab workshops. Though students often initially doubt that they can pick up any information from touching an object, they are generally surprised at how easy it is. During our practice sessions, I ask each student to bring in a small object and secretly put it into a basket. I pass the basket around, and each student selects an object, then holds it in their palms to connect with its field of energy. Without exception, students bring all kinds of information related to their items: names of people connected to it, places it has been stored, feelings of people who have used it — you never know what you are going to get. Having another person in the class to validate the impressions makes this one of the most valuable, and simple, practices for witnessing the quantum field in action. You can even try this at home yourself with friends or family members.

Psychometry is a natural part of your everyday life. You have likely experienced it without consciously knowing it. For example, I could never put my finger on why I had a general aversion to antiques. I didn't want antique furniture in my home, and I often felt uncomfortable in vintage or antique stores. Today, with the understanding that we are sensitive to the energy and information stored in the local field of material objects, it makes sense that objects owned by other people convey energy that we may not resonate with.

Not only do you participate in the psychometric process by picking up on energy from the field, but you also *add* to the information field of material objects you interact with or own. Have you ever had a favorite piece of clothing that, after a while, you just didn't like wearing anymore? Maybe you put it on, and now it just doesn't feel right. This often happens when you outgrow a certain energy in your life — especially when you upshift your vibration. Suddenly, the energy field of the clothes you used to wear is embedded with an outdated energy imprint — one that is no longer aligned with your vibration. This feeling is a cue that it is time to clean out your closet, give away those old-vibration clothes, and keep only the items that resonate with you energetically. It feels good to purge because you are releasing energy in the fields around you that no longer support your growth and expansion.

EXPERIMENT: PERSONAL PSYCHOMETRY

Tuning into the energy of the objects in your life can help you keep the energy of your inner space clean and uplifted. Consider setting an intention to pay attention to the way your clothes, furniture, home décor, and other local items intuitively influence your state of mind or mood. Here are some ways you can work with the energy of your personal items:

- Furniture: If you have old furniture, be sure that its energy feels good to you. Even your own personal old furniture carries the record of any trauma or discord that occurred within its field. Getting new furniture can be cleansing if you are starting a new phase of life.

- Home design: If a room in your house is feeling energetically heavy consider rearranging your furniture. The energy flow within rooms can become trapped, so practices like feng shui are helpful in opening up those fields and releasing residual energetic debris.

- Clothes: Have you ever had an item of clothing or jewelry from a partner, parent, or loved one that makes you feel good when you wear it? You can feel the love and harmonic vibration when the possessions of those you love are close by. Whether it is your partner's favorite sweatshirt, a special ring from a family member who passed, or even your child's stuffed animal, personal items from those you love can bring comfort and fill your inner space with nurturing energy.

Going Interdimensional: Past Lives, Alternate Realities, and Life after Life

One of the biggest questions in our exploration of consciousness is, *Where is the mind itself?* You and I are both conscious and aware, viewing the world through the lens of brainpower, but where is our consciousness actually held? Old-school science tells us that the mind is the brain, and when the brain ceases to function, so do we; brain death equals our death. Though this model makes sense from a materialistic perspective, it does not make sense from a quantum perspective, where the law of conservation of matter clearly states that nothing can be truly created or destroyed. There is no death, only change.

If consciousness isn't in the brain, where is it? More clues were revealed to me in 1993, when I had quite an extraordinary experience. It was a hot summer night, so I decided to sleep with my head at the foot of the bed, which was closer to the air conditioner. I drifted off in good spirits after a lovely day. Then, the next thing I remember is waking up with my face next to the headboard — where my feet should be. My first thought was *I can't be here. I am sleeping at the other end of the bed!* Then, I thought, *I must be having an out-of-body experience.* Then, finally: *I should turn around and look at myself!* Instantly, with that single focused intention — by turning to observe — I woke up in a rush of energy, my heart thumping and the entire lower half of my body tingling and prickling with energy. Even stranger, every time I drifted off, I felt a magnetic pull drawing me out of my sleeping body. I remember clenching over and again throughout the rest of the night to consciously *hold myself in my body.*

Hold myself in my body? That sounds absurd. But it happened again and again. This was the second time in my life that my fully aware consciousness was located in a separate place from my physical brain. And in both cases, I was conscious, alert, and able to make decisions. And, in both cases, the act of thinking brought me back into myself. Everything I had been taught until that point in my life told me that what had happened to me was impossible, but I had no doubt what I experienced was real. In terms of quantum mechanics, it makes perfect sense. I wasn't dreaming or hallucinating; I was exploring the nonlocal field.

Your mind is not your brain — your mind *uses your brain* to interface with material reality. The real home of your mind is the quantum field. Your human brain is the quantum computer your consciousness uses to navigate the material dimension. Knowing this, mysterious phenomena — such as out-of-body experiences, near-death experiences, past-life recall, interdimensional or time travel, lucid dreaming, and even life after death — become possible. László explained, "Consciousness is not generated by the brain: it is only transmitted by it.... The brain is a transceiver; it receives and transmits consciousness. The fact is that consciousness is a local manifestation of a universal phenomenon. Consciousness is universally present in space and time."

 Consciousness is a function of the quantum field, not the brain.

Like remote viewing, the idea of nonlocal travel caught the eye of the government in the early 1980s when the CIA conducted the study *Analysis and Assessment of Gateway Process* — a formula for altered states of consciousness popularized by Robert Monroe in the 1970s. The report, authored by Lieutenant Colonel Wayne M. McDonnell, provided a scientific framework for understanding and expanding human consciousness, out-of-body experiences, and other altered states of mind. In an attempt to rationally explain the reality of such widely experienced and potentially useful psychic phenomena, the report uses quantum mechanics to explain the functioning of human consciousness and the space-time dimensionality that is transcended by it.

Understanding that the universe is an interconnected holo-gram of energy-information, we can imagine consciousness itself as the fundamental body of all existence — not a byproduct of our local biological brain. Not only are we capable of *knowing* nonlo-cal information beyond our material reality (precognition, remote viewing, etc.), but we are also capable of *personally experiencing* realities beyond our own. It is estimated that one in ten people have had some kind of out-of-body experience, which can happen as a natural byproduct of your expanding consciousness or can be spontaneously induced by trauma, psychedelic drugs, or other energy-shifting activity. As our energy shifts — intentionally or unintentionally — so can our range of perception, giving us greater access to nonlocal dimensions of the quantum field.

To understand how nonlocal experiences are possible, we need to reimagine the role of the human brain. We can no longer look at it as either the generator or storage device of consciousness. It is a transmitter of a consciousness that far exceeds our local band-width. Going into the field is not an anomaly or freak accident. It is a return to our true nature, giving us a sneak peek at the reality behind reality and our true home. You do not need your brain to be conscious; you need it to consciously interact with the physical dimension. We often forget that biology is a quantum phenome-non — and that, as such, our quantum nature quite naturally ex-tends beyond the body.

Out of Body: Nonlocal Travel through Space

Going out of body is just an expanded state of consciousness — one where you are local and nonlocal at the same time. Being self-aware — and unencumbered by a material body — your conscious mind moves freely, traveling by thought alone. In the quantum field, when you think of a place, you are instantly there. The zero-point mind moves in no time at all. If you are wondering whether you have ever ventured into the quantum field, here are some common experiences you may have had:

- Awareness of the room where you are sleeping, almost as though you are awake
- Perception from unusual or impossible perspectives, like a bird's-eye view or inside walls, closets, furniture, or objects
- A sense of flying, along with the urge to avoid power lines, trees, or other objects your mind is trained to physically avoid
- Spontaneous presence in another place or the home of a loved one
- Encounter with interdimensional beings, wildlife, or ancestors

There are all kinds of life-forms in the universe. Some you may recognize; others you may not. Humans, animals, plants, fish, bugs, microbes — any physical life you see in the material world has a counterpoint in the quantum world. The invisible world of nonlocal interdimensional life exists all around you, even if your mind perceives only what it experiences locally (more on this in chapter 7).

As you open your mind and expand your vibrational awareness, you can perceive *more of reality*. You may gain the ability to see, hear, feel, or sense things that previously you were entirely unaware of; you might even perceive things that other people do not notice. Awakenings of consciousness initiate you into a deepened understanding of the world and the things you encounter in it. Extrasensory perception is a byproduct of the expansion of consciousness.

The gifts of inner illumination are earned through personal

growth. Don't be surprised to notice that extraordinary things happen during periods of upshift or awakening. Though transcendental experiences can be incited or forced by outside means, including psychedelic drugs (like ayahuasca, mescaline, or psilocybin "magic" mushrooms) or biofeedback or brainwave stimulation techniques (like binaural beats), these can be shortcuts to a mindset that is designed to be developed through authentic life-expanding experiences. *Life will show you the truth as you grow into it.* Field experiences are bound to your state of being and part of your meaningful relationship with the universe. To authentically experience the transcendent reality, you must enter it wholly — with your whole heart and mind centered on the truth within.

Other Lives: Nonlocal Travel through Time

Physicist Evan Harris Walker once referred to the brain as "the 'hosting hardware' of human consciousness." If that's the case, might your local consciousness not only conceal the vast possibilities of nonlocal inner space travel but also conceal the realities of nonlocal time travel? Might the reduction valve of your personal mind have only enough storage to host your memories from this local life — your current experience in space and time? Might there be a host of your past, present, and future lives stored in the universal databank of the quantum field? And if so, might we all carry within us — in our deep energetic dimension — information from beyond the walls of this lifetime?

To time travel with quantum consciousness, you don't need a time machine. In 1904, Dorothy Eady was born in London, and — after a childhood near-death experience at the age of three — she developed strange behaviors, including speaking with a foreign accent, developing a fascination with Egyptian culture, and asking to be "brought home." Her family and schoolteachers could make no sense of her obsession with ancient culture, especially as time passed and she began to share extraordinary information about the lost civilization. She began to have dreams of meeting with Pharoah Seti, where he imparted memories of a past life with her ancient Egyptian family. She was so deeply connected to this experience that she studied Egyptian history and eventually moved to Cairo to work for the Department of Egyptian Antiquities. On her first arrival to Egypt, she knew she had been there before. She later adopted the name Omm Sety and dedicated her life to helping archaeologists excavate the Temple of Seti I — where she had unexplainable knowledge of the location of long-buried gardens and buildings. Her work was so extraordinary that it couldn't be refuted by Egyptologists. Carl Sagan said that she was "a lively, intelligent, dedicated woman who made real contributions to Egyptology. This is true whether her belief in reincarnation is a fact or fantasy."

This is just one of countless stories that point us to the extraordinary nature of human consciousness. Edgar Cayce, during states of hypnotic sleep, gave accounts of over 2,500 past-life — or, in the timeless sense, other-life — readings. Even the Buddha recounted over five hundred other lives, known as Jataka tales, or the stories of his other existences. Do we all, like Omm Sety, hold a treasure trove of other lives within us — lives that may be affecting us in this very moment? Might a near-death experience or personal awakening open up more storage in our "local hosting hardware" to enable us to expand our awareness to nonlocal lives? If there is no such thing as time in the quantum dimension, then surely we must also hold information about future lives — even parallel lives, as well. Might we all be time travelers living with amnesia about our other lives in other times?

My personal suspicions about this grew stronger when my daughter was just two years old, as she started telling strange stories of another time when we lived together. "Mommy," she said one day out of the blue. "Last time we were together, I was the mom." Then she went on to describe a different time in the past when her dad, sister, grandmother, and I lived together, musing about her father being her brother and how we were "dead in the trees." She started telling this story as soon as she could talk and was very matter-of-fact about it. She spoke as if she was simply reciting a memory. To this day, she attests to the story, reflecting that her young mind couldn't fully comprehend the death scenario that she now understands as a hanging. Could it be true? If so, how could we find evidence to prove it?

Many of us have had intuitions about our own past lifetimes. Could there be ways to get validations in this life that confirm our other-life experiences? I brought that question to IntuitionLab several years ago, and we began to conduct other-life mastermind groups for our students. During this crowdsourced intuition share, individuals took turns tapping into the nonlocal field to pull down other-life information for their peers. What we discovered was exciting! Not only do individuals generally find it surprisingly easy to access other-life memories, they are consistently able to provide evidence of them through various means:

- Multiple individuals (who had no prior contact with each other on the subject) describe the same or similar other-life situations or objects for a specific person.
- Individuals describe other lifetimes that occurred in places where the person has lived, visited, or had meaningful experiences in this lifetime.
- Individuals describe other lifetimes in which the person has had similar talents or abilities as they do in this time (like sharing that the person was once in a military drum corps — only to find out that they are the drummer for a band in this life).

- Individuals describe geographic locations or events from a previously unknown personal perspective that can be validated historically (like describing the layout of a town they have never visited or details of a battle they have never heard of).
- Individuals describe an other-life physical injury or illness that is reflected in the person's body in this life. My daughter's story of a hanging in our past life is a great example of this: Not only was I born with a red birthmark on the back of my neck, I had cervical spinal fusion surgery at age forty. My daughter, too, has since developed neck problems.

Many people don't realize that it is possible to consciously validate other-life information, but group intuition shares offer undeniable evidence through both synchronicity and shared discovery. But the best other-life validations can be found right here in this life. To find out who you really were in a past life, just look at the interests, talents, vocations, and relationships in your life today. All of it is connected. Just like in the case of Omm Sety, who had a passion for all things Egyptian, your passions and life themes are likely rooted in another time as part of the great parade of your lives. Other lives are more than interesting stories, they are part of your story — the great journey of your consciousness.

Because you remain entangled with experiences beyond local boundaries of time and space, other-life information correlates to some dimension of your present life. Peter Smith called this *intanglement*: "Intanglement is about the internal connection to all other selves that exist in the different realms of our personal universe. Every age we have ever been or will be is stored in our energy field. Our alternate realities are within reach and our parallel lives available for exploration." Because you are inwardly entangled with your other lives, you have access to their information, no matter when and where you are in time or space.

FIELD WORK STORY:
CHILDHOOD MEMORIES OF OTHER LIVES
by Jen, customer success manager

Jen's story is another example of how we may have access to other-life memories as children, before we spend too long in this world, and forget.

One evening I was driving in the car with my three-year-old son when, out of nowhere, he asked me, "Do you remember that time a long time ago when we lived in that blue house?" Since we never lived in a blue house, I was curious what he meant and asked him to tell me more. "It was a long, long time ago, and you weren't my mommy then. We lived in a blue house far away." I started to get chills and goosebumps as he spoke. "A man broke into our house and shot you in the belly. I tried to save you and I couldn't. I'm sorry I couldn't save you."

A rush of emotion suddenly came over me as I wondered if he could be remembering something from another life. He was so matter-of-fact about it, continuing to reiterate that there was a time that we lived together when I wasn't his mother. Interestingly, I've had ongoing stomach issues for most of my present life. And to this day, he still talks about our life in the blue house.

Five Ways to Validate Other-Life Information

Cross-life entanglement, or "intanglement," gives you the ability to find evidence that confirms your intuitions about your transcendental travels. For this reason, working with a partner or group is especially helpful in intuitive field work. You can be sure you are not *just making stuff up* when you exchange insight with people you don't know. Whether you are working with someone else or tuning into your own inner field, here are some ways to confirm intuitive data about your other lives:

1. **It feels personal.** We experience an other-life scenario as though we are part of it. Since consciousness records its personal experience in the quantum field, you naturally read the data as a personal experience. Whatever happens will be happening to you; you feel it, you sense it, you know what's going on around you. Unlike watching a movie from a detached point of view, other-life information is immersive, like a mental virtual reality experience. You feel as though you're in some way reliving it.

2. **The location is meaningful.** Oftentimes, people have connections to places they have lived in another life — along with attractions or aversions. When location information comes up, ask yourself what connections or feelings you have about that specific place. Many times during our IntuitionLab research, people have traveled to, lived in, or had an ancestral linkage to the places in their other lives.

3. **There are consistent evolutionary themes.** Your life is a work in progress, so it's no surprise to think that in another life you may be working on the same unresolved issues. For example, if money is a theme in your life, you may witness lives where you were wrestling with being rich or poor. You can have recurring themes around health, career, family, love, and so on. Whatever dynamics you discover in a past life, you will most likely find active at some point in this life as well.

4. **You recognize people.** It's not just evolutionary themes that follow you from life to life, people do too. You become entangled with other people as you help each other to

grow — through loving relationships and also challenging ones. You may recognize the energy of someone in your life with a different name and face. You might also notice them working with you on the same evolutionary theme, like standing up for yourself, overcoming fear, or achieving something important.

5. **You have natural talents or gifts.** Talent, since it is an intuitive gift, is one of the few things you can take with you across lifetimes. Do you have any special gifts that you didn't have to work hard to develop? Any natural abilities where you excel without a lot of training? Evidence suggests that we carry developed talents and intuitive skills (like creativity) from life to life. For example, when I was a young artist, much of my early art was bright, colorful, and mosaic — similar to stained glass. It was quite interesting when, years later in our IntuitionLab work, a student (who had never seen my early art) referenced that, in a prior life, I was a stained-glass maker.

When we recognize talent as a kind of portal to the nonlocal field, the mysteries of child prodigy and genius can be seen in a new light. Acknowledging that we have had other lives to develop skills and talents explains how it is possible to be gifted with abilities without training. Ervin László, who was both a scientific and musical genius, described his prodigal piano ability as "living myself into the music" and recognized the deep intuitive connection to his field-sourced talent. Whether it is Mozart composing symphonies as a child, Picasso creating his first oil painting at age nine, or Pascal becoming a mathematical genius at age twelve, the untaught brilliance of great minds suggests that we store a wealth of cross-life information in the quantum field.

INVESTIGATION: YOUR OTHER LIVES

Take a moment to reflect on your life: can you find any clues about another life? To find out, see if you answer *yes* to any of the questions below:

- Have you ever felt called to visit a faraway place for no apparent reason?
- Do you have an unexplainable fascination with another culture or time period?
- Do you seem to have recurring karmic relationships with certain people in your life?
- Do you have any natural talents or abilities you possess without any formal training?

In your journal, record any intuitive resonance you feel with people, places, and times that may be entangled in your journey of consciousness. Pay close attention to the thoughts and feelings that make no sense or don't have an apparent source; they are most likely from an interdimensional source in the quantum field. Unexplained intuitions may be nonlocal memories touching you from across the universe.

Life after Life

Each day, living in a material world, we are immersed in a cycle of beginnings and endings. We live in a pageant of transformation fueled by the friction between somethingness and nothingness, as the sun rises and sets each day. What appears to be an end, or a death, is a new beginning in disguise. Each autumn, nature appears to die with the falling leaves — only to be reborn each spring. Relationships, passions, careers, friendships — they may end, but new ones follow. We may think we live in a world of life and death, but truly, we live in a world of rebirth.

Dr. Eben Alexander attested to the reality of life after life in his book *Proof of Heaven*: "As a practicing neurosurgeon...my [near-death] experience showed me that the death of the body and the brain are not the end of consciousness, that human experience continues beyond the grave." Life after life is no longer considered impossible, even according to many theories in contemporary science. Einstein's theory of special relativity — in which the famous equation $E = mc2$ comes into play — proves that energy cannot be created or destroyed, only changed in state. Matter and energy are interchangeable, just different forms of the same fundamental substance: information. We are all beings of matter, energy, and information — a trifecta of manifested consciousness. Locally, our bodies, hearts, and minds may change states, but our nonlocal identity exists without beginning and without end.

Your body (matter), your heart (energy), and your mind (information) are different states of one indestructible consciousness. What we call death is a transformation, not an end — a transfer of information from one state (manifested matter, energy, and consciousness) to another (manifested energy and consciousness). When we transition, we shed our material skin to transcend the vibration of matter and return to our home in the eternal, unified, heavenly field. We don't *go anywhere* when we die; we only change form. A byproduct of this transformation is the "tunnel of light" experience, so often described by individuals who have had a near-death experience or undergone deep hypnosis.

Michael Newton, a master hypnotherapist and author of the *Journey of Souls* series, became one of the world's leaders in between-life exploration after he inadvertently led patients into nonlocal experiences during therapeutic regression. Over many years of research and practice, he wrote extensively about people reawakening their immortal identity, explaining that the tunnel of light is "the initial gateway of their journey into the spirit world. Most now fully realize they are not really dead but have simply left the encumbrance of an Earth body which has died.... The most common type of reaction I hear is a relieved sigh followed by something on the order of, 'Oh, wonderful, I'm home in this beautiful place again.'" The quantum field, it seems, is more than a data-storage bank; it is alive and filled with unearthly wonders.

It is not possible to lose our consciousness when our consciousness is part of the very fabric of the universe. If anything, we should expect the separation from the confines of material reality to feel more like liberation than nonexistence; death is but a portal to the boundless, nonlocal dimension — a place where light, energy, and information are abundant. Near-death experiencers often report that this reunion with our cosmic dimension comes with the gifts of peace, happiness, and even all-knowingness.

Michael Talbot explained that "some NDEers [near-death experiencers] discovered that in the presence of light they suddenly had direct access to *all* knowledge." Not surprisingly, these people often experience a sense of instantaneous understanding and clarity as they enter into a state of light. It is as though, through our nonlocal merging with the light, energy, and information field, we regain our expanded intuitive access to its wisdom. Our awareness is no longer limited by time or space. Might that also explain the proverbial "life-passing-before-your-eyes" scenario, reported by countless people who nearly died? On the completion of our life's journey, do we instantaneously experience the whole of our life through a single moment of intuitive understanding?

Since there is no such thing as time in metareality, when you leave the time field, you can behold your life in its entirety — everything all at once. This colossal moment of intuitive insight is just one of the many ways we continue to rely on our intuition even

beyond this life. Intuition is the one true language of consciousness — one that transcends the boundaries of time, space, and
individuality. All of life speaks the same language of intuition. It
is how we read the code of the field, speak without words, and
direct our energy to expand with the universe. The whole universe
is intuitively entangled across the vast distances of time and space
and even across the boundaries of life and death.

ILLUMINATION KEY #6

I AM EXTRAORDINARY

There are no ordinary people.
You have never talked to a mere mortal.

— C. S. LEWIS

One of the most exciting things about the quantum revolution is
that it shows us just how extraordinary we are. We are at the beginning of a great journey of discovery where, though we may not
yet be able to time travel or turn water into wine, we can find the
deep magic in small, extraordinary moments. Once you begin to
experience even the smallest impossible things — like knowing
something you should have no way of knowing or being aware of
something before it happens — a whole new world of possibility
opens before you.

Stepping into this new world requires a shift to the quantum
mindset. You are so much more than an individual person living
in a material bubble in space-time; you are part of a dimensionally
interwoven universe participating in coexisting planes of reality.
The heavens are not in the sky; they are all around you. You might
not be able to perceive the deeper realities from the physical plane,
but a part of you is always in connection with it. Your being is

a magnificent powerhouse that rises from the deep dimension; your conscious reality is just the tip of the iceberg — a single point emerging from the depths of our collective worlds, alternate dimensions, and parallel universes, often called the *multiverse*.

The idea that we live in a multiverse — a universe of universes — is integral in theoretical physics today. It suggests that multiple and alternate realities exist beyond the perception of our observable universe, a vast collection of separate realms that invisibly interpenetrate our own. Included in the multiverse are parallel realities, divergent timelines, and alternate worlds.

The many-worlds interpretation envisions a collection of realities where every possible outcome of an event actually occurs, creating a fractal with every outcome as a branch of another reality. Every observation or decision you make theoretically creates a new branch and, ultimately, a multitude of parallel universes. You and I are living in a "patchwork quilt of separate universes all bound by the same laws of physics." Though it may seem impossible to participate in the seemingly separate worlds of the ever-present metareality, we are all a part of the great tapestry of space, time, matter, energy, information, and potentiality. With each decision you make in your life, you create a new field of potentiality — a new branch on the tree of your life's path. Theoretically, there may be countless branches, or alternate lives, for those choices you did not make and for the cascading ripple of lives not lived.

The beautiful life that you create is a singular journey through infinite potentiality, lived out through the never-ending present moment, and existing beyond local time, space, and dimensionality. "In the quantum consciousness realm," explained Peter Smith, "we have come to understand that our consciousness is active in many apparent times and places on this planet, all unfolding in unison." Still, all the information in all realities is still part of the one unified quantum field. This means that the other realities, like all things in the nonlocal field, are reachable by your intuition. A part of you knows the outcome to every road not taken. Intuitively, you can explore other realities.

Immense power and potential exist all around you, ready to be explored by your intuitive mind. The otherworldly realm is its true domain. Your quantum intelligence can transcend time and space in our reality, but it can also transcend *this reality* itself. Just as your true being exists beyond the limits of time and space, the real you is made for somewhere beyond this reality.

A SPECIAL FIELD WORK STORY: PARALLEL REALITIES by Whitley Strieber (excerpt from *A New World*)

While consciously witnessing alternate dimensions is still exceptional, extraordinary people, like author Whitley Strieber, one of the world's foremost interdimensional experiencers, give us clues as to what could be possible for us all.

I had been invited to a small conference at the All Nations Gathering Center on the Lakota Sioux Pine Ridge Reservation in South Dakota....I had not been on the reservation for more than a few hours before I began to feel it. And when I say feel, I am not talking about something vague — some sense of unusual energies. Far from it. On my first morning there, when I happened to close my eyes during a drive of half an hour or so, I saw movement behind my closed lids — what looked like shadowy trees and rolling hills, but not the ones we were passing. Surprised, I opened them immediately. I couldn't understand why I'd been seeing anything at all. When I closed them again, what I saw simply took my breath away. I sat there watching an entire second landscape flow past the car. Although it seemed to be twilit rather than sunny, the effect was so vivid it was like wearing a virtual reality headset. I was flooded with strong, poignant and yet contradictory emotions. There was at once a sense of homecoming and homesickness. It wasn't as if I was in two places at once, but rather looking out the windows of my heart into two worlds that have been locked forever in a secret embrace and seeing that wonderful, sweet thing for the first time.

ILLUMINATION KEY #6
empowers you to do impossible things.

Once you embrace the quantum nature of your reality, you can move deeper into your own extraordinary existence. When so-called impossible things happen, you can now accept them — and work with them — as a natural part of your evolving consciousness.

In the sixth lab, you have the opportunity to personally experience things that should traditionally be impossible. There are many ways to enter and explore the quantum field; the section ahead offers you a few ways to get started right now.

Key #6 Activation: Accepting the Impossible Is Possible
Expand the Limits of Your Mind

To begin your practice of nonlocal exploration, let's get into a quantum state of mind. Remember, you are not a human being made of flesh and blood; you are an indestructible, limitless being of energy and light wearing what appears to be a physical body. In the lab ahead, you can practice reading the illuminating codes of the nonlocal realm and investigating other worlds. You can use your intuition to go beyond the confines of this reality so you can discover more about your true home — and the magnificent journey of your consciousness.

Venturing Inward

Use these five affirmations to remind yourself of your unlimited nature as you begin to explore your inner dimension:

- *I can know both the future and the past.*
- *I can know what is happening in other places.*
- *I am entangled with lives beyond this one.*
- *My consciousness is held in the field, not my body.*
- *My consciousness can travel to other times, other places, and other worlds.*

If you are thinking that there is no way you can do these things, trust me — you are capable of more than you know. As you venture inward, be patient with yourself, and be open to the universe — you never know what gifts it has in store for you.

LAB #6
TRAVEL BY THOUGHT
Experiencing Your Limitless Mind

In this lab, you have the opportunity to explore your inner realm and transcend the boundaries of time, space, and even this reality. Using your quantum intelligence, you can use the practice of remote viewing to see what is happening in other times, places, and other lives. The thoughts, feelings, and sensations of your intuition can put you in touch with any place in the world, any time in the past or future, and all other realities via the holographic information embedded in the quantum field.

Getting Started

For the practices ahead, be sure to select unfamiliar subjects for your nonlocal information exploration. Subjective bias can be a challenge when remote viewing, so you want to be sure that your mind has no information about any target you select. For example, you would not want to remote view your grocery store because your mind has already recorded a ton of information about it — memory information that you could conflate with intuitive data. This is called *front-loading* and can invalidate any evidence from your intuitive download. Instead, select a place, time, or experience you have never consciously interacted with. This will prove to yourself that any synchronicities, intuitive hits, or insights are genuine evidence of your connection to the field.

Open a No-Mind Portal

Prior to beginning any of the exercises ahead, be sure to do your usual practice to quiet the mind and get into your intuitive zone. A short meditation or drop into a no-mind portal will:

- create a state of calm where intuition flows.
- relax your body and energetically raise your vibration.
- increase your resonance with the quantum field and its information.

Create Your Six-Step Remote-Viewing Practice

You can use this framework for each of the three practices in this lab.

1. **Select your target:** Set your attention on a nonfamiliar target so that you have no observation bias. On a piece of paper, write down or describe your target.
2. **Entangle with your target:** Send energy into the field to connect with your target, moving into a state of resonant vibration with the idea of it.
3. **Turn on your inner receiver:** Open your mind to receive any data from your target. Let it download bits and bytes of its information into your mind.
4. **Record your impressions:** Write down or draw any information you receive — images, words, sounds, colors, feelings, scenarios, anything that bubbles up in your field of awareness.
5. **Go deeper:** After the initial download, follow your sense of resonance to go deeper and retrieve additional information around the target.
6. **Get validation:** When you are finished, view the target and record any evidence that validates your insights.

Here are some tips that will help with this process:

- Don't let your rational mind edit or filter out information that you don't understand. This is usually the best kind of information and where you will get the biggest validations.
- Remember that the data you receive often does not perfectly describe the target. You will most likely get bits and bytes of information about it, or you may get an impression of something similar in your own life. For example, if the target is a red ball, you may get an impression of a red ball you had as a kid, even if it looks different from the exact target. Your intuition naturally uses information stored in your memory field to convey its messages.

Nonlocal Experiment 1: Remote Viewing with a Partner

For our first remote-viewing session, I invite you to try this with a friend or family member. Practicing with another person is the best way to get validation of your intuitive hits because you can get verifiable outside data. You know you aren't making things up when you access information that you should have no way of knowing. To fully trust your intuition, you have to believe in it. Exercises like this help you build trust in your inner guide and prove the reality of its influence in your life.

To begin, partner up with another person who can practice with you in a separate location, ideally a place where neither of you have visited. To avoid subjective bias, make sure you are in a place that your friend doesn't know about and vice versa.

Some potential remote-viewing locations include:

- a room or place in your home that your partner has never seen
- a public place, like a library or coffee shop
- an outdoor space with a lot of activity, like a monument or park

Then follow these steps to start your remote-viewing experience:

1. **Time:** Set up a specific time to conduct the activity with your partner.
2. **Location:** Each partner picks a secret place to conduct the exercise, ruling out any places that the two of you have been together. If you don't want to leave home, try it from a room in your house that your partner has never seen.
3. **Practice:** Use the remote-viewing framework above, with your partner as the target. Then intuitively tap into any and all information around them to get a sense of their

location and the objects nearby. See how much informa-tion you can each draw from the nonlocal field.

4. **Validation:** When you are both finished, take turns sharing your information and matching the intuitive im-pressions with their counterpart in reality. You can do it right away over live video or the phone. You can also take pictures of the locations to be sure you are getting all the validations.

When placing information for your partner, be sure to use your own intuition to validate their impressions, remembering that they may not use exact descriptions. Since we are still at the early stages of our intuitive development, we likely will not get a full vision of objective reality; instead, we can get pieces of it that are often delivered according to our own personal frame of ref-erence. For example, if your partner says, "I see a fish," but there are no fish in the room, consider other fish-related objects. If you are wearing a Phish tour T-shirt, that's a hit! Why? Because your partner's intuition got them to say exactly the right words: "fish" could mean "Phish" in this instance. Remember, the impressions from the field are right-brained, so they are often symbolic, visual, or metaphorical — they are very often *not* literal. Be sure to keep your mind open for your partner when placing their insights so you don't miss any of the hints their intuition is sending.

Nonlocal Experiment 2: Time Traveling to the Future

You can use remote viewing to explore all kinds of places around the world, but you can also use it to explore the past and future. When we started practicing remote viewing in our Intuition-Lab sessions, we were surprised at how often students picked up on past versions of places — the way they used to look years or even decades before. People would remote view houses with old wallpaper or different paint colors than the current version. Since we did not set a specific intention to connect with data from the present moment, like reading a map with only half the coordinates, we connected with the place but in an array of different times.

 Prophecy is remote viewing the future.

In essence, when you *see the future*, you are simply viewing a nonlocal place in a relative future time. When seers and diviners of old described scenes from our future, they were remote viewing. From biblical prophets like Isaiah and Ezekiel to the oracles of ancient Greece or famous clairvoyants like Nostradamus and Cayce, they were simply accessing the nonlocal quantum field and sharing its information with us. What makes time-based remote viewing tricky is that, unlike space, which is manifested, time exists in potentiality. Remember, life is not predestined, so with future-viewing there is always the possibility of change interference. Remote viewing a future path is a game of potentiality, but you can play with the future field in some interesting ways:

1. **Target:** Set your intention on remote viewing a future happy scene in your life. Close your eyes and let your intuition take you there.
2. **Practice:** Use the remote-viewing practice above to access as much information as possible about the place and time of this happy event. Ask yourself questions like, *What is happening in this place and time? Where is this place? What is the purpose of this celebration? Which people are present?*
3. **Record:** Make sure to record everything you experienced, and file it away somewhere safe for future validation.

Note: Future fieldwork is a time investment because obviously you don't get instant validation. You may need to wait days, months, or even years to witness your impressions come to life. Consider setting an intention for a happy time and place in the near future for quicker validation.

You can create your own variations of this practice, adding various targets:

- Remote viewing future places of residence
- Remote viewing future job or business locations
- Remote viewing a future relationship
- Remote viewing future travels
- Remote viewing future global dynamics

As always, be sure to conduct all field work in a high-vibration, illuminated frame of mind to be sure that you are aligning with the best and clearest potentialities.

Nonlocal Experiment 3: Remembering Your Other Lives

Our final practice in the "Impossible Things" lab unites the nonlocal and local experience. When you practice remote viewing for different times and places, you use your intuitive imagination to observe a nonlocal scenario. You are remote in that you feel separate from the situation and can view it like a picture or movie. However, you can take this process to a deeper level by not just *observing* the scenario but also by *participating* in it.

When you tap into another life, for yourself or another person, you are doing more than focusing on a point in time or space — you are immersing yourself in an experience. You don't just view a situation, you become part of it. You understand it, feel it, and can learn from it. Past- and other-life exploration is a valuable way to gain insight about your journey of consciousness — to understand your life purpose, grow into your authentic self, and overcome past challenges. What you don't resolve in one life, you carry forward to the next in a continuing lesson. What you cultivate in life — talents, strengths, even relationships — you also carry forward. Your trials and triumphs coalesce, life to life, in a beautiful symphony of human experience. Through intuitive communion with the nonlocal field, you can hear that song from any time or place.

Three Types of Other Lives

Here are three types of other lives that we can tap into:

- **Past lives:** Past lives are other lives that happen in a time prior to the present moment, relative to our current position in space-time. This is the most common type of other-life experience. It is most easily accessible because you can directly trace connections to the current life.

- **Parallel lives:** Parallel lives are other lives that are happening in the present moment. Technically, this includes all other lives — past and future — since we understand that beyond our reality there is no such thing as time, and everything happens all at once.

- **Alternate lives:** There are also alternate and future paths for the present life, determined by different choices and potentialities. These are your doppelgängers, the other versions of your life that exist from roads not taken or from various potentialities.

Past-Life Exploration Practice

You can use the practice below to explore your other lives. In this lab, we will explore a past life because it gives you the greatest opportunity for validation.

1. **Activate your other-life entanglement.** Set an intention to become aware of a past life that is currently affecting your present life. Your attention activates the energetic

line that connects your past and present lifetime — and the learning lessons they share.

2. **Enter your no-mind zone.** Close your eyes, relax your mind and body, and smile. Let your smile light you up inside as you shift into a high-vibration headspace. Embody the radiant inner peace of your beautiful smile. When you are ready, visualize the steps below.

3. **Merge with the field.** In your mind's eye, imagine your consciousness ascending into a brilliant cloud of radiant light — the all-knowing light that holds all the information of the universe. Understand that this light holds the record of all your life journeys. Soak up the light and be one with it. Take a deep breath. Feel the light and all its wisdom interpenetrate every cell of your body. Feel it illuminate your mind and light up your heart.

4. **Open a nonlocal portal.** Reaffirm your intention to merge with a helpful past-life memory stored within the field. Imagine a portal before you — a brilliant and glowing doorway, an interdimensional portal immersed in pure light. On the other side of it is a past-life scenario. When you are ready, step across the threshold.

5. **Intuitively explore.** Be present in this place. Notice whatever is around you in this other dimension — the landscape, architecture, people, or events. Let your imagination intuitively move you, and go along with whatever scenarios arise in your field of vision. Let a story unfold. Notice how you feel and anything that resonates or feels familiar. Ask yourself:

   o   Where am I?
   o   Who am I?
   o   What is happening?
   o   Who is here with me?

Trust the information that flows into your field of consciousness and go with its flow, without judgment or analysis. Allow your intuition to reveal the significance of this moment in time. If uncomfortable feelings or situations arise, you can pull back from them anytime. You have complete control. Past-life experiences are often deeply emotional and can relate to pain points in your present life experience. Notice any thoughts or emotions that arise as you feel the connection to people, places, or life themes that are part of your current experience.

6. **Close the portal.** Once the story has played out, take a deep breath and a moment of gratitude for the information you received. You can come back to this place whenever you like. Envision yourself stepping back through the light portal into local time and space, then close the door behind you. Return to this moment in space and time, then open your eyes.

7. **Connect your lives.** Take a moment to ask yourself:
   o   Why was this life shown to me?
   o   How does it connect to my life today?
   o   What am I to learn from this situation?

8. **Journal your insights.** Take a moment to record your experience and write down any insights, impressions, or memories that came to light.
   o   List any material from your past life that connects to your present life (people, places, ancestry, talents, interests, recurring life patterns, etc.). Are there any parts of your life now that obviously connect to those things?
   o   Write down any resonant feelings that connect you to that past-life scenario. Does it feel familiar to you? Does it feel like a real memory on some level?

o   What does this other life show you about your current life? Did it reveal a continuous karmic relationship with someone in your life? Did it reveal any life themes or patterns you are continuing to work through today?

9. **Find the meaning.** After completing your past-life investigation, contemplate its overall message for you. You were shown this life for a reason. It holds a key to something important in your life today.

Lab #6 Workbook: Remote Viewing across Space, Time, and Lives
Recording Your Inner Adventures

Record your various remote-viewing experiences — of other locations, times, and lives — in your journal or workbook using the framework below.

Remote Viewing: Other Locations

   Impressions and downloads: _____
   Validations: _____

Remote Viewing: Other Times

   Impressions and downloads: _____
   Validations: _____

Local Remote Viewing: Other Lives

   Other-life scenario and impressions: _____
   Connections to current life (patterns, themes, locations, people, objects, talents, vocations): _____

   _____

CONCLUSION

Activating Key #6 of the illumination code proves
the impossible is possible.

The sixth key unlocks the boundaries of time, space, and reality so you can venture deep into the magic of the nonlocal field. Once you have known the unknowable and experienced the impossible, there can be no doubt of a higher reality.

Key Principles

- The whole universe is entangled.
- The mind is a function of the field, not the body.
- You can perceive beyond time, space, and the material world.
- Your consciousness does not begin and end with its container of local reality.
- Extrasensory perception is a byproduct of your expanding consciousness.

Key Applications

- Use your intuition to explore information in the quantum dimension.
- Get evidence of the quantum field with remote-viewing practices.
- Prove the limitless nature of your consciousness with past-life and other-life exploration.

As you continue your inner ventures, remember that all things reveal themselves in due time. If there is information you are not meant to know right now, you will not be able to know it until the time is right. True illumination comes when you trust the universal process of unfolding.

CHAPTER SEVEN

Guiding Forces

*The "Mind of God," which Einstein wrote eloquently about,
is cosmic music resonating throughout hyperspace.*

— MICHIO KAKU

You and I are part of a magnificent cosmic unfolding and interplay of simultaneous realities, colliding fields of consciousness,
entangled relationships, and the dynamic energy it all creates. But
the most important part of this extraordinary existence is not the
science that explains it — it is the fact that it is *meaningful*. Every
bit of information, every thought, every choice is an integral part
of the expansion of a conscious universe. Life is more than a playground; it is a journey guided by the deeper awareness within you.

Your inner guidance system would not exist if life were not
purposeful. The fact that we have built-in intuition, higher callings, gut feelings, and an inner sense of what is right or wrong for
us is evidence that the choices we make in this life *matter*. We are
part of something bigger than we know. And we are supported
by an array of guiding forces that point us in the right direction,
enlighten us, and give us clues about the eternal nature of our existence. The quantum field *is* awareness, the guiding force that illuminates our life journey.

At the heart of everything that we have explored in this
book — reality, metareality, time, space, the field of intrinsic

awareness, the illumination code, and impossible things — exists the *one*. The unified field of everythingness invites you into the mystery of your true being, and our last illumination key offers you entry into it. The final frontier of existence leads you to your true and everlasting home. And your intuition, informed by the illuminating code of the quantum field, guides you there.

The zero-point field is the proverbial unmoved mover: it is whole in its totality, and we are moved to expand into that totality. With every insight, we become more like the mind of the universe — enlightened, aware, and united with all other things. Life in our material world is a *becoming*. Since the moment you passed through the portal of your mother's womb and arrived into this holographic reality, you have held a powerful gift: the gift of time — which gives you the ability to change your state. What is time but a measurement of change, of energy in motion? Deepak Chopra put it well: "Eternity is timeless.... After death we become timeless. Literally without time in the 'zone of eternity' where souls abide. But why wait for an afterlife? If time is an illusion, we should be able to step out of it whenever we want, simply by living in the present moment — then the value of going to Heaven will be achieved."

The change of state we naturally crave is our return to wholeness. We long to lift the blinders of our limited reality and know the deep dimension within us — to return to a state of coherence and communion with life itself. When we are young, we long to find ourselves. But this is more than just a desire to find the right profession or life partner; it is a calling to discover our extraordinary nature — to find out who we really are and what we are made for. When you live in connection with your inner field, you don't need to go anywhere to make those discoveries. You only have to change your state of mind.

The urge to find yourself is the unconscious longing to return to a state of unity with the cosmos. In this final chapter, we explore some of the guiding forces that light your way on the ultimate journey home — the return to yourself. You are moved by these forces in subtle, often unnoticeable ways, both internally and externally. Though part of the magic of this world is our free will — our ability to creatively manifest from the great field of potentiality — if we look close enough, we can find clues that guide us to do that in the best possible way. People often joke that life doesn't come with an instruction manual; but actually, it does. The guide to life is coded into you — and the reality you live in. You live in a meaningful universe, and there are guiding forces everywhere.

Signs from the Universe

The whole world, inside and out, is filled with the illuminating cosmic code. You receive guiding information internally as intuitive impressions; and you receive guiding information externally as signs, serendipity, and other meaningful experiences in material reality. Remember, from a universal perspective — just like there is no such thing as time or space — there is no such thing as *inside us* or *outside us*. These dualities are just a product of relativity as you live in localized space-time. The world outside you is just an extension of the world *perceptively* inside you; both are part of the same one that guides and informs you.

 Signs are how the universe pays attention to *you*.

The meaningful signals life brings you every day are an invitation to build a conscious, living relationship with the universe. Just as you are entangled with the universe, the universe is entangled with you. *It knows you personally* because you are a part of it — and it is the part of you that knows everything. It holds you in its loving embrace, using intuitions and signs to communicate with you on a regular basis. External signs are coded into your reality and can appear in many ways, including:

- **Synchronicities:** Meaningful coincidences that defy rational explanation
- **Numbers:** Recurring patterns that get your attention at an important moment
- **Dreams:** Lucid dreams that serve as a meeting point between realms
- **Opportunities:** Unexpected positive events or opened doors that offer a path forward
- **Nature:** The appearance of natural phenomena (like feathers, wish flowers, shooting stars, rainbows) that highlight something significant
- **Electricity:** Electrical interferences, like static on a radio or a computer glitch, that signal the presence of quantum energy exchange
- **Animals:** Seeing specific animals in an unusual context that catches your eye in a serendipitous moment
- **Déjà vu:** A spontaneous merging with the quantum field that feels like a memory

Déjà vu is simply a sudden union with the intuition memory field. During its connection with the field, you are both local and nonlocal — reading the local reality code around you while also processing its nonlocal data from the cosmic memory field. This is why during déjà vu, you often feel like you are experiencing the situation from outside yourself or from a different perspective. These fleeting moments are a glimpse of our all-knowing nature.

Like déjà vu, signs from the universe point you toward the deeper dimension of your reality. When you tune in to the subtle messages coded into your life, you can find guiding information hidden in seemingly random and mundane situations. As Chopra also explained, "Synchronicity is choreographed by a great pervasive intelligence that lies at the heart of nature and is manifest in each of us through intuitive knowledge." Illuminating signs and synchronicities often show up in unexpected moments or just when you need them, with the common purpose of guiding you from the deep dimension.

Here are some examples of signs and synchronicities:

- You are thinking about taking a new class, then you meet someone who invites you to it.
- You get a big idea to try something new, then glance at the clock to see it's 5:55.
- You are going through a hard time in your life, and randomly find a rose on your car windshield.
- As you are considering moving to a new place, you then get invited there for a trip.
- Ever since your friend passed on from this life, you see their favorite flower everywhere.

When the time is right, life will use whatever it can to get your attention. The purpose is multifold — sometimes as a validation that you are moving in the right direction, sometimes to comfort you, sometimes just to remind you of the meaningful nature of life and that you are not alone.

The key to finding the meaning in a sign is paying attention to what you are doing when the sign shows up. Nothing is random. What were you thinking or doing or discovering when the universe waved you down with one of its signals? With synchronicity, context is everything. Author Laura Lynne Jackson explained in her book *Signs*, "Carl Jung coined the term synchronicity to describe a seemingly meaningful coincidence. Jung was fascinated with the idea that the events in our lives are not random, but rather express the reality that we are all part of a deeper order — a unifying, universal force he called the unus mundus, Latin for 'one world.'" Synchronicity is a manifestation of the interconnectedness of all things — the underlying deep order of cosmic consciousness and a sign of your entanglement with the universe.

Secrets of the Signs

Signs are how the universe communicates *personally* with you. A sign starts a conversation, then you respond to it with your attention and/or action. You can think of a sign as an *external intuitive impression* that the universe drops into your life out of nowhere. You then use your *internal intuitive process* to decode its purpose or meaning. In this way, life guides you from both the inside and the outside. Here are two secrets to help you understand your sign language:

1. **The more you pay attention to your signs, the more they happen.** As we have learned via quantum mechanics, the more you observe something, the more energy you send to it. The more energy you send to it, the more you entangle with it, and the more it flows within you (insights and feelings) and around you (signs and synchronicities). For example, if, you start to notice the clock at 11:11, accept it as a genuine communication signal, and open energetic space for more signals to come. It won't be long before you are noticing number patterns on the hour around the clock.

2. **You can create your own signal to start a conversation with the universe.** You don't just have to wait for the universe to give you a sign; you can start your own conversation with life by creating your own signal. I call these *tokens* — intentionally created symbols that represent

your connection to the universe. A token can be any object, symbol, number, animal, song, or words that the universe can use to signify its presence in your life. For example, I have been using my token — a white daisy — for nearly thirty years. Whenever a white daisy shows up, I know my intuition is at work. You will have the opportunity to get — and activate — your own token in the lab at the end of this chapter.

Recognizing the wisdom of life's serendipitous signals is an integral part of your quantum intelligence. Though the subtle world of imagination and intuition can often feel nebulous, external signs serve as real, verifiable manifestations of the deep dimension. Since they are observable phenomena, they can be witnessed by multiple people and provide all kinds of validations, like some of the situations we regularly experience in IntuitionLab:

- People repeatedly attest that they experience an uptick in signs and synchronistic number patterns during times when they are actively practicing with their intuition.
- When using insight card decks, people often pull the same one card over and over, even though there are fifty-two cards in the deck.
- People regularly pull an insight card that has objects or scenarios that directly relate to a previous intuitive download.
- In breakout groups, people are randomly paired with partners who shared similar life experiences and could help each other.

These phenomena are evidence of an elevated state of entanglement between people and the quantum field — a state created by shared energy and intention. Synchronistic patterns are codes that help you understand what is going on in the world around you. By

intuitively reading the signals life is sending your way, you can decode its secret messages and consciously interact with the beyond.

EXPERIMENT: RECEIVING YOUR COSMIC SIGNALS

As you use your quantum intelligence more and more, you may
start to notice more signs of entanglement and synchronicity. This
happens because your relationship with the universal field is deep-
ening. Here are some signals to look out for as you grow into your
deep dimension:

- **Time signs:** One of the most common signals the universe gives is through numbers that show up around the
  clock — numbers or patterns you see repeatedly. These
  could be any numbers — 1:23 or 9:11 or the classic 11:11
  or 5:55 that many folks call "angel numbers." Your consistent apprehension of these patterns is a sign of alignment
  with the deep dimension.
- **Song signs:** Have you ever had a song come on the radio
  and you feel like it is speaking to you in the moment?
  Streaming your music on shuffle opens space for life to DJ
  synchronistic messages through your music. Songs that
  resonate or repeat are often sharing a message of support
  or guidance from the universe.
- **Travel signs:** Many signs can show up when you are out
  on the road. Since you are often in a relaxed state of attention when driving, it's easy for the universe to catch your
  eye. Here are some details to look out for:
  o Recurring numbers on mile markers (randomly no-
     ticing 111 or 222 or 333)
  o Streetlights going off or coming on just as you drive
     by them

o Random messages that you happen to notice on bill-
   boards, tractor trailers, or other signage that seem to
   have a personal message for you
o Close encounters with flying birds or other animals

Just be sure to pay attention to what you are thinking or
talking about when the sign appears. These are usually punctuation marks for important moments in your life.

Life beyond Life

The universe is teeming with life. In the material world, you are
surrounded by all kinds of life — some that you perceive and some
that you don't. You and I can see a planet, a bird, or even a tiny
gnat, but we cannot observe the world of microscopic life — like
cells, microbes, fungi, and viruses. Human beings make up only
0.01 percent of earth's life. Scientists also estimate that more than
70 percent of the world's life is made up of microscopic organisms;
this means that even on earth, we can't physically perceive more
than half of the life around us.

Just as we are immersed in a sea of material life that is undetectable to our limited-range physical sensors, an immaterial
world of energetic life surrounds us as well. Your physical body is
designed to sense other physical states — and your quantum body
is designed to sense metaphysical states. With your intuition, you
can sense energetic states that elude physical perception, including
a whole spectrum of universal life. Since the quantum world exists
at a frequency above physical reality, the higher your consciousness vibrates, the greater the range of life you can perceive.

I was in shock the first time I caught a glimpse of the imperceptible dimensions of the field. After a big awakening and vibrational upshift, I began to see things that other people could not.

At first I thought I might be losing my mind. But with time, I realized that this new experience was a byproduct of expanding my range of perception. Mostly, I could now see energy forms in the air around me. They felt like individual beings, yet they were amorphic, more plantlike than humanlike. I remember thinking it looked like they were floating in an ocean. In the daylight, they look like a subtle oasis; in the darkness, they softly flicker like static on a television. The special ones glow and seem to convey information telepathically. They can appear and dissolve into thin air. Others fly through the air and make a loud *pop* as they pass through physical materials, like a wall, window, or piece of furniture. Behind my desk, I have a drum that plays itself on a daily basis and greets me with a tap when I start my workday or walk into the room. Friends and family have witnessed these events around me so often they are no longer surprised by them.

Breakthroughs into cosmic consciousness are unique from person to person, but the outcome of initiation into expanded fields of reality often includes the ability to perceive life beyond our own. The high-vibration superconscious realm is home to vast ecosystems of interdimensional life, many of which we cannot begin to comprehend. Great spiritual masters have seen them and reported them; but regular people like you and me can see them, too, when we open up to our extraordinary intuitive nature.

ARCHETYPES OF INTERDIMENSIONAL BEINGS

Spiritual traditions around the world teach that we coexist with a host of energy-based life. Human history is rich with an array of archetypes that describe the life we encounter when we transcend the walls of this reality:

- Angels
- Gods and goddesses
- Ancestral spirits
- Aliens and extra-
  dimensionals
- Ascended masters
- Spirit guides
- Orbs
- Ghosts

- Fairies
- Animal spirits
- Nature spirits and
  elementals
- Djinn or genies
- Devas and devis
- Kami
- Orishas
- Valkyries

In the 1700s Swedish scientist Emanuel Swedenborg under-
went a spiritual awakening that led him to a life-changing series
of paranormal experiences. He wrote extensively about his experiences, many of which foretold discoveries made by contemporary
physics. Explaining the fundamental role of intuition in the universal realms, he explains that all the information of a person's life
is recorded through the nervous system of their spiritual body —
and that, in "the heavens," matter is replaced by information as
the source of sustenance. In the timeless metareality, intuitive
information-sharing is foundational. He states that "there is a single
language for everyone in all heaven," explaining that people intuitively communicate through thought alone, regardless of their native
tongue.

Swedenborg preemptively described the holographic universe,
with clusters of thought information or, as Michael Talbot put it,
"telepathic bursts of knowledge as a picture language so dense with
information that each image contains a thousand ideas." Furthermore, Swedenborg believed that "despite its ghostlike and ephemeral qualities, heaven is actually a more fundamental level of reality
than our own physical world. It is, he said, the archetypal source
from which all earthly forms originate, and to which all forms return." As such, we can understand the nonphysical dimension as

something more than an alien landscape full of strange and unknown beings; instead, it is a familiar place — a home that we return to — filled with beings that we know and love.

One of the greatest gifts the quantum field has to give us is an understanding of the continuous nature of life. Since everything is conserved in the field, nothing is ever really gone — including those we love. Years ago, my youngest sister, Jennifer, passed away unexpectedly, when she was only twenty-five years old. Within hours of her departure from the material world, strange things started to happen around her close friends and family members: Her best friend reported hearing her voice call to him. Her personal items would show up in bizarre places around our house (my mother once found her favorite ring in the dishwasher). I even woke up to my two-year-old daughter giggling in her crib at 2 a.m., saying, "Mom! Aunt Jenny is driving me crazy!" One time, when I was unpacking after a visit home, I found a note that Jennifer had written to me when she was nine years old zipped into the mesh lining of my brand-new suitcase! One thing was certain: though my sister is no longer here in flesh and blood, she is very much alive. And very talented at interdimensional activities!

FIELD WORK STORY: WHEN MIND MOVES MATTER
by Scott, travel blogger

Scott's story is an example of how we stay connected with the people we care about and how it is possible to reprogram our reality code to communicate across the quantum field.

I grew up with Kim and was pretty much a fixture in her house since seventh grade. I was even there on the day her sister Jennifer was born. When we were teenagers, we started a Chestney family tradition: each Christmas, we would take a "family" picture in front of the tree — with me, Kim, and her two sisters. Year after year, we would take a new photo of the four of us. Even after we all grew up, I still kept one of those photos framed in my apartment.

I usually get my intuition through dreams. When I dream of someone, they often show up in my life shortly after. Not long after Jen passed, she visited me in a dream. I had just moved, and most of my stuff was still in boxes. A couple days after the dream, something strange happened as I was getting ready for work. I opened my sock drawer and, low and behold, that framed Christmas photo was lying right there in front of me — on top of my clothes. I couldn't believe it. The photo had been packed away during the move, so there was no possible way it had been there prior. I think Jen found it and put it there as proof she'd come to see me…and to say, "See ya later."

Your inner guidance shows up as thoughts and feelings that arise from nowhere; your *outer guidance* — or signs — shows up as physical events and happenings with no apparent cause. It can be hard to believe in the reality of external signs until you experience them personally. How is it possible for a force in the nonphysical dimension to affect our physical reality?

Once we realize that there is no fundamental difference between matter and energy, that question becomes easier to answer. If everything is built of information — manifesting in different physical or energetic states — then all realities must be informed by a common code. All consciousness has access to this code, whether it has a physical body or not.

The field has already shown us that we can affect reality with our thoughts. The cosmic womb of the zero-point field makes the creative power of manifestation and the law of attraction possible. It only makes sense that we should have this same power wherever our consciousness travels. Furthermore, if we can manifest change in our entire life situation, why should we not be able to manifest change in a small piece of matter? If we can use our creative power to reprogram our personal reality on a grand scale — intentionally manifesting from the quantum field of potentiality — isn't it possible that we have the latent power to reprogram the location or attributes of material assets in that manifested reality?

Psychokinesis (a.k.a. telekinesis) is the ability to move objects without any physical contact. Theoretically, it does not go against the new laws of physics: if all the world is made of the mind, then the principle of mind over matter may, on some level, apply across dimensions. If everything is fundamentally made of information, might we all, at a certain level of consciousness, be able to recode that information with our intention? Remote viewer Ingo Swann, who was part of the Stargate Project with the US government, conducted research that showed that his thoughts could affect a magnetometer during concentration. Thought, it seems, can move things.

Could emerging exploration in subjects like quantum teleportation be the key to explaining psychokinetic phenomena, like my sister's uncanny ability to move physical objects in our reality? Quantum teleportation is a phenomenon in quantum mechanics related to entanglement; it allows for the nonlocal transfer of quantum information from one location to another — without actually physically moving the particles themselves. Deepak Chopra and Menas C. Kafatos explained in their book *You Are the Universe*,

> Recently experimenters have found a way to move photons from one position to another without passing through the space in between, the first example of true teleportation. Because the photons skip from point A to point B instantaneously, no time elapses. The speed of light isn't actually

exceeded; it's made irrelevant. We may say that time is bypassed. In fact, teleportation unravels the neat pop-up picture of space, time, and matter. Teleporting photons have enormous implications.

We may not be ready to build a *Star Trek* transporter just yet, but with so much evidence from paranormal phenomena, we can speculate the possibilities.

Whitley Strieber — author of a classic documentation of extradimensional life, the book *Communion*, and one of the foremost experiencers of other worlds in our time — has been exploring interdimensional phenomena for most of his life. On multiple occasions, I have had the opportunity to talk with him about his extraordinary experiences and what contact with "the visitors" reveals about the nature of our own reality. Explaining how nonphysical beings can affect physical reality, he says they "rearrange atoms" — that they "think first in math" and may "see the underlying truth first, then — and only if necessary for some functional reason — the outcome. This would mean that they would see first the forces and math that lies behind the apple, and only if necessary the actual form." Could this math be part of the code of reality? Part of the same code that informs us from the quantum realm? Could it be possible for otherworldly beings to make changes in our material reality like computer programmers altering an algorithm?

Strieber explained that our relationship with interdimensional beings "only begins with what we now know as the physical.... The physical is only part of a huge tapestry of reality.... It is a process of contact that is intended to lead to the deep inner sharing that is communion." Connection, it seems, is everything. Becoming one with each other, one with other worlds, one with the illuminating information in the field, one with the universe — beyond time, space, and the boundaries of this reality.

Could it be our destiny to develop our quantum intelligence so that we can transcend the illusory container of physical life, commune with all beings, and experience the ultimate triumph over death? "Right now, we cannot reliably engage with our dead. Our whole religious journey is, at its core, an effort to ensure that the death of the body does not mean annihilation," Strieber concluded, suggesting that eventually "the barrier between us and our own dead is going to fall. Empirical evidence will emerge that enables us to escape the trap of believing that physical life is the only life. On the other side of the wall of death, there lies a new freedom and a new life, and along with them opportunities for enrichment that are presently almost beyond imagination."

This idea validates countless experiences from people all around the world throughout all of history who claim to have been visited by loved ones who have passed on — showing up in dreams, visions, near-death experiences, and even mediumship. Like the epic love story between Sam and Molly in the movie *Ghost*, maybe we all carry our bonds from this world to the next. Maybe those who leave before us really do guide us, give us signs, and share information with us through intuitive lines of communication. Ancestral veneration is a common practice in many religions and indigenous cultures. They hold a deep reverence for the consciousness of their ancestors who they believe watch over them from the next world. Devotion to one's entangled elders is a sacred practice that affirms the continuing nature of life — without fear of it.

INVESTIGATION: YOUR INTERDIMENSIONAL ENTANGLEMENTS

Though you many not consciously realize it, your community of friends and loved ones is not limited to your little bubble in the space-time dimension. You travel, life to life, with kindred spirits, and you are supported by an array of often imperceptible guiding forces — interdimensional points of consciousness that we recognize as our ancestors, loved ones, guides, teachers, and other sacred beings. If you look closely, you can find evidence that they are with you and see the signs they send to guide you.

Take a moment to reflect on your life. Have you ever felt the presence of someone who had passed on from the material world? Have you ever witnessed strange, serendipitous events that felt like a communication from beyond? Thanks to our understanding of the quantum field, we no longer have to meet these kinds of occurrences with fear or incredulity. Instead, we can embrace the mysteries of life beyond life with natural curiosity and wonder. Here are some ways to recognize the invisible presence of your interdimensional entanglements, the ones that remain connected to you beyond time and space:

- Thoughts of a person that come to mind out of nowhere
- A scent that has no apparent source and reminds you of someone
- Changes in the air, like a cold spot or a wisp of air on your skin
- Physical objects making sounds, like subtle pops, pings, or vibration
- Vivid dreams that feel as though you were talking with someone in real life
- Objects that are moved or show up in a place to get your attention
- Electronic disruptions, like a radio, light, or television turning on or off

These are all ways that interdimensional consciousness can easily interact with the field of our reality and give us signs of their existence.

FIELD WORK STORY: A VISIT FROM BEYOND
by Beth, editor and writer

Beth's story shows us how we remain connected with our entanglements beyond this life, even if we don't realize it.

One evening, during an online remote-viewing workshop with Kim, I couldn't believe my eyes. Looking back at me through Kim's webcam, I saw Dr. L, a physics professor and former mentor from my college years. The thing is, Dr. L had died of old age a few months earlier.

At some point after Kim and I met, we discovered that, serendipitously, we both knew Dr. L, even though he lived hundreds of miles from where we were both living in Pittsburgh. He was the father of her childhood best friend and, though Kim and Dr. L hadn't seen each other in years, they had spent over a decade together as dancers at a ballet school in Kim's hometown.

On this day, Dr. L was with Kim again. He gave her shoulder a fatherly squeeze, his eyes crinkling with joy, then disappeared in an instant. *Did I really just see that?* Every hair on my arms stood on end. The air felt electric. Then, as we went around the room sharing our remote-viewing impressions, a fellow student, Elizabeth, began to describe a man that sounded just like Dr. L! She perfectly described his tall, lean physique and signature blue eyes; she also reluctantly shared that, though she couldn't explain why, she was seeing Kim and this man spinning around together.

Putting the pieces together, I suggested we all meet up after class. When I told Kim that I had seen Dr. L, she looked at me quizzically, obviously not realizing that he had passed. Then her eyes lit up as something clicked inside. "That explains it!" Kim was dumbfounded. "That's why

I had been making his special pancakes all week!" It turns out that, when she had sleepovers with her best friend, Dr. L would make them his special, all-natural pancakes with yogurt and maple syrup, which became a comfort food for Kim. All week, Kim had been strangely craving those pancakes; she even started making them daily — and had eaten one right before the workshop! The magic was capped off by Elizabeth's "spinning" vision: one of her most vivid ballet memories is her and Dr. L dancing and spinning as they shared a performance in *The Nutcracker.*

Coherence: God, Love, and the Return to Yourself

In quantum mechanics, the state of coherence is one of synchronized energy, where different parts of a quantum system work together in coordination as one. Imagining the universe as a great symphony of individual players — playing their part together — we can see that coherence occurs when everyone plays in sync, with all rhythms, notes, and chords perfectly in tune. If the beat or tune is off, the symphony becomes incoherent.

Coherence is the state of union within existence. It can be so powerful that it awakens you to new levels of consciousness as you expand in harmony with the quantum field. You can experience the state of coherence as a kind of transcendence, bliss, or rapture of the spirit. The sense of peace and power that comes with coherence can even feel like a state of grace, where you are filled with the knowledge, peace, and power of the deep dimension.

In quantum physics, when subatomic particles are in a coherent state, they can cooperate and communicate with each other. Through resonant wave patterns, individual waves and particles get into phase and behave like one united wave-particle system.

You can see an example of this when you look at different types of light. Coherent light is constant in both frequency and phase with a single frequency and wavelength, and incoherent light has inconsistent frequencies and waves.

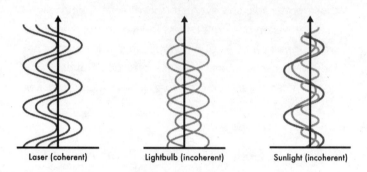

Laser (coherent)   Lightbulb (incoherent)   Sunlight (incoherent)

The difference between coherent and incoherent states.

Lasers and fiber optics work with forms of coherent light, with waves being so tightly knit that they can travel vast distances without diffusing. You see incoherent light in incandescent and fluorescent lightbulbs and flashlights. Even the sun, with its large full-spectrum bandwidth, is very incoherent. Light waves that travel in coherence are much more efficient and can carry impressive amounts of information. This is why coherent light is used ubiquitously in technology. Laser light can reach the moon and beyond — beaming endlessly into space. The fiber-optic cables that we use to run our global information network carries information-light-energy so fast that it travels at about 70 percent the speed of light. Coherent states travel in flow and exhibit great power from their unification.

Knowing this, why should light behave any differently in our own bodies? The guiding information-light-energy of the quantum field flows more efficiently into our consciousness when we are in a coherent state — when we meet it on its own wavelength. When you are on the same wavelength as the universe, you are attuned to its energy and flow of information. Coherent union is a return to wholeness as individual consciousness moves into a state of coherence with the field, becoming one with the vast, unified field of cosmic consciousness.

 Coherence is a state of oneness with the universe.

When you live in a coherent state, you live in the flow of life. You play your own special tune in the great song of the universe — with perfection. Your mind and heart are attuned to the information and energy that informs you, arising from the oneness of your inner field. When you live in this state, your mind is at peace and your heart is full. You are just where you are meant to be — and you recognize that. The way naturally unfolds before you, and doors open just when you need them to. Like an individual wave flowing along with the great wave of existence, you live each day in tandem — in trust — with the outpouring of life itself.

On the other hand, when you live in an incoherent state, you feel as though you have fallen out of sync with life, like you are playing the wrong notes at the wrong time in our cosmic symphony. You may feel confused or emotionally overwhelmed — cut off from the guiding flow of your inner field. When you live in this state, you can feel like you are in a rut or frustrated with your life path — like you are lost, stressed, fearful, or anxious. Incoherence steals your peace of mind. Once-opened doors now close to redirect you back into coherence.

The quantum field is constantly pulling you back into a state of coherence with it. As though life itself cannot rest in zero-point peace until you — and all the other minds in the universe — re-unite with it, it perpetually calls you home. It uses your inner guidance system to bring you back into alignment with its flow. *As much as you crave reconnection with life, life craves reconnection with you.* Every wave of incoherent energy is magnetically called back to join the unified field. No matter how incoherent life gets — no matter how hard the ups, downs, pains, and losses — your guiding powers of insight and resonance lead you, like a compass, back to your true north.

Finding coherence is a necessary step in the expansion of consciousness. It is also the optimum state for your intuition. Dr. Rollin McCraty, the director of research at HeartMath Insti-tute, has done extensive scientific studies on coherence, explaining, "We also found that if people get themselves into what we call a coherent state — a heart coherent state — that facilitates neural communication in intuition experiments. It's increasing our access to our intuitive capacities by even just sitting in a coherent state for a few minutes." Simone Wright explained, "Coherence indicates connectedness, cooperation, and a holistic balance in a system that has many individual moving components, all of which synchro-nize so that the whole is greater than the sum of the parts."

INVESTIGATION: THE MUSIC OF YOUR BEING

Growing up as a teenager, "What kind of music do you like?" was one of the first questions we asked a new friend. The music you like is a reflection of where you find coherence in the field — the song your life is attuned to. It is no wonder that music can be such a defining force for young people seeking to find themselves in the world. As you look back over your life, can you recognize your in-tuitive connection with music during different stages of your life? Ask yourself:

- What kind of music do you feel coherent with?
- What music uplifts, energizes, or resonates with you now?
- Do you feel a deep sense of connectedness when you listen to music?

Next time you play a favorite song, feel the coherence it brings you. Let it lift you up or take you away. When you go to a concert or show, notice how the shared experience of music bonds you to those around you. When you let the music of life move you, both literally and figuratively, you can feel your personal connection with the oneness of all things.

Just like the hypnotic dance of the starlings — where thousands of birds fly in unison, creating coherent forms that wax and wane effortlessly in the sky — we are all individual beings entangled with the greater whole. The question is, *Are you flowing with life?* Are you living in a state of coherence, like the flock of birds, with the dance of the universe? László explained why this is so important:

> Individual consciousness is not something separate, belonging only to the brain of the individual who manifests it. Individual consciousness is a cluster of information deriving from information that is universally present in space and time. Schrödinger was right when he said that there is no such thing as consciousness in the plural. There is one consciousness, one supreme set of information in the universe. Individual consciousness is a projection of that set, its features selected by the particular needs and capacities of the individual brain and organism.

Though coherence can be a powerful spiritual state of union, it also has practical applications in your personal life. Intuitively, you can sense coherence — as truth, alignment, even love. You feel coherence with your kindred spirits — the people who walk the same path as you. You feel coherence when you fall in true love, when nothing in the world could divide you and your beloved. Coherence can also be a litmus test for the energy you encounter in your life and is especially helpful for recognizing untruth. Truth is a coherent state that creates resonance, while untruth is an incoherent state — a misalignment or disconnection with the truth — and creates dissonance. You can intuit the difference by paying attention to the subtle cues you receive from the quantum field.

EXPERIMENT: THE LUMINESCENCE TEST

Coherence with the field brings a kind of inner radiance that speaks louder than words. Learning to recognize coherence is an invaluable life hack. You can intuitively distinguish a person's coherent or noncoherent energy by tuning into their inner luminosity. Sensing coherence can help you:

- recognize when someone is lying or being untruthful.
- recognize when someone is uncomfortable or upset, even when they say otherwise.
- recognize when someone is insincere or inauthentic.

You can easily sense coherence because it draws you in with its radiant presence. It resonates with you. On the other hand, untruths and deceptions are naturally incoherent with the field and emit a dissonant energy. Below is a simple practice to tune into the coherent or incoherent energy. When you want to do a vibe check on someone, try tuning into their state of coherence:

1. Don't listen to the words they say. Listen to how their energy speaks to you.

2. Tune in to their vibe. Despite what you *think*, how do they make you *feel?*
3. What do they radiate? Does their energy feel resonant or dissonant? Do you see the radiant light in their eyes, or do they avoid eye contact? Are they open and loving, or is there something that doesn't feel right?

You can use this technique to vet new relationships, choose business partnerships, find the right teachers, or even guide your children as they grow up. The ability to lie is a byproduct of a separation from our shared inner field, where there can be no lies and where everything coexists in a state of truth. The mind can imitate states of coherence to appear as truths, but intuition, as the knower of all truth, can see right through them.

The Loving Embrace of the Universe

You can understand coherence as a scientific term for the state of love. Coherence with another person creates an unbreakable bond, an entangled union, in the flow of shared experience. Much like the feeling of being in love, you are empowered by coherent personal connections that make you feel alive, reconnected, and part of something bigger than yourself. Focused within, coherence is self-love — the intuitive call to authentically reconnect with life and fully self-actualize. Through inner coherence, you can reconnect with a deep wholeness that revitalizes and illuminates you with qualities like:

• clearer, visionary thinking
• a peaceful sense of calm and trust in life
• increased intuitive flow and awareness
• a strengthened energy field and sense of vitality
• confidence and resilience

- creativity, ingenuity, and inspired action
- an expanded capacity to love

Growing into deeper coherence with life is the true aim of spiritual growth, personal evolution, and the path to enlightenment. All the signals you receive from the quantum field — all the information, energy, insightful thoughts, and resonant feelings — stream 24/7 with the sole purpose of reuniting you with the whole truth of life. The more coherence you establish with your inner dimension, the less you will be troubled by the pain of incoherent states. The high-vibration waves of cohesive consciousness are unaffected by rogue incoherent waves of untruth, fear, distress, or confusion.

Do you feel that you are living in coherence with your true nature? That your life and actions are in sync with who you really are? When we have inner coherence, we don't have to pretend to be something we are not. We live true to our self. Inner coherence comes with an abiding sense of peace, power, and trust in life. When you live in this state, tuned in to the frequency of the deep dimension within you, you are in a state of love with life. This is why so many spiritual awakenings are accompanied by feelings of bliss and joyful reunion with life — the synchronization of energy between your individual being and the ever-present universe generates a coherence that can be felt as a powerful rapture of love. *Coherence is the loving embrace of the universe.*

Love is the ultimate state of coherence. It is the all-powerful force that reunites you with the quantum field, your inner dimension, the universe, God, and your true and whole being. All the clichés we have learned about love turn out to be true, even through the scientific lens. *All you need is love. God is love. Love will conquer all.* We are living in a very incoherent world — full of strife, confusion, and suffering. The return to coherence puts an end to all of that because all of those things are byproducts of living out of sync with the universe. The ills of our world are symptoms of our inner disconnection — of seeing the *other* instead of the *one*. Coherence draws you back into union with life and the quantum field so you can live each day by the inherent wisdom held there.

The endgame to life — what we have all been looking for — is the return to inner coherence, to reunite with the deepest part of yourself. Your quest for self-actualization can take wrong turns if you look for yourself in the wrong place — in the wrong people, vocations, aspirations, or material possessions. By turning within, you slough off the false parts of yourself and strip down to the pure, authentic truth of who you are. This can be an uncomfortable process at first and feel more like you are *becoming no one* than becoming the *someone* you thought you should be. As you recalibrate into union with the zero-point field of nothingness and everythingness, you are taking the greatest step on the journey of life — the return to yourself.

ILLUMINATION KEY #7

I Am the One I Am Looking For

We must always go beyond, always renounce the lesser for the greater,
the finite for the Infinite; we must be prepared to proceed from
illumination to illumination...to reach the utmost transcendence
of the Divine and its utmost universality.

— Sri Aurobindo

Human beings are, by nature, seekers. From youth to old age, our seeking calls us forward — searching to understand the world and trying to find friendship, true love, peace of mind, prosperity, happiness, wisdom, truth, and experiences of all kinds. In our quest, we encounter many teachers, guides, and wisdom keepers, but all beacons of light exist to guide you to the same destination: to the truth held within you. *You* are the teacher you have always been looking for. You hold all the answers within you. Truth whispers to you in the ever-present wisdom of your inner dimension, and it guides you in the call of your heart. You are a singular point in the great presence of the universe — the omnipotent living conscious- ness we call God, the limitless and undefinable "I am," intrinsically informed by the collective shared being of all existence.

With the realization that all of life's mysteries are revealed through communion with the omnipresent wisdom of your deep dimension, you are the one and only thing you ever need to find. You don't need to go to faraway places to find yourself. You don't need to study with illustrious gurus or masters. You don't need spirit guides or angels to show you the way. The greatest guides exist only to point you within yourself, to the one thing you can trust — your intuitive coherence with a living, guiding, and ex- panding universe.

Together, your inner wisdom and guiding forces help you nav- igate the illusions of the mind-made world. Knowing this, people often ask, *How do I know the difference between my own intuition and a thought or feeling imparted upon me by a guiding force?* For example, if you get an idea to call your mother, is your internal receiver picking up information about her due to your personal entanglement? Or could it be a guiding force, like an interdimen- sional loved one, nudging you to do something helpful? Here are some ways to understand how information arrives in your mind from the quantum field and detect the presence of a guiding force:

Intuition from Your Inner Field	*Intuition from Signs and Guiding Forces*
• Intuitive insights that naturally arise from the space between your thoughts	• Sudden thoughts that grab or direct your attention to something
• Subtle resonant feelings that move you into awareness or action	• Sensations or feelings that have no apparent source
• General imagination, inspiration, and creativity that flow as you merge with the field	• Impossible things, coincidences, or external signs that originate outside you
• Abiding truth that remains constant, held in the timeless wisdom of the nonlocal information field	• Supernatural or metaphysical experiences that connect you to a particular guiding force

A classic example of a guiding force experience is Maria's story from chapter 5, when she heard a voice call her to pull over so she would avoid a car accident. Guiding forces often show up in emergency situations and carry with them a sense of urgency or power. In this supernatural experience, Maria's father was able to break through her attention and guide her to safety. You can also intentionally interface with your guiding forces through meditation and visualization practices, which we will explore in the final lab ahead.

In the end, all information you receive arrives from the same unified field of oneness. Whether you intentionally download it or receive it from a guiding force, all that really matters is that the information is received. The teachers, guides, loved ones, and angels are all, like you, manifestations of *the one*. The true power exists behind all individuals and archetypes in the zero-point self that unites all things — the one and only truth. Every guiding bit of information in the field has the same source: the part of you that knows everything.

ILLUMINATION KEY #7
guides you to the ultimate truth of who you are.

With the final key, you can recognize the internal and external manifestations of a universal guidance system designed to guide you home to your true being and oneness with life.

When you activate the final key in the illumination code journey, you discover that the one and only truth of life is found within you. You no longer have to seek for anything out there. All the answers are within you.

Key #7 Activation: Creating an Inner Light Sanctuary
A Space to Commune with Your Inner Dimension

To know the illumination code — to know truth, yourself, and the guiding forces of the universe — is to know *the light*. Light is the master key to the world. We know it from ancient wisdom and now also from contemporary science; all roads lead back to the light. Whether you find it in the holographic light, information, and energy of quantum field; the inner light of your illuminated consciousness; or in the light of God — guiding light is fundamental to all our existence. In this world, we use different words to describe a singular experience, but everyone is on the same quest to become one with the light inside us.

Time and again, throughout history, humanity has told stories of the divine connection to light: Moses and the burning bush, Jesus glowing with the light of transfiguration, the Hindu god Brahma as the light of creation, the Native American sun dance to commune with the Great Spirit, and in many traditions, a glowing halo as the sign of holiness. Near-death experiences, too, are nearly always associated with a tunnel of light or invitation into the light — a light that brings with it understanding, comfort, and a loving presence. Not only can we see the light, we can know it and feel it too. The light of truth touches us on every level of our being.

The Inner Light Sanctuary: Your Interface with the Quantum Field

To begin our final lab, let's create a place to commune with the light, a kind of inner sanctuary where you can explore the light and move into deeper states of coherence with the universe. Your inner light sanctuary is a place of conscious interface with the guiding light of all the quantum field. To create and enter into your sanctuary, find a quiet space where you won't be disturbed, and relax into a quiet state of meditation.

1. With your eyes closed, take a few deep breaths to calm your mind and relax your body, releasing any heaviness or dissonant energy. Breathe in light; breathe out any tension, stress, or fears.
2. Greet yourself with a gentle smile. Let that smile lift you up and light you up from the inside out. Feel the upward vibrational shift as you embody this true, beautiful smile.
3. Next, feel the light of that smile wrap around you, infusing every cell in your body with its light and revitalizing energy. Take your time, and soak up the light. This light is filled with information — the truth of the universe. Absorb the light, and let its guiding wisdom interpenetrate your heart and mind.

4. As you begin to embody the all-knowing light, feel it start to shine through you, radiating in all directions. Imagine it forming a luminous bubble that gently holds you in its loving embrace. Be present in this communion for as long as you like.

5. Gradually, notice your circle of light expanding and taking on the form of a physical space — a sacred area made just for you. A beautiful inner sanctuary comes into form — a place where you can consciously meet the universe whenever you like, no matter where you are. (This sanctuary can take the form of any place you imagine: a glowing white room, a field of daisies, a mountaintop, a chapel, a meditation studio, whatever feels good to you.)

6. The most important feature of your sanctuary is how it feels. Fill your space with light, love, and transcendent peace, where you welcome a joyful connection to the universe. This is a high-vibration space where you move into coherence with the high-vibration information, energy, and light of the quantum field.

7. Rejuvenate yourself in this space. Your sanctuary can be a healing place as well as a guiding place. Like a decompression chamber between worlds, this sanctuary acclimates you to the high-vibration light and energy of the quantum field. Know that once you have created this space, you can return here anytime.

8. When you are ready, take a deep breath and repeat this inner light mantra twice, either out loud or to yourself:

    "I trust the wisdom of my inner light to inspire and guide my life. I trust the wisdom of my inner light to inspire and guide my life."

9. With a smile, open your eyes.

Now, you are ready for your Illumination Journey.

LAB #7
THE ILLUMINATION JOURNEY
Discovering Your Pathway to the Deep Dimension

Our final lab is a guided visualization journey that allows you to consciously access the part of you that knows everything and interact with various manifestations of the quantum field. During this journey, you can forge a path into the deep dimension and create a sacred space where you can intentionally interface with your higher self and personal guiding forces (interdimensional teachers, guides, archetypes, and loved ones). At the end of our journey, you receive a token — a gift from the universe to validate your experience. You can use the framework below to lead you through your journey.

To begin, find a quiet and comfortable space where you won't be disturbed for the duration of your journey. You may also want to light a candle, lower the lights, or use your favorite intuition-enhancing tool to create a relaxing atmosphere. You can also keep your intuition cards nearby if you want to pull a card at the end. Be sure to hold space for ten to fifteen minutes after your journey to journal your experiences.

1. Sit or lie down in a comfortable position. Then, close your eyes, and take a few deep breaths to calm your mind and relax your body.
2. Set your intention on connecting with the deeper part of your being. Ask the universe to bring you higher awareness of your life's journey or purpose.
3. Smile and visualize a peaceful and powerful white light lifting you up into your inner light sanctuary. Imagine yourself there, noticing the forms, sounds, feelings, and vibrations of this sacred space. Be here for a moment as you soak in the light, love, and high-vibration presence around you.

4. When you feel uplifted, with a clear mind and an open heart, imagine a closed door appearing before you some-where within your sanctuary room. Walk up to this door. Notice how it looks and feels. Then, reach out and pull the handle, gently opening the door. Someone is waiting for you on the other side.

5. Open the door. *Who is standing before you?* Observe any feelings, sensations, or awareness that arise as you meet your guide. Remain for a moment in shared connection. You may want to greet them, say hello, or even hug. Do whatever moves you.

6. Next, your guide has somewhere to take you. Follow them. Notice the path you take or what surrounds you as move toward this next destination. Where do you end up?

7. Look around and explore the scenario around you. Per-haps it is another time in your life; perhaps it is another place, or even another lifetime. Intuitively feel your way through this place until you recognize its connection to your life.

8. When you are ready, you can ask your guide why you have been brought to this place. Listen. Allow them to speak to you with words, feelings, and inspired thoughts. Notice the understanding that arises.

9. Trust your intuition, and let the experience unfold nat-urally, receiving any information with an open heart and mind. You can ask questions to your guide — who they are, what you are meant to learn, or any other guidance.

10. Soon, you notice that your guide is holding a golden box — one that you intuitively recognize as a gift for you. They hold it in their palms, with their arms outstretched toward you.

11. Remove the lid from the box and look inside it. *What object do you see?* Accept whatever object appears in your mind. It may have a personal significance to you, or it could also be something that seems random. This object is a token: a symbol that commemorates your journey and serves as an ongoing connection between you and the universe. You will bring this token back from your journey and into your life.

12. When you are ready, accept your token gift. Hold it close to your heart, or tuck it into your pocket. Thank your guide for their gift and ongoing guidance.

13. Then, together, you and your guide walk side by side, retracing your steps back to your inner light sanctuary. There, at the threshold, you say your goodbyes, and step back through the doorway into the white light of your inner space. Be present there for a moment.

14. Finally, slowly open your eyes. Take a deep breath and feel yourself reconnected to the earth.

15. Journal your experiences immediately so you do not forget them. Write down a detailed description of your guide and token. Now is also a good time to pick an insight card to find deeper understanding and synchronistic connections.

16. To seal your journey, use the framework in the Lab #7 workbook to activate your token for ongoing validation and guidance in your life.

Tips for Your Illumination Journey

Here are some important points to help you get the most of your Illumination Journey:

- Remember to go with whatever intuitively comes to you, even if it feels like your imagination. Imagination is a gateway to your intuitive field.

- Don't try to analyze or overthink anything as you go. Just go with the flow, and digest the information after the journey is over.

- Regarding your guiding force, anything is possible. You could meet a loved one in spirit; a religious figure, saint, or ascended master; an animal; your inner child; a version of yourself in the future; even a ball of light — be open to whatever comes.

- The same is true of your token. It could be a piece of jewelry, an animal, a number, a word, a symbol, a name. Trust the first impression that abides and resonates with you.

- If any dissonant or uncomfortable energy arises, simply release it. Pay it no mind. The thinking mind often uses this tactic to maintain control and override intuitive perception. Just smile and intentionally shift back into the high-vibration light.

- Finally, if you are stuck at first or your mind feels blank, don't worry. Just relax. Go with the flow, and eventually your mind will surrender to your intuition. Or, if you aren't in a clear, calm mindset, you can come back and try another time.

What Is Your Guiding Force and Token?

The last step of your Illumination Journey is discerning its purpose and activating your token through self-reflection:

- **Your guiding force:** The guide that came to you in this journey is a manifestation of your higher self. They can show up as an ancestor, guiding teacher, animal, friend,

or other transcendent being. In all cases, they are an actu-
alization of the part of you that knows everything. They
exist outside of time and space, so they can be anyone
from anywhere. As such, they are always there to support
you. You can continue to call on this guide for wisdom in
your daily life and return to your inner sanctuary to intentionally reconnect with them.

- **Your token:** The object that you received is a symbol — a
  kind of souvenir that allows you to stay connected with
  your guide. This object-symbol is now your own personal sign from the universe. When you notice your token
  showing up in your life, it can be a sign that the universe
  is with you. For example, if your token is a butterfly, it can
  show up as an actual living butterfly but also as objects
  such as a photo of a butterfly, a butterfly emoji, a butterfly
  figurine, or even a song about butterflies. Whenever you
  recognize your token, take pause. Life has drawn your attention to this moment. What meaningful thing are you
  doing or thinking? Your token can often be a punctuation
  mark for something important, as well as a reminder that
  you are not alone.

Lab #7 Workbook: Your Inner Travels
A Record of Your Illumination Journey and Token Gift

Write down all the details you can remember in your journal or
Illumination Workbook using the following framework.

Description of my guide: _____

What happened when I met my guide: _____

Where we traveled: _____

What I discovered: _____

Validations: _____

1. How the appearance of this guide meaningfully relates to my life (personal connection, symbol, resonant feelings, etc.)
2. Signs and synchronicities that demonstrate connections to this guiding force (coincidences or moments of serendipity)
3. Significance of this guiding force showing up in my life today

Description of my token: _____

Activating and Charging Your Token

From this day forward, you can keep your token as a sign that the universe is with you. The secret to getting your token to work is giving it your relaxed attention. If you forget about it, so will the universe. On the other hand, if you look for it too hard, you will never see it. Here are some activities to help you energize your token without overthinking:

1. **Own your token.** Ask yourself what it could represent or what it means to you. You can think of it like a personal mascot or as a symbol of your inner guidance. Make it an extension of yourself.
2. **Post your token.** Like a vision board, you can use trinkets, pictures, or downloaded images of your token to keep it top of mind. Place reminders of it around your home or office. Make it a part of your life.
3. **Charge your token.** Bring your token to mind during your meditation, mantras, or prayers to vitalize it with high-vibration energy.
4. **See the signs.** With time, you will likely notice synchronicity and patterns in the way your token comes to you.

You may notice it starting to show up more in your life suddenly, or you may even get intuitive flashes of it during important moments. Whatever the case, you can develop your own special relationship with it — one that can grow into something reliable and deeply insightful in the years ahead.

Your Token Experiences

Record when and where you notice your token. Over time, look back for repeating patterns, themes, and connections for deeper insight. The more you charge your token with personal energy and relaxed attention, the more often it will show up.

Where I saw my token: _____
What I was doing at the time: _____
Its message for me right now: _____

CONCLUSION

Activating Key #7 of the illumination code moves you into coherence with the guiding force of the universe.

The final key opens a conscious pathway to the part of you that knows everything. With this key, you can open up an intentional relationship with your guiding forces and create a lifelong communication system with the universe.

Key Principles

- The quantum field *is* awareness.
- Synchronicity is a byproduct of your entanglement with the universe.

- We live in a meaningful universe, supported by an array of guiding forces.
- Light is the measure of all good things.
- Coherence is a state of oneness with life and the cosmos.
- All seeking is a longing to return to coherence with the universe.

Key Applications

- Start building a sign language with daily synchronicities.
- Explore your guiding forces and how they support your life.
- Activate your token to energize your connection to the universe.
- Get into deeper states of coherence with life so you can expand your awareness into the quantum field and transcend the boundaries of this world.

With this final illumination key, you can unlock the real magic of the universe. Recognizing that your existence is a meaningful part of life itself, you can live each day insightfully and in coherence with the guiding forces within you. Your inner light is an essential, local point of consciousness — a single ray in the endless shine of universal light — that holds everything you seek. *Follow the light. It is illuminating the way home.*

Journey Onward and Inward

Owing to our immortal consciousness, we have always been here,
and will always be here — a real, existent entity in the universe. Our life
need not be a preparation for death; it can be a celebration of eternal life.

— ERVIN LÁSZLÓ, *THE WISDOM PRINCIPLES*

Awareness of the continuous nature of life changes everything. With it, you face your own limitlessness — the part of you that knows everything, that lives forever and is a vital part of the indivisible one. There is no language to fully describe how you are both part of the one *and the one itself*, though you can intuitively realize it in the magnetic pull that draws you deeper into coherence with cosmic consciousness. You can feel it in the power of unconditional love, you can know it in moments of intuitive enlightenment, and you can sense it in the breathtaking perception of natural splendor — the wide-open skies, the whispers of nature, and the way the light flickers off dancing leaves on a warm summer day. You may not know exactly what it is, but it feels a little bit like peace and a little bit like *belonging* — a deep joyfulness laced with a hint of a nostalgia that feels like home.

When you discover your field of intrinsic awareness and the magnitude of its power, how can the world ever be the same? You now see that you are more than a carbon-based life-form that lives and dies. In this life, your persona is a beautifully crafted avatar — a singular manifestation of the *great you*, a consciousness that transcends all beginnings and ends, all times and places. This life is but a moment in an endless parade of moments, and the end of it is only a new beginning. This life is not an end in itself; it is a preparation for a new life — one that awaits us all in the new frontiers of metareality.

Seeing the infinite nature of the world fills every day with a sense of wonder and reveals clues about our ultimate human destiny. Will we embrace the unity of the field, rise above our differences, and come together as the one that we truly are? Or will we fail to see past the limitations of material reality and its divisions to fall further out of coherence with each other and life itself? Our collective intuition is calling us to reunite — to break down the illusory barriers of the physical world, including the walls built by our egos and the wall of so-called death. Maybe one day, the barrier between life and afterlife, too, will blur as our minds expand to know all worlds. There is no such thing as death, really. Only change. Maybe one day, that change will be a welcomed milestone in the journey of our lives — like the caterpillar transforming into a butterfly, a star reborn, or the Christ resurrected.

We can no longer deny our infinite nature. There is just too much evidence showing us that we are truly immortal beings. Our individual mind meets this idea with resistance because it is not capable of understanding the beyond. Like our inability to conceive of what existed before the big bang, it has no frame of reference. But our intuitive mind can catch glimpses of our infinite nature in both profound and fleeting moments of enlightenment. Each experience of inner revelation — of guiding wisdom, joyful communion, or selfless love — is a calling card of the deep dimension, a sign that the eternal dimension is coming alive within you.

Is this world a kind of incubator, a safe space where we can grow, develop, and bring our true potential to life? Might we all, with time, move into deeper coherence with our true nature — embracing the magic of life and living in harmony with all things? This seems to be the real test of life: whether we own our limitless nature and oneness in the unified field or we destroy each other in the process. Brian Greene, author of *The Elegant Universe*, once wrote, "As our generation marvels at our new view of the universe — our new way of asserting the world's coherence — we are fulfilling our part, contributing our rung to the human ladder reaching for the stars."

The divisions that create *otherness* — separation and opposition to one another — also create a dissonance that threatens our future. Though no outcome is ever certain, we can collectively align our energy with the highest frequency outcomes from our current field of potentiality. We can each bring light — illumination — to the path ahead, both for our personal growth and for sustained, vibrant human life on this planet. We can each do our part to add to the coherence of the world. The collective energy of uplifting meditation, prayer, and visualization has had a documented effect on conflict resolution. Not only is this shift felt through subtle, internal channels, it manifests as a reprieve in societal dissonance that includes an observable reduction in violent crime and aggravated assaults. The power of thought and intention is more real than we once imagined. We make a difference in the world with the energy — and light — we put into it.

PRACTICE: A LIGHT OFFERING FOR THE WORLD

You can use this simple practice to bring a little more light into your world:

1. Begin by finding a quiet space and entering into your inner light sanctuary, where you are surrounded by the interpenetrating universal wisdom of the quantum field.

2. Feel the light growing stronger and stronger within you, pulsating with the heartbeat of the universe and flowing into you in deep coherence with life itself.

3. Imagine the light radiating outward from your core being — a brilliant illuminating light shining its rays into the world.

4. Gradually, visualize the light expanding. Radiate coherent, love-infused healing light to every place in your body. Then, expand it further to your home and loved ones, filling them each with the peace and power of cosmic truth. Continue to radiate the light through you, expanding even further into the world — to strangers, faraway places, people, and all the earth — and sending light to all the dark places.

5. Send light to every person, place, and time on earth. Send it to the past, and send it to the future. Send it into all the dark hearts, and fill the world with illuminating light. Envision our beautiful planet growing into a state of coherent oneness.

With the seven keys of the illumination code, you now have a framework for your inner expeditions. You can use whatever practices that resonate with you to expand into the heights and depths of your whole being. To know the mystery for yourself. To do impossible things. To recognize, once and for all, the potentiality you hold within. The revelations of our new science have shown how implicitly our consciousness is connected to the world — how the energy, information, and light of our inner field informs our reality, guides the way forward, and leads us to create a better world.

Human evolution is more than a physical process; it is a shared participation in the expansion of the universe. The next step for us in this universal progression is to *change the way we think*. It's time for us to use our untapped quantum intelligence to intuitively re-harmonize with the great cosmic symphony of life — to reconnect with each other and expand into the enlightened consciousness that calls us inward and onward.

Acknowledgments

I am so grateful for all the beautiful lights that came together to bring *The Illumination Code* into the world. First and foremost, thank you to New World Library for its continued vision and dedication to bringing forth emerging ideas that can change the world. To my editor, Georgia Hughes, for her brilliance and ongoing belief in my work, and to the brightest of lights, Kim Corbin, for shouting this message far and wide. Thank you also to my agent, Wendy Keller, for pushing me out of my comfort zone and without whom this book would not have been born.

Thank you to the illuminating thought leaders who have paved the way for this book and took time out of their lives to explore these new frontiers with me: Dr. Ervin László, Whitley Strieber, Peter Smith, Dr. Jude Currivan, Dr. Helané Wahbeh and the Institute of Noetic Sciences, Ira Israel, and Simone Wright. It has been an honor to build upon the work of these brilliant minds.

To my IntuitionLab faculty and students, none of this would have been possible without you. Thank you from the bottom of my heart to everyone who experimented, failed forward, and explored these new frontiers with me. Deepest gratitude to our light leaders and story contributors: Beth Wojiski, Arlene Holtz, Walter Zemrock, Elizabeth Corvese, Carin Lockhart, Tove Engebø-Skas, Hesther Weisenberger, Marilyn Sawyer, Stephanie Miller, Jen Woodward, Chantal Konicek, Angela Sipe, Sara Kostelnik, Meagan Grant, Maria Brady, Melissa Turner, and Scott Green. Your excitement for intuition and your spirit of wonder has kept this work moving forward.

I owe everything to the support of my family — Jon, Eva, and Lily — the lights of my life.

Experiments, Investigations, and Practices

Notes

Introduction: The Final Frontier Is the Inner Frontier

p. 1 *"Spiritual practitioners don't use sophisticated"*: Thich Nhat Hanh, *Your True Home* (Boston: Shambhala, 2011), 298.

p. 1 *Rung in each year by the Lord Mayor*: Wikipedia, s.v. "Hull Fair," last modified May 8, 2023, https://en.wikipedia.org/wiki/Hull_Fair.

p. 4 *my grandmother Wakefield's eighth-great-grandfather*: Wikipedia, s.v. "List of Mayors of Kingston upon Hull," last modified September 7, 2023, https://en.wikipedia.org/wiki/List_of_mayors_of _Kingston_upon_Hull.

Chapter One: A Part of You Knows Everything

p. 15 *"Intuitive realization is the king of sciences"*: Paramahansa Yogananda (website), accessed September 23, 2023, yogananda.com.au.

p. 19 *In America, about 75 percent*: Robyn Rapoport and Kyle Berta, *Methodology Report: American Fears Survey July 2018*, Chapman University, https://www.chapman.edu/wilkinson/research-centers /babbie-center/_files/fear-2018/fear-V-methodology-report-ssrs.pdf.

p. 19 *Furthermore, 67 percent of Americans*: Taylor Orth, "Two-Thirds of Americans Say They've Had a Paranormal Encounter," YouGov, October 20, 2022, https://today.yougov.com/topics/society /articles-reports/2022/10/20/americans-describe-paranormal -encounters-poll.

p. 19 *Whether these people are encountering*: David w. Moore, "Three in Four Americans Believe in Paranormal," Gallup, June 16, 2005, https://news.gallup.com/poll/16915/three-four-americans-believe -paranormal.aspx.

p. 20 *a consciousness-infused universe*: Ervin László, *The Wisdom Principles: A Handbook of Timeless Truths and Timely Wisdom* (New York: St. Martin's, 2021), Kindle, loc. 485.

p. 21 *"The most fundamental feature of the universe is information"*: Ervin László, *The Akashic Experience: Science and the Cosmic Memory Field* (Rochester, VT: Inner Traditions, 2010), Kindle, loc. 212.

p. 21 *Wheeler notoriously coined the phrase "It from bit"*: Anil Ananthaswamy, "Inside Knowledge: Is Information the Only Thing That Exists?,"

NewScientist, March 29, 2017, https://www.newscientist.com /article/mg23431191-500-inside-knowledge-is-information-the -only-thing-that-exists.

p. 21 *"The world 'runs' on information"*: Ervin László, *The Immutable Laws of the Akashic Field: Universal Truths for a Better Life and Better World* (New York: St. Martin's, 2021), 6.

p. 23 *"God was and is light"*: Wighard Strehlow and Gottfried Hertzka, *Hildegard of Bingen's Medicine* (Rochester, VT: Bear, 1987), xvii.

p. 23 *"The photons that make up light have no mass"*: Deepak Chopra, *The Seven Spiritual Laws of Success* (San Rafael, CA: Amber-Allen, 2015), 29.

p. 26 *"A new concept of the universe is emerging"*: Ervin László, *Science and the Akashic Field: An Integral Theory of Everything* (Rochester, VT: Inner Traditions, 2007), 81.

Chapter Two: The Field of Intrinsic Awareness

p. 41 *"Nonlocality...is an expression"*: Paul Levy, *The Quantum Revelation: A Radical Synthesis of Science and Spirituality* (New York: Select-Books, 2018), 90.

p. 43 *"omnipresent, all-penetrating existence"*: Swami Vivekananda, "The Complete Works of Swami Vivekananda/Volume 1/Raja-Yoga /Prana," Wikisource, last modified July 2, 2022, https://en.wiki source.org/wiki/The_Complete_Works_of_Swami_Vivekananda /Volume_1/Raja-Yoga/Prana.

p. 43 *Even popular psychics, like Edgar Cayce:* "Akashic Records," Free Dictionary, accessed September 23, 2023, https://encyclopedia2.the freedictionary.com/Akashic+field.

p. 44 *"the most translucent" fifth element*: Wikipedia, s.v. "Aether (Classical Element)," last modified September 26, 2023, https://en.wikipedia .org/wiki/Aether_(classical_element).

p. 44 *Nikola Tesla, too, was fascinated*: László, *Akashic Experience*, loc. 204.

p. 44 *"today's physics allows for the existence"*: Larry Dossey, *The Power of Premonitions: How Knowing the Future Can Shape Our Lives* (Dutton, NY: Hay House, 2009), 182.

p. 45 *"Mystics and sages have long maintained"*: László, *Science and the Akashic Field*, cover.

p. 46 *"Science calls it the unified field"*: Simone Wright, *First Intelligence: Using the Science and Spirit of Intuition* (Novato, CA: New World Library, 2014), 36.

p. 51 *Recent studies show that 58 percent*: Vanessa Mae Rameer, "US

Loneliness Statistics 2023: Are Americans Lonely?," Science of People, https://www.scienceofpeople.com/loneliness-statistics/.

p. 51   *"The compulsive thinker, which means almost everyone"*: Eckhart Tolle, *The Power of Now: A Guide to Spiritual Enlightenment* (Novato, CA: New World Library, 2004), 15.

p. 54   *"the soul's power of knowing God"*: Swami Kriyananda, ed., *The Essence of Self-Realization: The Wisdom of Paramahansa Yogananda* (Nevada City, CA: Crystal Clarity, 1990), 43.

p. 54   *"The kingdom of God is within you"*: Luke 17:21.

p. 55   *"Do you then also see the lovely significance"*: Richard Rohr, *The Universal Christ: How a Forgotten Reality Can Change Everything We See, Hope for and Believe* (New York: Convergent, 2019), 60.

p. 55   *"I take refuge in the seminal point"*: *The Tibetan Book of the Dead* (New York: Viking Press, 2006), 13.

p. 56   *"All these principles of intelligence"*: Wright, *First Intelligence*, 39.

Chapter Three: Metareality

p. 67   *"Everything we call real is made of things"*: "Niels Bohr Quotes," Goodreads, accessed September 23, 2023, https://www.goodreads .com/author/quotes/821936.Niels_Bohr.

p. 69   *"The old ideas of science led us to believe"*: Wright, *First Intelligence*, 37.

p. 70   *matter itself isn't quite as ubiquitous*: Brian Clegg, *Dark Matter and Dark Energy: The Hidden 95% of the Universe* (London: Icon Books, 2019), Kindle, loc. 12.

p. 71   *Both the object and your body may seem real and solid*: Trevor English, "Due to the Space inside Atoms, You Are Mostly Made up of Empty Space," Interesting Engineering, February 28, 2020, https://interestingengineering.com/due-to-the-space-inside-atoms -you-are-mostly-made-up-of-empty-space.

p. 71   *"Atoms are mainly empty space"*: Carl Sagan, *Cosmos* (New York: Ballantine, 2013), 230.

p. 71   *But, most interesting of all*, space is not actually empty: László, *Akashic Experience*, loc. 212.

p. 71   *"The world is not 'material'"*: László, *Immutable Laws*, 224.

p. 73   *"According to quantum cosmology, we have evolved"*: Ervin László, *What Is Reality? The New Map of Cosmos, Consciousness, and Existence* (New York: SelectBooks, 2016), Kindle, loc. 798.

p. 76   *"Quantum physics has defied logic"*: Bernard Marr, "15 Things

Everyone Should Know about Quantum Computing," Bernard Marr & Co, accessed September 23, 2023, https://bernardmarr .com/15-things-everyone-should-know-about-quantum-computing/.

p. 77   *"Sitting on your shoulders is the most complicated object"*: Alison Ebbage, "Neurology: Thinking Outside the Box," Institution of Engineering and Technology (blog), February 20, 2020, https://eandt .theiet.org/content/articles/2020/02/neurology-thinking-outside -the-box/.

p. 77   *Bridging the gap between reality and metareality*: Frank Landymore, "Scientists Suggest Our Brains Work Like Quantum Computers," Byte, Futurism, October 20, 2022, https://futurism.com/the-byte /brains-work-like-quantum-computers.

p. 79   *"The manifest world is a set of clusters of coordinated vibration"*: László, *What Is Reality?*, loc. 690.

p. 79   *"Consciousness is fundamental"*: Ervin László, "Ask Ervin Laszlo Series: What Is Consciousness?," László Institute, YouTube video, September 4, 2022, https://www.youtube.com/watch?v=2PWwtg9 P434.

p. 80   *"We know that interactions between things in the physical world"*: László, *Immutable Laws*, loc. 500.

p. 83   *"Man's dilemma — now and always"*: David R. Hawkins, *Power vs. Force: The Hidden Determinants of Human Behavior* (Sedona, AZ: Veritas, 2013), Kindle, loc. 510.

p. 85   *Human beings can see only about 0.0035 percent of reality*: "Visible Light: Eye-Opening Research at NNSA," National Nuclear Security Administration, October 17, 2018, https://www.energy.gov /nnsa/articles/visible-light-eye-opening-research-nnsa.

p. 86   *"That which cannot be seen is called invisible"*: Wayne Dyer, *Living the Wisdom of the Tao* (Carlsbad, CA: Hay House, 2008), 28.

p. 87   *"The fundamental reality is not matter but energy"*: László, *What Is Reality?*, loc. 651.

p. 87   *"Everything we call physical reality"*: Jude Currivan, *The Cosmic Hologram: In-Formation at the Center of Creation* (Rochester, VT: Inner Traditions, 2017), 19.

Chapter Four: The Mind Matrix

p. 97   *"Mind is the matrix of all matter"*: Gregg Braden, *The Divine Matrix: Bridging Time, Space, Miracles, and Belief* (Carlsbad, CA: Hay House, 2008), 56.

p. 98   *Information in the universe cannot be canceled or obliterated*: László, *Immutable Laws*, 302.

p. 101   *Einstein was one of the first scientists*: Deepak Chopra and Menas
C. Kafatos, *You Are the Universe: Discovering Your Cosmic Self and
Why It Matters* (New York: Harmony, 2017), 75.

p. 101   *"For eternally and always there is only now"*: Gary Kowalski, *Science
and the Search for God* (New York: Lantern, 2003), 23.

p. 101   *For as long as a person is alive*: Chopra and Kafatos, *You Are the
Universe*, 82.

p. 103   *"an eerie feeling"*: Ron Southwick, "Three Mile Island Accident Was
Eerily Foreshadowed by a Hollywood Blockbuster Days Before,"
NPR, March 18, 2019, https://whyy.org/articles/three-mile-island
-accident-was-eerily-foreshadowed-by-a-hollywood-blockbuster
-days-before/.

p. 104   *"magic show, an illusion where things appear to be present"*: James G.
Lochtefeld, *The Illustrated Encyclopedia of Hinduism: A–M* (New
York: Rosen, 2002), 433.

p. 104   *"I want you to realize that there exists no color"*: Deepak Chopra and
Rudolph E. Tanzi, *Super Brain: Unleashing the Explosive Power of
Your Mind* (New York: Harmony, 2012), 275.

p. 105   *"An advanced civilization should reach a point"*: Melvin M. Vopson,
"Expert Proposes a Method for Telling If We All Live in a Computer Program," Science Alert, November 22, 2022, https://www
.sciencealert.com/expert-proposes-a-method-for-telling-if-we-all
-live-in-a-computer-program.

p. 105   *"light can embed vast amounts of information"*: Currivan, *Cosmic
Hologram*, 63.

p. 105   *"pixels…are the single points"*: Currivan, *Cosmic Hologram*, 35.

p. 106   *we are microcosmic cocreators in a living, loving, nonlocally unified*:
Author conversation with Jude Currivan, October 23, 2023.

p. 106   *"The phenomena we encounter in the world"*: László, *What Is Reality?*,
loc. 863.

p. 106   *"All the information that codes the system"*: László, *Immutable Laws*,
loc. 192.

p. 107   *extrasensory perception, telepathy, and other paranormal phenomena*:
Wikipedia, s.v. "Michael Talbot (Author)," last modified June 1,
2023, https://en.wikipedia.org/wiki/Michael_Talbot_(author).

p. 108   *"The Akashic Records might seem"*: László, *Akashic Experience*, loc. 454.

p. 109   *"The unified field is a space-filling medium"*: László, *Akashic Experience*, loc. 217 (my italics).

p. 109   *"telepathy-like interconnections between organisms"*: Wikipedia, s.v.
"Rupert Sheldrake," September 14, 2023, https://en.wikipedia.org
/wiki/Rupert_Sheldrake.

p. 109   *"collective unconscious"*: Steven Gimbel, "Carl Jung and the Concept of Collective Consciousness," Wondrium Daily, October 14, 2020, https://www.wondriumdaily.com/carl-jung-and-the-concept-of-collective-consciousness.

p. 112   *"The individual human mind is like"*: David R. Hawkins, *Power vs. Force: The Hidden Determinants of Human Behavior*, author's official authoritative edition (Carlsbad, CA: Hay House, 2013), xxvii.

p. 112   *The universal field contains everything*: Lynne McTaggart, *The Field: The Quest for the Secret Force of the Universe* (New York: Harper Perennial, 2008), 35.

p. 112   *"universal* information-and-memory *field conserves"*: László, *Immutable Laws*, 340 (my italics).

p. 112   *"There is empirical evidence supporting"*: László, *Immutable Laws*, 370.

p. 113   *"We simply have to remember"*: Author conversation with Peter Smith, March 2023.

p. 117   *"to find the secrets of the universe"*: "Nikola Tesla: How This Energy Visionary Changed Our World," Just Energy (blog), accessed September 23, 2023, https://justenergy.com/blog/nikola-tesla/.

p. 118   *"When our mind is calibrated"*: Wright, *First Intelligence*, 98 (my italics).

p. 119   *These wave interference patterns are a highly efficient*: McTaggart, *The Field*, 85.

p. 122   *"In ordinary perception"*: McTaggart, *The Field*, 136.

p. 122   *"request for resonance"*: Author conversation with Peter Smith, March 2023.

p. 125   *"We are here to find that dimension"*: Eckhart Tolle, "We are here to find that dimension within ourselves which is deeper than thought," Facebook, June 21, 2019, https://www.facebook.com/Eckharttolle/photos/a.191110401216/10157138592481217/.

p. 126   *"Yogis and spiritual masters"*: László, *Immutable Laws*, 370.

Chapter Five: Quantum Intelligence

p. 145   *"What intellect is to the physics of yesterday"*: Kim Chestney, *Radical Intuition: A Revolutionary Guide to Using Your Inner Power* (Novato, CA: New World Library, 2020), 14.

p. 147   *Einstein's best ideas came when he was aimless*: Ephrat Livni, "Albert Einstein's Best Ideas Came When He Was Aimless. Yours Can Too," *Quartz*, June 8, 2018, https://qz.com/1299282/albert-einsteins-best-ideas-came-while-he-was-relaxing-aimlessly-yours-can-too/.

p. 147   *"If you want to experience the supernatural"*: Joe Dispenza, *Becoming*

Supernatural: How Common People Are Doing the Uncommon (Carlsbad, CA: Hay House, 2019), 29.

p. 147 *"In truth, the present moment never ends"*: Chopra and Kafatos, *You Are the Universe*, 76.

p. 148 *"The present necessity of communicating"*: W. Brugh Joy, *Joy's Way: An Introduction to the Potentials for Healing with the Body Energies* (Los Angeles: Tarcher/Putnam, 1979), 116–17.

p. 148 *"You mean to say that you think"*: Peter Smith, *The Transcendence of Celeste Kelly* (Foxground, NSW: AIA Publishing, 2023), 19.

p. 160 *"decisions made on the basis of feelings"*: Dylan Walsh, "We're More Likely to Stick to Decisions Rooted in Emotions," *Yale Insights* (blog), Yale School of Management, June 23, 2020, https://insights.som.yale.edu/insights/we-re-more-likely-to-stick-to-decisions-rooted-in-emotions.

p. 164 *Other studies showed that microscopic crystal solutions*: Joy, *Joy's Way*, 52.

p. 165 *"The choice of where we put our attention"*: Russell Targ, *Limitless Mind: A Guide to Remote Viewing and Transformation of Consciousness* (Novato, CA: New World Library, 2004), 170.

p. 167 *As soon as the photon or electron is observed*: Chopra and Kafatos, *You Are the Universe*, 19.

p. 167 *"In the act of observation"*: McTaggart, *The Field*, 85.

p. 167 *"A key feature of this view"*: Dossey, *Power of Premonitions*, 191.

p. 169 *"The real knowledge is free"*: "Carlos Barrios, Mayan Elder and Ajq'ij of the Eagle Clan Quotes," Goodreads, accessed September 23, 2023, https://www.goodreads.com/quotes/482534-the-greatest-wisdom-is-in-simplicity-love-respect-tolerance-sharing.

p. 182 *"Beauty is truth, truth beauty"*: John Keats, "Ode to a Grecian Urn," https://www.poetryfoundation.org/poems/44477/ode-on-a-grecian-urn.

Chapter Six: Impossible Things

p. 183 *"Quantum behavior forces us to be"*: Chopra and Kafatos, *You Are the Universe*, 32.

p. 183 *"The materialistic focus"*: Mario Beauregard et al., "Manifesto for a Post-Materialist Science," *Explore* 10, no. 5 (July 2014): 1–4, https://www.researchgate.net/publication/264463775_Manifesto_for_a_Post-Materialist_Science.

p. 184 *"What the future holds remains to be seen"*: Nick Pope, *Ancient*

Aliens, season 14, episode 16, "The Alien Brain," aired October 11, 2019, on History Channel.

p. 184   *"Much that was considered normal"*: Ira Israel, *How to Survive Your Childhood Now That You're an Adult: A Path to Authenticity and Awakening* (Novato, CA: New World Library, 2017), 105.

p. 185   *"spooky action at a distance"*: Wikipedia, s.v. "Quantum Entanglement," last modified September 24, 2023, https://en.wikipedia.org/wiki/Quantum_entanglement.

p. 185   *"When two quantum entities interact"*: Levy, *Quantum Revelation*, 86.

p. 185   *"at very deep levels, the separations"*: Dean Radin, *Entangled Minds: Extrasensory Experiences in Quantum Reality* (New York: Paraview Pocket, 2009), 14.

p. 185   *"Today we know that entanglement"*: Radin, *Entangled Minds*, 14.

p. 188   *"When particles are entangled"*: Lynne McTaggart, foreword to *The Holographic Universe: The Revolutionary Theory of Reality* by Michael Talbot (New York: Harper Collins, 1991), xiii.

p. 190   *"We often dream about people"*: Carl Jung, *Synchronicity: An Acausal Connecting Principle* (Princeton, NJ: Princeton University Press, 2010), 8.

p. 191   *"Although they shared no common language"*: Nina Strochlic, "A Forgotten Adventure with a Telepathic Tribe," *National Geographic*, November 29, 2016, https://www.nationalgeographic.com/magazine/article/amazon-encounter-explorer-photographer.

p. 192   *"Many people claim that they have"*: Rupert Sheldrake, *A Sense of Being Stared At* (New York: Crown, 2003), chap. 1.

p. 192   *"Telepathy is real; it does happen"*: Upton Sinclair, *Mental Radio* (Project Gutenberg), chap. 2, https://www.gutenberg.org/files/63693/63693-h/63693-h.htm.

p. 193   *When you understand these principles, one thing is for certain*: László, *Science and the Akashic Field*, 224.

p. 193   *"In Buddhism, these are not miracles"*: Alan Wallace, quoted in Dean Radin, *Supernormal: Science, Yoga, and the Evidence for Extraordinary Psychic Abilities* (New York: Random House, 2013), 103.

p. 194   *"Between 1621 and 1631"*: "Venerable Mary of Agreda: The Bilocating, Flying Nun," Chapel of the Good Shepherd (blog), August 13, 2020, https://www.goodshepherdlatinmass.com/post/venerable-mary-of-agreda-the-bilocating-flying-nun.

p. 196   *"Life is like a movie"*: Mark Anthony, *The Afterlife Frequency: The Scientific Proof of Spiritual Contact and How That Awareness Will Change Your Life* (Novato, CA: New World Library, 2021), 153.

p. 197 *"There is really no before and after for the mind"*: László, *What Is Reality?*, loc. 355.

p. 197 *"According to this venerable rule"*: Dossey, *Power of Premonitions*, 106.

p. 203 *"The Force is 'an energy field created'"*: Helané Wahbeh, *The Science of Channeling* (Oakland, CA: New Harbinger, 2021), 17.

p. 204 *A remote viewer goes into the quantum field*: Wikipedia, s.v. "Remote Viewing," last modified August 19, 2023, https://en.wikipedia.org/wiki/Remote_viewing.

p. 204 *"If we could see remote places"*: McTaggart, *The Field*, 159.

p. 205 *"The idea that extrasensory abilities"*: Ingo Swann, *Everybody's Guide to ESP: Unlocking the Extrasensory Power of the Mind* (New York: J. P. Tarcher, 1991), 14.

p. 208 *"Virtually every single process"*: Jack Fraser, "How the Human Body Creates Electromagnetic Fields," *Forbes*, November 3, 2017, https://www.forbes.com/sites/quora/2017/11/03/how-the-human-body-creates-electromagnetic-fields/.

p. 208 *"electromagnetic fields of energy"*: Gaia News, season 5, episode 18, "Mind-Body Healing with the Biofield," https://www.gaia.com/video/mind-body-healing-with-the-biofield.

p. 211 *"We operate and exist"*: Wright, *First Intelligence*, 148–49.

p. 213 *"Maybe I know where the water is"*: John Steinbeck, *East of Eden* (1952; repr., New York: Penguin, 2002), 167.

p. 218 *"Consciousness is not generated by the brain"*: László, *Wisdom Principles*, loc. 463, 471.

p. 218 *The report, authored by Lieutenant Colonel Wayne M. McDonnell*: Thobey Campion, "How to Escape the Confines of Time and Space According to the CIA," *Vice*, February 16, 2021, https://www.vice.com/en/article/7k9qag/how-to-escape-the-confines-of-time-and-space-according-to-the-cia.

p. 219 *It is estimated that one in ten people*: "First Out-of-Body Experience Induced in Laboratory Setting," ScienceDaily, August 24, 2007, https://www.sciencedaily.com/releases/2007/08/070823141057.htm.

p. 221 *"the 'hosting hardware' of human consciousness"*: Anthony, *The Afterlife Frequency*, 261.

p. 221 *"brought home"*: Wikipedia, s.v. "Dorothy Eady," last modified August 7, 2023, https://en.wikipedia.org/wiki/Dorothy_Eady.

p. 222 *a lively, intelligent, dedicated woman*: Wikipedia, s.v. "Dorothy Eady."

p. 222 *Edgar Cayce, during states of hypnotic sleep*: Edgar Cayce, *Edgar Cayce's Story of Jesus* (New York: Berkley Books, 1976), cover.

p. 222 *Even the Buddha recounted over five hundred other lives*: Britannica, s.v. "Previous Lives of Buddha," accessed September 23, 2023, https://www.britannica.com/biography/Buddha-founder-of -Buddhism/Previous-lives.

p. 224 *"Intanglement is about the internal connection"*: Peter Smith, *Quantum Consciousness: Journey through Other Realms* (Carlsbad, CA: Hay House, 2018), 66.

p. 227 *"living myself into the music"*: Ervin László, "Simply Genius! Where Does Talent Come From?," Heal Your Life (blog), June 30, 2011, https://www.healyourlife.com/simply-genius.

p. 227 *recognized the deep intuitive connection to his field-sourced talent*: Conversation with Ervin László, March 2023.

p. 229 *"As a practicing neurosurgeon"*: Eben Alexander, *Proof of Heaven: A Neurosurgeon's Journey into the Afterlife* (New York: Simon & Schuster, 2022), 9.

p. 230 *"the initial gateway of their journey"*: Michael Newton, *Journey of Souls: Case Studies of Life between Lives* (Saint Paul, MN: Llewellyn, 1994), 19.

p. 230 *"some NDEers [near-death experiencers] discovered"*: Talbot, *Holographic Universe*, 251.

p. 231 *"There are no ordinary people"*: C. S. Lewis, *The Weight of Glory* (New York: Harper One, 2001), 14–15.

p. 232 *"patchwork quilt of separate universes"*: Frank Swain, *The Universe Next Door: A Journey through 55 Alternative Realities, Parallel Worlds and Possible Futures* (London: New Scientist, 2017), 12.

p. 232 *"In the quantum consciousness realm"*: Smith, *Quantum Consciousness*, 114.

p. 233 *"I had been invited to a small conference"*: Whitley Strieber, *A New World* (San Antonio, TX: Walker & Collier, 2019), 70, 72.

Chapter Seven: Guiding Forces

p. 247 *"The 'Mind of God,' which Einstein wrote eloquently"*: Michio Kaku, *Parallel Worlds: A Journey through Creation, Higher Dimensions, and the Future of the Cosmos* (New York: Anchor Books, 2005), 18.

p. 248 *"Eternity is timeless"*: Chopra and Kafatos, *You Are the Universe*, 76.

p. 251 *"Synchronicity is choreographed"*: Deepak Chopra, *The Spontaneous Fulfillment of Desire* (New York: Harmony, 2004), 14.

p. 251 *"Carl Jung coined the term synchronicity"*: Laura Lynne Jackson, *Signs: The Secret Language of the Universe* (New York: Dial Press, 2019), Kindle, loc. 207.

p. 255 *Human beings make up only 0.01 percent of earth's life*: Hannah

Ritchie, "Humans Make Up Just 0.01% of Earth's Life — What's the Rest?," Our World in Data, April 24, 2019, https://ourworld indata.org/life-on-earth.

p. 257   *Explaining the fundamental role of intuition:* Talbot, *Holographic Universe*, 258.

p. 257   *"there is a single language":* Emanuel Swedenborg, *Heaven and Hell* (1758; repr., New York: Swedenborg Foundation, 1979), chapter 27, section 236.

p. 257   *"telepathic bursts of knowledge":* Talbot, *Holographic Universe*, 258.

p. 257   *"despite its ghostlike and ephemeral qualities":* Talbot, *Holographic Universe*, 238.

p. 260   *Remote viewer Ingo Swann, who was part of the Stargate Project:* McTaggart, *The Field*, 147.

p. 260   *"Recently experimenters have found a way":* Chopra and Kafatos, *You Are the Universe*, 87.

p. 261   *"rearrange atoms":* Strieber, *A New World*, 24–25.

p. 261   *"only begins with what we now know as the physical":* Strieber, *A New World*, 8.

p. 262   *"Right now, we cannot reliably engage with our dead":* Strieber, *A New World*, 21.

p. 266   *The fiber-optic cables that we use:* "What Is Fiber Internet?," Century Link (blog), accessed September 23, 2023, https://www.century link.com/home/help/internet/fiber/what-is-fiber-internet.html.

p. 268   *"We also found that if people get themselves":* Rollin McCraty, "This Mind-Boggling Research from the Institute of HeartMath Shows That Your Heart Might Be the Key to Intuition and Precognition," Beautyfull Life (blog), accessed September 23, 2023, https://the heartrevolution.org/magazine/heart/heartmath-intuition -research-your-heart-is-key/.

p. 268   *"Coherence indicates connectedness, cooperation, and a holistic balance":* Wright, *First Intelligence*, 62.

p. 269   *"Individual consciousness is not something separate":* László, *Wisdom Principles*, loc. 472.

p. 273   *"We must always go beyond":* "Surrender to the Divine Will," Sri Aurobindo Ashram Trust, vol. 20, 315, https://library.sriaurobindo ashram.org/mother/cwm14/chapter/22.

Conclusion: Journey Onward and Inward

p. 287   *"Owing to our immortal consciousness":* László, *Wisdom Principles*, loc. 498.

p. 289 *"As our generation marvels at our new view"*: Brian Greene, *The Elegant Universe: Superstrings, Hidden Dimensions, and the Quest for Ultimate Theory* (New York: Vintage Books, 1999), 387.

p. 289 *Not only is this shift felt through subtle, internal channels*: Alvin M. Saperstein and Gottfried Mayer-Kress, "A Nonlinear Dynamical Model of the Impact of SDI on the Arms Race," *Journal of Conflict Resolution* 32, no. 4 (December 1988), https://journals.sagepub.com/doi/10.1177/0022002788032004003.

Index

Keats, John, 182
knowing feeling, the, 150–57
knowledge, implanted, 55, 59

lab exercises: to awaken quantum
    thinking, 33–38; catching the
    code, 59–63; illumination
    journey, 279–85; intuition and
    memory codes, 131–40; limit-
    less mind, 235–45; metasenses,
    89–94; sacred seeing, 174–80
Lao-tzu, 86
lasers, 266
László, Ervin, 20, 21–22, 26, 45, 71,
    73–74, 79–80, 87, 106, 108–9,
    112–13, 126, 218, 227, 269, 287
Lectio Divina, 28–29
Levy, Paul, 41, 185
Lewis, C.S., 231
life: infinite nature of, 288; purpose-
    fulness of, 247–49
light: coherent vs. incoherent, 266;
    and encoded wisdom, 106–7;
    energy and self-actualization,
    106; inner light sanctuary,
    276–78; inner light show ex-
    periment, 24–25; light-themed
    words, 25; and luminous mind,
    22–24
linear thinking, 19
Lloyd, Seth, 105
locations and biofields, 212–13
loneliness, 50–51
love: and coherence, 265, 270; as
    energy, 54; soulmates, 187–90,
    201; as ultimate coherence,
    271–73; as vibrational state of
    mind, 123

luminescence, 270–71
luminous mind, 22–24

*Manifesto for a Post-Materialistic
    Science*, 184
Marr, Bernard, 76
Mary of Ágreda, 194–95
Matter and Memory (Bergson), 109
Mayoruna people, 191
McCraty, Rollin, 268
McDonnell, Wayne M., 218
McIntyre, Loren, 191
McMoneagle, Joseph, 205
McTaggart, Lynne, 122, 167, 188,
    204–5
Meltdown: Three Mile Island (film),
    102–3
memory: accessing, 114–24;
    contrasted with intuition,
    113–14; cosmic memory bank,
    112; future memory, 196–97;
    local and nonlocal memory
    exercises, 135–38
metacognition, 146–48
metaphysics, 19–21, 44
metareality: cosmic consciousness,
    77–81; duality of reality vs.
    metareality, 74–75; everyday
    miracles, 81–83; illumination
    key, 83–88; lab exercises with
    metasenses, 89–94; noth-
    ingness and somethingness,
    72–77; physical/metaphysical
    phemonena, 67–70; taste
    experiment, 88–89; world
    beyond the world, 70–72
metasenses, 85–88, 89–94, 110
mind, reprogramming, 30–32
mindfulness practice, 127–28

THE ILLUMINATION CODE

About the Author

Kim Chestney is a globally recognized author and intuition expert whose work leads individuals into deeper awareness of their intuitive nature and the power that it holds. Working for nearly twenty years in the tech sector, she has led initiatives with some of the top thought leaders, technology companies, and universities in the world — raising awareness of insight, creativity, and ingenuity as vital forces in the progression of society and culture. The *Pittsburgh Post-Gazette* named Kim as an innovation leader "on the vanguard of a movement to unearth the genius within," and her work has been featured by an array of leading-edge organizations, including *ABC News*, SXSW, *Coast to Coast AM*, *Success Magazine*, *Women's World*, Carnegie Mellon University, the Omega Institute, the Shift Network, the Edgar Cayce Association for Research and Enlightenment, *Dreamland*, and Americans for the Arts. She is the author of multiple books published around the globe since 2004, including *Radical Intuition: A Revolutionary Guide to Using Your Inner Power* and *The Psychic Workshop: A Complete Program for Fulfilling Your Spiritual Potential*. Kim is the founder of IntuitionLab, a thriving international intuition community dedicated to exploring the inner frontier and bringing its magic into everyday life.

Learn more at KimChestney.com and Intuition-Lab.com.